Francis Bourdillon

The Parables of our Lord Explained and Applied

Francis Bourdillon

The Parables of our Lord Explained and Applied

ISBN/EAN: 9783744792622

Printed in Europe, USA, Canada, Australia, Japan

Cover: Foto ©Lupo / pixelio.de

More available books at **www.hansebooks.com**

THE

Parables of Our Lord

EXPLAINED AND APPLIED.

BY THE REV. FRANCIS BOURDILLON, M. A.
RECTOR OF WOOLBEDING, SUSSEX.

PUBLISHED BY THE
AMERICAN TRACT SOCIETY,
150 NASSAU-STREET, NEW YORK.

PREFACE.

THE aim of this work is not critical elucidation, but simple, practical explanation and application. The chapters are intended to be read, either privately, or in any of the various ways in which plain family sermons are found to be useful. In each parable the main scope has been regarded, rather than those more minute points, which, in many cases at least, must be looked on as mere accessories; nor has the author gone into those refinements of application in which an ingenious fancy is apt to indulge, but which often tend to draw away the mind from the great lesson intended to be taught. Long words and involved sentences have been avoided, and the author's aim has been to use "great plainness of speech," in the earnest hope that the book may be of use to the poor and unlearned, as well as to those of more cultivated minds. And now he sends it forth with the humble prayer that it may be blessed by God for the setting forth of the teaching of our Lord, and for the extension of "the kingdom of heaven."

The words, "the kingdom of heaven is like," or similar words, are found at the beginning of a large number of the parables; and if this work were to be read through continuously, it might have been enough to explain, once for all, what those words mean. But as each chapter is meant to be read by itself, and independently of the rest, it has been thought necessary to give a short explanation of these words almost as often as they occur. Occasional repetitions will therefore be noticed, for which allowance is asked on the ground just stated.

As a general rule, the parables have been arranged in the order in which they may be believed to have been spoken; not, however, without exception, when there seemed any good reason for departing from this plan. Indeed, strict accuracy in this respect is not attainable, nor is it of any great moment.

CONTENTS.

INTRODUCTION. The Nature and Design of our Lord's Parables ....PAGE 7
    I. Fields White to the Harvest 13
   II. The House on the Rock, and the House on the Sand— 20
  III. The Two Debtors 27
  IV. The Foolish Rich Man 35
   V. Servants Waiting for their Lord 42
  VI. The Unfruitful Fig-tree 51
 VII. The Sower ; in four parts :
      1. The Seed that Fell by the Wayside 57
      2. The Seed that Fell on Stony Ground 63
      3. The Seed that Fell among Thorns 67
      4. The Seed that Fell on Good Ground 73
VIII. The Tares of the Field 79
  IX. The Seed, the Blade, and the Ear 85
   X. The Grain of Mustard Seed 92
  XI. The Leaven in the Meal 98
 XII. The Hidden Treasure 104
XIII. The Pearl of Great Price 109
XIV. The Gospel Net 114
 XV. The New Cloth, and the New Wine 118
XVI. True Defilement 125
XVII. The Blind Leading the Blind 130
XVIII. The Unforgiving Servant 135
XIX. The Good Samaritan 142
 XX. The Importunate Prayer 150
XXI. The Father's Gift 156
XXII. Christ, the Door 162

CONTENTS.

XXIII. The Good Shepherd .... PAGE 170
XXIV. The Strait Gate, and the Shut Door 178
XXV. The Guest who Chose the Chief Rooms 186
XXVI. The Great Supper 192
XXVII. The Man without a Wedding Garment 203
XXVIII. The Tower-Builder 208
XXIX. The Lost Sheep, and the Lost Piece of Silver 213
XXX. The Prodigal Son 221
XXXI. The Unjust Steward 229
XXXII. The Rich Man and Lazarus 239
XXXIII. The Unjust Judge 248
XXXIV. The Pharisee and the Publican 253
XXXV. The Laborers in the Vineyard 259
XXXVI. The Pounds 269
XXXVII. The Talents 278
XXXVIII. The Two Sons 286
XXXIX. The Wicked Husbandmen 290
XL. The Budding Fig-tree 298
XLI. The Wise and Foolish Virgins 301
XLII. The Vine and the Branches 310

INTRODUCTION.

The Nature and Design of our Lord's Parables.

Our Lord taught much in parables; and many of his most important and solemn lessons are in this form. There is, however, considerable difference of opinion as to what is a parable and what is not; and some who take the stricter view would confine the parables of our Lord to a comparatively small number. The author of this work has gone on a wider principle, and has considered as parables all those parts of our Lord's teaching in which religious lessons are conveyed under the form of a history, a tale, or a similitude; excluding, however, those similitudes which are mere figures of speech or illustrations. It is difficult to draw the line exactly. He has preferred the wider principle, as furnishing a greater variety of spiritual truth, and as giving a more comprehensive view of the figurative teaching of our Lord.

The reason for which our Lord made use of this way of teaching seems to have been twofold.

First, his hearers were accustomed to figurative speaking, for it was much in use at that time, and in that part of the world. They would therefore be more likely to be attracted by it than by direct instruction. Indeed, in many cases a truth is more easily understood by people in general when set forth by means of a simple figure. And perhaps in all cases a figure or parable, when once its spiritual meaning and application are perceived, greatly helps the memory to retain the lesson, and tends also to fix the impression on the heart. One reason, therefore, why our Lord taught by parables was, that he might draw attention, and be more easily understood, and that his teaching might make a more lasting impression.

But this was not all. There was a second, and, as would seem at first sight, a contradictory reason. But it was not contradictory really; nothing that our Lord did or said was so. If he used parables in part to make his teaching more interesting and plain, he certainly did so also to veil or conceal his meaning. This we learn from his own words. When he had ended the parable of the sower, which was spoken to the multitude at large, his disciples said to him: "Why speakest thou unto them in parables?" His answer was in these words: "Because it is given unto *you* to know the mysteries of the kingdom of heaven, but to *them* it is *not* given. For whosoever hath, to him shall be given, and he shall have more abundance: but whosoever hath not, from him shall be taken away even that he hath. Therefore speak I to them in parables, because they seeing see not; and hearing they hear not, neither do they understand. And in them is fulfilled the prophecy of Esaias, which saith, By hearing ye shall hear, and shall not understand; and seeing ye shall see, and shall not perceive: for this people's heart is waxed gross, and their ears

INTRODUCTION.

are dull of hearing, and their eyes they have closed; lest at any time they should see with their eyes, and hear with their ears, and should understand with their heart, and should be converted, and I should heal them." In St. Mark the words are given yet more strongly: "That seeing they may see, and not perceive; and hearing they may hear, and not understand; lest at any time they should be converted, and their sins should be forgiven them." And the passage in St. Luke is in the same form: "That seeing they might not see, and hearing they might not understand."

Having given this answer, our Lord went on to explain the parable fully to his disciples; not however without a gentle rebuke, as if *they* too were in a measure gross in heart and dull of hearing: "Know ye not this parable? and how then will ye know all parables?"

Our Lord, therefore, in this and other parables, concealed the meaning from some, while he explained it to others. To the former, the parable was a mere tale or figure, the spiritual meaning being hidden; to the latter, the meaning was made known, and the lesson was all the more deeply impressed on their minds from being taught by way of parable.

But who were these last? The disciples. All who really wished to learn were taught plainly. Not only the twelve apostles, but the far larger number of the disciples; for this number comprised those who had joined themselves to our Lord, and placed themselves under his teaching: the very word means learners or pupils. Now our Lord never turned away any who wished to become his disciples. "Him that cometh to me," said he, "I will in no wise cast out." On the contrary, he invited all to come and learn of him: "Come unto me all ye that labor and are heavy laden, and I will give you rest. Take my yoke upon you, and learn of me." "*Learn* of me;" it is the very same word as *disciples;* learn of me, become my learners or disciples.

None, therefore, were shut out from the knowledge of the truth but by their own fault. If any one from among the multitude who heard the parable of the sower, for instance, had come humbly to Jesus as a disciple or learner, seeking instruction, doubtless he would have received it. The meaning of the parable would not have been kept hidden from him. He would at once have become one of those of whom our Lord said: "Blessed are your eyes, for they see; and your ears, for they hear." It was because the people did *not* do this that they remained in ignorance. They were like those of whom the prophet spoke. Their heart was gross, and their ears dull of hearing, and their eyes they had closed. They did not seek, and therefore they did not find. Some things indeed our Lord said so plainly that all who heard them could understand them; and often what he said seemed to make a general impression. On one occasion, just after he had spoken one of the parables, "the people," we read, "were astonished at his doctrine, for he taught them as one having authority, and not as the scribes." But few were so much impressed as to become his disciples and to seek further instruction. The multitude remained the multitude still; the disciples were still but a few, though doubtless

INTRODUCTION. 11

some did from time to time join themselves to the number.

The words, "Whosoever hath, to him shall be given, and he shall have more abundance," throw great light on the subject. Whosoever hath in him, through grace, the beginning of true religion, an awakened conscience, a desire for spiritual instruction, a spirit of sincere inquiry, to him shall be given. That light and knowledge of which he stands in need shall not be withheld from him. He shall receive, and receive abundantly. The word of God will not be a dark word to him. The more he searches, the more will he find. God himself will teach him.

This applies as much to us as to those who heard our Lord. What are we with regard to his teaching? Are we *disciples*, or are we only of the *multitude*? If we are careless about spiritual things, or if we hear or read the word of God merely as a matter of form or custom, or only because the *mind* is interested in it, as distinguished from the *heart*, then we are like the multitude who heard our Lord's parables. Even though the word may reach the understanding, there is no spiritual impression made on the heart. In this state we are little likely to receive a blessing. But if, on the other hand, we place ourselves as learners at our Saviour's feet, and come to the word of God with an earnest desire to be taught, then we are *disciples*, as much as they who went about with him from place to place to hear his words; then he reckons us among those who take his yoke upon them, and learn of him; and he will bless us, and teach us, and give us the light of his truth in " more abundance." Let us be disciples indeed. Let us be humble and diligent learners of Christ our Lord. We cannot go about with him from place to place, but he has left us his word and the means of grace, and has promised us the Holy Spirit. Let us make full use of all that he has given.

The parables of our Lord differ greatly from one another. Some are short and plain, others much longer and more difficult. Some teach a simple moral lesson, others a deep spiritual truth. A large number of them relate to "the kingdom of heaven," or "the kingdom of God." These form a class by themselves. They represent to us God's government on earth under the gospel in a great variety of points. They show what takes place now, and what is to take place hereafter. They set forth the first beginning of the gospel on the earth, its spread, its hinderances, its success, and what will happen at the end. They show how God deals with men under the gospel dispensation, and how men receive the message of salvation, and how they act with regard to the Saviour. They declare very solemnly what will take place at the end of the world, the close of the present dispensation. This class of our Lord's parables, therefore, is most solemn and important; and perhaps it is to this class especially that the distinction between "the multitude" and "the disciples" applies. Let us give earnest heed to them. In causing us to live in gospel times and in a Christian land, God has given us a deep, personal concern in "the kingdom of heaven." There is not a parable on this subject that does not contain some lesson of vital consequence to us.

THE

PARABLES OF OUR LORD.

I.

Fields White to the Harvest.

"Say not ye, There are yet four months, and then cometh harvest? behold, I say unto you, Lift up your eyes, and look on the fields: for they are white already to harvest. And he that reapeth receiveth wages, and gathereth fruit unto life eternal: that both he that soweth and he that reapeth may rejoice together. And herein is that saying true, One soweth, and another reapeth. I sent you to reap that whereon ye bestowed no labor: other men labored, and ye are entered into their labors." JOHN 4:35-38.

THIS short parable was spoken by our Lord to his disciples just after his conversation with the woman of Samaria, and while she was gone into the city to tell the people of the wonderful things she had heard.

It was winter time, answering perhaps to our November or December, for it wanted four months to harvest; and in that country the harvest is much earlier than with us. The fields bore no appearance of harvest yet; they were not even green; the seed was probably but just sown; for four months is about the time there between sowing and reaping. Every one knew this. So our Lord said, "Say not ye, There are yet four months, and then cometh harvest?" But then he added, "Behold, I say unto you, Lift up your eyes, and look on the fields; for they are white already to harvest." What did he mean? Did not the very appearance of the fields contradict his words?

He meant not the natural harvest, but the harvest of souls. In the natural harvest there is always a time of waiting between sowing and reaping. It is so generally in the spiritual harvest too, but not always. It was not so in this case. Seed had been sown, and the harvest was about to follow directly. Jesus had spoken to the woman of Samaria the words of eternal life, and she had received them. And now she had gone into the neighboring city, to tell to others what she had heard. Jesus knew what would follow. He knew that the Samaritans would come out to him at the word of the woman, and hear the gospel from his lips. He knew that many would believe on him for the saying of the woman, "He told me all that ever I did;" and many more because of his own word. No sooner did they hear his word than they believed it. No sooner did he come to them, than they received him, and begged him to stay with them. Here was indeed a speedy harvest. Here was a field ripe as soon as sown.

Our Lord drew the attention of his disciples to

this. "Lift up your eyes," said he, "and look on the fields; for they are white already to harvest." They were to observe the readiness of the Samaritans to receive the gospel. But that was not all. This was but one field; there were other fields equally ripe for the sickle. The disciples were to go forth to their work of preaching the gospel, with the encouraging belief that souls were ready to hear and to believe. They were to take what happened among the Samaritans as a sample of the success which would follow their labors among other people. There was great need of the gospel. Souls were perishing for lack of knowledge. In great numbers there was a work of preparation already going on. From among both Jews and Gentiles many would hear and receive the word. There was a great field for the disciples to labor in, and there was every thing to encourage them. Let them put in the sickle of the gospel, and gather in souls to Christ, for the harvest was ripe.

Other men had labored before them—other teachers had prepared men's minds for the gospel. The ancient prophets, the Jewish teachers, John the Baptist, had all done so. And now the disciples, the preachers of the gospel, were to go forth and finish what they had begun, and thus to enter into their labors. "One soweth, and another reapeth," was a proverb. It was to be fulfilled in this case. Those other teachers had sown; the preachers of the gospel were to reap.

The fields were white for the harvest then, and the same may be said now. The greater part of the world is still without the gospel. But the need of the gospel, as God's appointed instrument for bringing souls to him, is still as great as ever; and in every part of the heathen world there are some at least who are prepared to receive it. In every quarter of the world there are now openings for the gospel; and to no heathen land do our missionaries go without finding some to welcome their message.

The field is wide indeed. The heathen and Mohammedans together are reckoned at not less than seven hundred millions in number. Here and there in this great field some labor has been bestowed, some seed has been sown, and some firstfruits have been gathered in—enough, at least, to stir up and encourage the sowers and the reapers. In some parts of the world the people are eagerly asking for the word of life; in others, old hinderances are being broken down and old prejudices are becoming softened; while others have not yet been reached by the gospel at all. True, there are many hinderances and difficulties still; yet never was the way so open, never did the fields seem so white to the harvest.

Our Lord bade the disciples lift up their eyes and look on the fields. In like manner he would have his disciples now to take notice of and care for the state of the heathen world. We are not to be indifferent to the case of the heathen. We are not to turn away our eyes from them, and attend only to home claims, as if our duty were confined to them. We are to lift up our eyes and look on other fields, on other lands beside our own. We are to care for souls wherever they are found. Though far off, yet the heathen are our neighbors in the sight of God. We must not pass by on the other side, or merely come and look at them; we must look and help.

For the disciples were not only to lift up their eyes and look on the fields; they were to go in and reap; they were to carry the gospel to those who were thus in need of it, and ready to receive it. Such is our duty too. As disciples of Christ, we are to acquaint ourselves with the state of the heathen, to take an interest in their state, to pity them, and to help them.

All may do something. At harvest time there is work for all. One reaps, another binds, a third loads the wagon. Men, women, and children work together. None need be idle. The old, whose reaping days are over, can yet help to gather up what is left; and even the little ones, whose working days have not begun, may be seen at harvest time returning from the field, each with his little bundle of gleanings. So it is in the spiritual harvest. The missionary who crosses the sea to carry the news of salvation by Jesus Christ to some dark land, *he* is the chief laborer in the field, the reaper in the harvest. But those who stay at home may be fellow-workers with him. The preacher, the speaker, the collector, the giver, the smallest contributor, are all engaged in the harvest field, each doing something in the great work. There is work for all, and to all the word comes, "Lift up your eyes, and look on the fields; for they are white already to harvest."

The reaper works for wages; and the laborer in the spiritual harvest has his reward too. Yes, a reward—yet not of works, but of grace; a gift, not a payment. But it will surely be received; for even a cup of cold water given for Christ's sake shall not go without a reward.

What is this reward? We are not told fully; but this parable throws some light on the subject. Part at least of the reward will be joy for souls saved. As there is rejoicing among us every year at harvest-home, so will there be joy at the great spiritual harvest-home. When the corn is all gathered in, and the last load has been brought to the barn, then the wages are paid, and all rejoice together, master and men, all who have had part in the harvest, from the highest to the lowest. So will it be in the harvest of souls. Even now there is joy in heaven over one sinner that repenteth. How great will be the joy when all the redeemed of the Lord are gathered in!

Happy then all who have labored for God— every sower, every reaper, every gleaner in the field of the world. What joy to have borne a part, however humble, in such a work, and now to see the fruit! What happiness to meet all fellow-workers, and rejoice with them! No jealousy now, no suspicion or distrust, no cold coöperation or doubting sympathy. Now all is love and joy. Now he who began in great discouragement, and saw but little fruit, meets him who came after him, and brought the work to a happy end. Now helpers at home, and preachers abroad, and those who have prayed, and those who have given, and those who have spent anxious hours in the cause—now they meet together and rejoice. They are happy, because the Redeemer is glorified—happy, because souls are saved—happy, because it has been their honor and blessing to bear part in such a work. Let none who know the preciousness of Christ refuse to bear a part, and thus neglect so plain a duty, so blessed a work, and lose a share in this joyful harvest-home.

II.

THE HOUSE ON THE ROCK, AND THE HOUSE ON THE SAND.

"Therefore whosoever heareth these sayings of mine, and doeth them, I will liken him unto a wise man, which built his house upon a rock: and the rain descended, and the floods came, and the winds blew, and beat upon that house; and it fell not: for it was founded upon a rock. And every one that heareth these sayings of mine, and doeth them not, shall be likened unto a foolish man, which built his house upon the sand: and the rain descended, and the floods came, and the winds blew, and beat upon that house; and it fell: and great was the fall thereof." MATT. 7:24-27; see also LUKE 6:47-49.

SUCH a thing might happen in our land; but it was much more likely to happen in that eastern country, in which our Lord spoke the parable.

For that part of the world is more liable to sudden storms and floods. Generally the climate is more dry than ours, and many of the streams are quite without water in the summer; but these dry water-courses are rapid rivers in the winter, and even at other seasons a change in the weather may suddenly fill them. The sky becomes overcast, the rain comes down in torrents, rivers overflow their banks, and spread themselves over the country, often doing great damage.

In this parable our Lord supposes two houses

to be built, both probably near a stream. The builder of the one was a wise man. Knowing that storms and floods were likely, he chose the firm rock for the site of his house, and there he dug deep for a foundation. The builder of the other house was not so wise. He was a foolish man. A level and pleasant situation on the sand presented itself, and there he built his house. The weather, we may suppose, was fine at the time; the sun shone, the air was calm, the neighboring stream was almost dry—no danger threatened. Why build on the hard rock when the sand was so much easier? Why dig into the ground for a foundation, when the house on that level surface would stand so well without one? He did not look forward, he thought only of the present. He made no provision for dangers that might come.

They did come. The fine season passed away, or the weather suddenly changed. The wise man had foreseen this, and prepared for it. "The rain descended, and the floods came, and the winds blew, and beat upon that house; and it fell not." "The stream beat vehemently upon that house, and could not shake it: for it was founded on a rock." Meanwhile, how did the other house fare? "The rain descended, and the floods came, and the winds blew, and beat upon that house; and it fell," "immediately it fell," "and great was the fall of it."

As long as the fine weather lasted, one house perhaps looked as strong and safe as the other. It was the storm that tried them. Then was seen the difference. The house on the rock stood it well;

and when the tempest was past, and the floods had gone down, there it stood, upright and safe. Not so the house on the sand. The same storm burst on it, the same winds blew, and the same torrent beat against it. When all was past, where was the house? Gone, swept away; nothing left but wreck and ruin. A foolish man, indeed; a fair-weather builder. What is a house worth that will not stand a storm? for storms are sure to come.

The wisdom of the one man and the folly of the other in this story are plain enough. But this is more than a story; it is a parable, a story with a spiritual meaning. We shall see wisdom and folly still more strikingly set forth in the application than in the story.

Our Lord does not, as he does in some cases, explain this parable at large. Yet he shows us how to understand it by what he says about the two men. By the wise man he represents "whosoever heareth these sayings of mine, and doeth them;" by the foolish man, "every one that heareth these sayings of mine, and doeth them not." This distinction is exactly the same as that contained in the words of St. James, "Be ye doers of the word, and not hearers only, deceiving your own selves."

But let none suppose that salvation by works is here taught. The contrast in this parable is not between grace and works, but between merely hearing the word on the one hand, and on the other believing, receiving, embracing it, and taking it as the guide of life. This last is called doing the word. Let us look a little more closely at both ways.

I. The man who is a hearer only, hears the word, but it makes no impression on his heart. He may hear it regularly, and even take pleasure in hearing it; but he hears it *only*. He hears it, not so much to learn from it, to receive good from it, to be guided by it, as to be interested and pleased. No wonder then, that it makes no change in his heart or life, that he is the same man after hearing it as he was before. He hears the word, and then he has done with it. There is nothing more of it till he hears it again.

Our Lord had many such hearers. Of the great multitudes who flocked to hear him from all parts of the country, numbers were hearers only, mere professors at the best, crying, "Lord, Lord!" but not doing the will of God, nor truly embracing the word.

There are many such hearers always. Every congregation has them. There is great danger of being hearers only, great danger of mistaking hearing for doing, and of being satisfied with being pleased without seeking to be profited. All hearers should look well to it that they be not hearers only. Such are like the foolish man, builders on the sand, builders without a foundation. Their building will not stand. Hearing and professing will never save.

II. The doer of the word is very different. His very hearing is a different kind of hearing; for he hears not merely to be pleased, but in order that he may learn the way of salvation and the will of God. And what he hears he humbly receives, believes it, feels it, and strives to follow and to practise it. He has not done with the word when it ceases to sound in his ears. It is both food and light to him. He remembers it, and treasures it up in his mind as his light and guide. And, just as we take food at meal times, and are afterwards nourished and strengthened by what we have taken, so is his soul fed continually by the word of God.

But there is a peculiar force in the figures here used—the rock and the foundation. Christ is the rock of our salvation. The believer's hope is built on him alone. "Other foundation can no man lay than that is laid, which is Jesus Christ." The doer of the word means, therefore, not merely a man who is sincere and in earnest in a general way, but one who truly believes on Jesus, builds every hope on him alone, and strives to show forth in his life the fruits of his faith. In other words, the doer of the word is a true and sincere Christian, taught by the word and Spirit of God.

The mere hearer and the doer may make the same profession, and bear in the eyes of men much the same character, as long as the day of trial does not come. As the two houses both stood firm while fine weather lasted, and one looked as safe as the other, so these two men may, to those who do not look very deep, or do not know them well, seem for a time much alike. But when the storm comes, how is it then? Ah, then the difference appears. The hearer only has no comfort laid up against the day of trouble. When affliction visits him, he knows not whither to flee for relief. When persecution arises, he is little likely to stand firm, for he has no foundation. If errors in doctrine spring up, and he becomes exposed to false teaching, he is liable to be swept away by the torrent, because he has no firm hold on the truth; it has not reached his heart, he is not rooted and built up in Christ. The doer of the word, on the contrary, knows where to seek help and comfort in all trouble and difficulty. To him, "to live is Christ." Christ is his life. He is joined to Christ by a living faith. He can do all things through Christ which strengtheneth him. He does not expect to be without trial. The very word which he has heard bids him look for it. But he meets it and bears it in his Saviour's strength. Thus he faces persecution, thus he meets false doctrine. His house is built upon a rock; it has a foundation; it will stand the storm. Christ is his rock.

But is this all? Does the parable point to no storms, no troubles, but such as these?

There is a fiercer storm coming, a greater trial. "Every man's work shall be made manifest; for the day shall declare it, because it shall be revealed by fire; and the fire shall try every man's work of what sort it is." What day is here meant? The great day, the day of the Lord, the last day, the day of trial and of judgment. In that passage the apostle is writing especially of ministers; but his words may well be applied to all. For that day will try not only the work of the minister, but the life and character and state of all. A different figure is used in the two passages. In the parable it is a storm, here it is a fire; but the meaning is much the same. Every man's house, his spiritual building, will be severely tried, tried to the uttermost, as by storm or fire. None will stand then, but those who are built upon Christ. No preparation for eternity will prove of any avail, except a true and living faith in Jesus, shown forth in the fruits of holiness. Religious knowledge, religious profession, a religious name, what will they do for the soul in that day? Nothing. Christ will then be all. They who are in him will be safe, but none else. All besides must see every hope fail them, every refuge swept away, and their house "brought to desolation" indeed.

How does *your* house, your spiritual building, stand? Has it a foundation? Is it on the rock? Look well to this matter.

If you feel any doubt, begin again from the very bottom. Take the house all down and build it afresh, rather than run the risk of its being swept away. It will be too late to make it safe when the storm comes. Now, in this calm and quiet season, now, while yet you may, look well to your foundation. Make sure of being in Christ by faith. Do not deceive yourself. Do not say to your soul, "Peace, peace!" when there is no peace. Let nothing satisfy you but a true and deep foundation in Christ, the Rock of Ages. Thus be you found among the wise, among those who are doers of the word, and not hearers only, deceiving their own selves.

III.

THE TWO DEBTORS.

"And one of the Pharisees desired him that he would eat with him. And he went into the Pharisee's house, and sat down to meat. And, behold, a woman in the city, which was a sinner, when she knew that Jesus sat at meat in the Pharisee's house, brought an alabaster box of ointment, and stood at his feet behind him weeping, and began to wash his feet with tears, and did wipe them with the hairs of her head, and kissed his feet, and anointed them with the ointment. Now when the Pharisee which had bidden him saw it, he spake within himself, saying, This man, if he were a prophet, would have known who and what manner of woman this is that toucheth him: for she is a sinner. And Jesus answering said unto him, Simon, I have somewhat to say unto thee. And he saith, Master, say on. There was a certain creditor which had two debtors: the one owed five hundred pence, and the other fifty. And when they had nothing to pay, he frankly forgave them both. Tell me therefore, which of them will love him most? Simon answered and said, I suppose that he to whom he forgave most. And he said unto him, Thou hast rightly judged. And he turned to the woman, and said unto Simon, Seest thou this woman? I entered into thy house, thou gavest me no water for my feet: but she hath washed my feet with tears, and wiped them with the hairs of her head. Thou gavest me no kiss: but this woman since the time I came in hath not ceased to kiss my feet. My head with oil thou didst not anoint: but this woman hath anointed my feet with ointment. Wherefore I say unto thee, Her sins, which are many, are forgiven; for she loved much: but to whom little is forgiven, the same loveth little. And he said unto her, Thy sins are forgiven. And they that sat at meat with him began to say within themselves, Who is this that forgiveth sins also? And he said to the woman, Thy faith hath saved thee: go in peace." LUKE 7:36–50.

WE know nothing of this Pharisee beyond his name, nor do we know why he invited Jesus to his house.

The woman some have thought to have been Mary Magdalene. But there seems no sufficient reason for thinking so. Mary is first mentioned in the following chapter; and there she is spoken of, not as one who had been a great sinner, but as having been heavily afflicted. This woman, on the other hand, had been of known bad character; probably living on the wages of sin.

But she was now greatly changed. Her conscience had been touched. She had been brought to true sorrow for sin, and to a belief in Jesus as able and willing to forgive her; and now, hearing that he was in the house of the Pharisee, she came and stood at his feet as he reclined on a couch at the meal, and wept, and kissed his feet, and anointed them with a precious ointment which she had brought with her for the purpose.

The Pharisee saw her, and knowing her character was much surprised—yet less, it seems, at her coming, than at Jesus' letting her come. He did not, however, say any thing, but only thought within himself. "This man," thought he, "if he were a prophet, would have known who and what manner of woman this is that toucheth him; for she is a sinner." From this it appears that this happened in some place where Jesus was a stranger, and that the Pharisee, (as might be supposed from his inviting him,) though not believing in him, had yet some doubt whether he were not a true prophet or teacher. But what he now beheld seemed quite against that. If he were really a prophet, would he not have known by his prophetic power what kind of woman this was? As for his letting such a woman come near him, knowing her character, even when she came in tears for her sins, such a thought seems not to have entered the mind of the Pharisee.

He did not speak aloud, but Jesus knew his thoughts, and answered them by the parable of the two debtors, addressing him personally: "Simon, I have somewhat to say unto thee." At the close of the parable he asked the Pharisee this question: "Tell me, therefore, which of them will love him most?" Simon's answer was ready, "I suppose that he to whom he forgave most." Our Lord approved of the answer; then turning to the woman, he thus continued, still speaking to Simon, "Seest thou this woman? I entered into thy house, thou gavest me no water for my feet: but she hath washed my feet with tears, and wiped them with the hairs of her head. Thou gavest me no kiss: but this woman since the time I came in hath not ceased to kiss my feet. My head with oil thou didst not anoint: but this woman hath anointed my feet with ointment. Wherefore I say unto thee, Her sins, which are many, are forgiven; for she loved much: but to whom little is forgiven, the same loveth little."

Thus did our Lord explain and apply the parable. God, even Jesus himself, was the creditor. The debtor who owed four hundred pence was the poor sinful woman, her sins were her debt; the debtor who owed but fifty was the Pharisee himself, in his own opinion far less sinful than she, and probably not guilty in truth of sins so many and so gross. In the parable both the debtors were forgiven, the one who owed much and the one who owed little. Neither could pay any thing; both were freely and fully forgiven. But was the Pharisee really forgiven? Our Lord did indeed first put the case as if he had been; but then he left it to him and to us to judge from his conduct whether he had been or not.

The debtor who had been forgiven much would, in Simon's own judgment, love more than he who had been forgiven but little. Following this out, one to whom nothing had been forgiven would not love at all. Now, how had these two persons, the Pharisee and the woman, behaved towards our Lord? The Pharisee had shown him no love at all, not even the usual civilities of a host; the woman, on the other hand, had given proof of the most devoted affection. The Pharisee had given him no water for his feet, a common attention in those countries; had not welcomed him, as was usual, with the kiss of friendship; had not paid him the customary honor of pouring oil upon his head. But the woman had supplied this neglect in a most remarkable manner. She had washed his feet with tears, and wiped them with the hairs of her head; she had humbled herself to kiss his feet, and that repeatedly; she had brought a most precious ointment, far more costly than the oil commonly used, and with it she had anointed not his head but his feet. The very lowest part of his person she thought worthy of all she could do and all she could give.

What did this conduct, so opposite, prove? The Pharisee, loving so little, had been forgiven little; nay rather, showing no love at all, could have received no forgiveness. The woman, on the other hand, loving so much, must have been forgiven much. If Simon had sought and found forgiveness, he *could* not have shown so great a want of love. Because the woman had been forgiven much, therefore she loved much. Her acts of love were a proof that she was forgiven.

This is the meaning of our Lord's words, "Wherefore I say unto thee, Her sins, which are many, are forgiven; for she loved much." They do not mean that the woman was forgiven because she loved, but that she loved because she was forgiven. First she was forgiven, and then she loved. She loved because she believed that she was forgiven. Her acts of love were thus a proof of her forgiveness. "Her sins, which are many, are forgiven, for she loved much." It was to Simon that our Lord spoke those words; and it was as though he had said to him, "Do not despise this woman, or wonder that I let her come near to me; do not suppose that I am not aware who and what she is. I know her well—far better than you do. I know all her past history. I know her present feelings, and her present state. She is penitent. She is forgiven. She loves me because I have forgiven her. You might have known the happy change in her by what you have seen her do. You have seen her show me every proof of affection. Nothing could have made her love me so but gratitude for sins forgiven. Her sins, which are many, are forgiven, for she loved much."

What follows shows clearly that this is the meaning; for, having thus spoken to Simon of the woman's conduct, he now exposes to him his own. "But to whom little is forgiven, the same loveth little." Did the Pharisee feel these words to apply to himself? Did his conscience remind him of his slighting treatment of Jesus? Did he see in his want of love a proof that he was not forgiven? And did he now learn his need, and seek and find pardon? We do not know; we are told no more about him. But for ourselves the lesson is plain. If our love is little, then we have been forgiven little. If our hearts are perfectly cold towards Christ, and we feel no gratitude and love to him at all, and are seeking to do nothing for him, then we have no proof whatever that our sins are pardoned.

A pardoned sinner loves his Saviour—not indeed as he wishes to love; but he does love truly, and the very sorrow that he feels for the coldness of his love, and his earnest desire to love more, prove that he does love in sincerity. Now if a man has nothing of this love, this sorrow, this desire, how can he have received forgiveness?

Our Lord has not spoken to the woman herself yet; but now he turns to her, and in the presence of all declares to her that she is forgiven. It was her hope, her trembling belief that she was forgiven, that made her love; now that hope and belief are fully confirmed: "Thy sins are forgiven." Could she want more than to hear her pardon from the Lord's own lips? He will give her even more. He will tell her how it was that she had received forgiveness. He will send her away in peace. For when those around murmured, then, lest an unbelieving doubt or fear should find a place in her heart, he added this, "Thy faith hath saved thee; go in peace."

Sorrow for sin, faith, pardon, love, peace; we see them all displayed in this case. What do we know of them ourselves?

This woman was "a sinner;" a gross sinner. We are all sinners; not sinners perhaps like her, yet sinners. Are we sorry for sin? Have we become convinced of sin?

She went to Jesus, she believed in him, she had faith in him. She had gone in heart before she went in person. Have *you* gone to Jesus? Have you believed in him? Have you faith in him? Have you sought his precious blood to take away your guilt?

He forgave her all. Her sins indeed were many; he himself said so: yet they were all forgiven, and that at once. There is forgiveness with him for all who go to him in faith and in sorrow for their sins. Have you received this forgiveness? Do you believe in it? Have you sought it, and that as a present blessing?

Love followed forgiveness. When she believed that she was forgiven, then at once she loved.

While yet that belief was faint and trembling, perhaps hardly more than a hope, even then she loved truly and deeply, and showed her love by all the means she could. Have you this proof that you are forgiven? Do you love Jesus? Do you do any thing to show your love?

Then followed a full assurance of forgiveness, which nothing need shake, and peace, the peace of God. It was not her works, not even her sorrow for sin, that had saved her; but her faith in Jesus. He was her Saviour, and her faith gave her a part in him. Therefore she might go in peace, and thenceforth live in peace. Have you this peace? Have you heard the voice of Jesus by the Spirit saying to you, "Thy sins are forgiven; . . . . go in peace?" He gave this peace to this woman; he left it as a legacy to his disciples; he would have every humble believer enjoy it. Seek it; seek it in faith; rest not content without it: "the peace of God which passeth all understanding."

IV.

THE FOOLISH RICH MAN.

"And one of the company said unto him, Master, speak to my brother, that he divide the inheritance with me. And he said unto him, Man, who made me a judge or a divider over you? And he said unto them, Take heed, and beware of covetousness: for a man's life consisteth not in the abundance of the things which he possesseth. And he spake a parable unto them, saying, The ground of a certain rich man brought forth plentifully: and he thought within himself, saying, What shall I do, because I have no room where to bestow my fruits? And he said, This will I do: I will pull down my barns, and build greater; and there will I bestow all my fruits and my goods. And I will say to my soul, Soul, thou hast much goods laid up for many years; take thine ease, eat, drink, and be merry. But God said unto him, Thou fool, this night thy soul shall be required of thee; then whose shall those things be which thou hast provided? So is he that layeth up treasure for himself, and is not rich toward God." LUKE 12: 13-21.

THERE was a great multitude of people gathered round our Lord at this time. This man was among them, and perhaps his brother was there too. We do not know which of them was in the right; but very likely he who spoke to our Lord was. But if he was in the right about the property, how wrong was the state of his heart. He could stand there and listen to those solemn words of our Lord, and yet be thinking all the while of nothing but the estate, and the dispute with his brother about it. If he was struck at all with what he heard, his only thought was that one who spoke with so much weight was just the person to prevail with his brother to do him justice. Whether right or wrong about the inheritance, he was clearly wrong in this, that his heart was more set on worldly than on spiritual things; so that, even while he heard Jesus himself speak, his chief interest was in the disputed inheritance.

Even we can see thus far from the account itself. But our Lord could read the man's heart, and doubtless saw much more clearly how worldly-minded and covetous he was. "Man," said he, "who made me a judge or a divider over you?" This was all his answer. Whatever the rights of the case might be, this was no question to bring to him. He came for a far higher work than to settle the rights of property. He came to save souls, and to teach men the knowledge of God. That was no time, and he was no person, for the things of this world.

Such was his answer to the man. But he then turned to the people around, who had doubtless heard what had passed, and gave them, in the form of a parable, a solemn warning against covetousness.

The parable is one of a peculiar kind, peculiar from its simplicity. There is no double meaning here, as in most of the parables. This is a plain story—a true story, for any thing we know to the contrary; at all events, a plain story of a covetous man.

He was not what would be called a bad man.

We are not told that he had got rich by wrong means. He was a rich man, and this year richer than ever, because his ground had borne such plentiful crops. So plentiful were they that he was even in a difficulty; he had not room for all. What should he do? He soon settled the question. He would pull down his old barns, and build greater, and there he would store up his property. Then he would make himself happy in the thought of his riches. In those great barns there would be corn enough to keep him in plenty for many years: he need have no anxiety; he would now enjoy life thoroughly, and indulge himself to the full. "Take thine ease," he would say to his soul, "eat, drink, and be merry."

But there was another concerned in this matter whom the rich man quite forgot. How solemn the words that follow. "But God said unto him, Thou fool, this night thy soul shall be required of thee: then whose shall these things be which thou hast provided?" The barns might be built, and the corn might be stored, and there it might last for years: but the man himself, the owner of it all, would be gone. He was about to die. Even while he thought and spoke, he was on the brink of the grave. Before to-morrow's sun should rise he would be a corpse. Whose would his wealth be then? Who would enjoy what he had laid up?

Now what was this man's fault? How was he wrong? for he *was* wrong, and foolish too.

Our Lord himself answers the question: "So is he that layeth up treasure for himself, and is not rich toward God." When his land brought forth so plentifully, his only thought was for himself. He did not consider what good he might do to others, what help he might give to the poor, what relief to the distressed. He had no intention of laying out any part of his riches in the service of God; all was to be spent on himself. "But," it may be said, "was not the corn his own? Did not his own land produce it? Was it not sown and reaped and gathered in by his own servants?" In one sense it was his own; in another it was not. It was not his own to use as he pleased, with no reference to the will of God. All that he had was given to him by God, and he was bound to use it as God willed. And it was not the will of God that he should spend all upon himself. He was but a steward, not an absolute owner.

Here is a great lesson. We are all but stewards, God's stewards, of what we have. We have no right to spend it all on ourselves. If we do so, we are unfaithful stewards, for God did not give us our goods to be spent so. Riches, and talents of every kind, bring a responsibility with them. We must account to God for their use. Alas, how many there are whose secret feeling with regard to what they have is just that of this man, "Soul, thou hast much goods laid up for many years; take thine ease, eat, drink, and be merry." How many are spending all on self, with no thought or aim beyond their own enjoyment or advancement! They lay up treasure, but it is all for themselves; they are not rich towards God. And a poor, miserable treasure it is; in danger of rust and moth and thieves; not "treasure in the heavens, that faileth not."

But this man was wrong in another respect also. "God said unto him, Thou *fool*," thou foolish man. How was he foolish? In this, that he overlooked the uncertainty of life, and laid his plans as if he were sure to continue to live. His barns were full, his riches were great; he forgot that he himself might be called away. And thus he lived all for the present life, with no thought of the future. This was foolish indeed, for eternity lay before him.

Are there none now who are foolish in the same way? None? Nay, are there not thousands, millions? At this very time, and never more than now, vast numbers are planning, and purposing, and toiling, with no object whatever beyond this world. Their faces become wrinkled with care, anxiety and over-work tell upon their bodily frame, restless desires deprive them of peace; and for what? That they may be richer and greater for a few years on earth. But meanwhile their time on earth is slipping away, life itself is passing, eternity is drawing near. And for eternity they are making no preparation. They give no thought to the awful change that death will make. They forget that death may overtake them at any moment, and must come soon. Are they not foolish, these thousands, these millions? Common as the folly is, is it not the greatest folly that can be?

In the parable the call was quick and sudden. It is not always so. More often the man of the world lives through the usual span of life, and dies at length from sickness or natural decline. He prospers perhaps in his plans, grows richer and richer, and surrounds himself with comforts. But by degrees he grows old, his power of enjoyment becomes less and less, perhaps mind and memory fail, and at length he dies. And this is all! This is what he has lived for and toiled for! Putting it at the very best, this is all. But do we never hear of sudden death now? Is it uncommon for a successful man of the world to be cut off in the midst of success, like the man in the parable? True, no message comes; but this does but make the case more awful, when, without any special message or warning, in the midst of worldly thoughts, cares, prosperity, success, the hand of God is laid upon the man, and in a moment he is taken away from all.

"Take heed, and beware of covetousness," said our Lord: "for a man's life consisteth not in the abundance of the things which he possesseth." Even the necessaries of life, such as food and clothing, are not *life;* far less are riches and luxuries. Life is more than this. Life is eternal. We are to live for ever. If we are not living now as if we were to live for ever, living for eternity, living to God, then, with all the wisdom we may show in other things, we are but fools after all. There is nothing that more hinders this than covetousness. A man's chief treasure cannot be both above and below. If it is below, then it is not above. "Take heed, and beware of covetousness." Let *all* take heed; not the rich only, but the poor also. A man may be covetous about a little as well as about much. A covetous *heart* is the thing to guard against.

There *are* true riches. Upon *them* we are to set our hearts, and for them we cannot be too desirous. They are "the unsearchable riches of Christ." Seek Christ himself for your portion, your treasure. Be willing to part with all to win him. Let this aim be first in your heart, far above all worldly gain or pleasure. Remember eternity; seek Christ; live to God, and spend your talents faithfully for him. This is to live indeed. Then you need not fear to leave earthly possessions, even should you be called away from them suddenly, for you will have a better inheritance waiting for you above, "a treasure in the heavens, that faileth not."

V.

SERVANTS WAITING FOR THEIR LORD.

"Let your loins be girded about, and your lights burning; and ye yourselves like unto men that wait for their lord, when he will return from the wedding; that when he cometh and knocketh, they may open unto him immediately. Blessed are those servants, whom the lord when he cometh shall find watching: verily I say unto you, that he shall gird himself, and make them to sit down to meat, and will come forth and serve them. And if he shall come in the second watch, or come in the third watch, and find them so, blessed are those servants. And this know, that if the goodman of the house had known what hour the thief would come, he would have watched, and not have suffered his house to be broken through. Be ye therefore ready also: for the Son of man cometh at an hour when ye think not. Then Peter said unto him, Lord, speakest thou this parable unto us, or even to all? And the Lord said, Who then is that faithful and wise steward, whom his lord shall make ruler over his household, to give them their portion of meat in due season? Blessed is that servant, whom his lord when he cometh shall find so doing. Of a truth I say unto you, that he will make him ruler over all that he hath. But and if that servant say in his heart, My lord delayeth his coming; and shall begin to beat the men-servants and maidens, and to eat and drink, and to be drunken; the lord of that servant will come in a day when he looketh not for him, and at an hour when he is not aware, and will cut him in sunder, and will appoint him his portion with the unbelievers. And that servant, which knew his lord's will, and prepared not himself, neither did according to his will, shall be beaten with many stripes. But he that knew not, and did commit things worthy of stripes, shall be beaten with few stripes. For unto whomsoever much is given, of him shall be much required: and to whom men have committed much, of him they will ask the more." LUKE 12 : 35–48.

THE men here spoken of are waiting for their master. He has gone to a wedding, probably his own wedding, to bring his bride home with him. It is night; for in that country weddings took place by night; and it is uncertain at what hour the master will come. These men are waiting therefore with their loins girded and their lights burning, so that, whenever he comes and knocks, they may be ready to open the door and go out to receive him with proper respect. They are not sleeping, and they are not misspending their time. Their thoughts are upon their absent master; their attention is fixed upon his coming; they are watching for him and expecting him. He must not come and find the house in darkness and the servants asleep, so they keep the lights burning. He must find them ready to meet him, and to do his bidding at a moment's warning, so they wait with their loins girded. Generally men used to ungird their long outer robe when they were at home, and gird it around them again only when they were actually setting out; but these men might be called to meet their master at any moment, so they wait for him with their loins ready girded.

What does this parable mean? It represents to us the way in which we, as the servants of Christ, are to wait for his return. He has gone away, and is coming back; but we know not when. We are to wait for him with our loins girded about, and our lights burning; that is, in a state of continual readiness, not putting off the getting ready till he comes, but being ready always. This is to be our state *now;* this is how we ought to be living to-day and every day. We do not know when he will come. We must be ready to welcome him whenever it may be.

We are to have our lights burning. Taking this in connection with what our Lord said elsewhere to his disciples, "Ye are the light of the world: .... let your light so shine before men, that they may see your good works, and glorify your Father which is in heaven," we may understand it to mean, that we are to be leading a consistent Christian life, adorning our profession as believers in the Lord Jesus Christ, not ashamed of him, not hiding our principles, but showing ourselves to be his disciples indeed, decided Christians, coming out from the world, taking up the cross and following Christ.

We are also to have our loins girded about. Thus we are to be ready to meet him when he comes. But we are also to be always ready for every call of duty; not idle, slothful, self-indulgent, but active and zealous; so that when he comes he may find us doing his work. Some people are always putting off the great concern; but this parable teaches us most forcibly that we must not put it off, that it is to be attended to *now*. "Let your loins be girded about, and your lights burning." Do not delay. Be not content with thinking, meaning, resolving. Let the care of your soul and a readiness for the Master's coming be a present thing with you, a thing of to-day, a thing of every day, and the most important thing of all. Let it be so in your esteem, for it is so really.

"Blessed are those servants, whom the lord when he cometh shall find watching." Blessed and happy would such servants be in the parable; more blessed still those servants of the Lord Jesus Christ who will thus be found ready when he comes.

Blessed, because they will not be taken by surprise. Sudden as his coming will be, sudden and awful, yet it will not come upon *them* unawares. It will be different perhaps from all their thoughts of it; far more solemn and overwhelming than they have ever conceived; yet it will not surprise them, for they have been long thinking of it, preparing for it, watching for it. To thousands and thousands it will come as a thief in the night, but not to *them*, for their loins are girded about and their lights burning. "Blessed are those servants."

They are blessed also, because they love their Lord, and are glad to see him come. He has been long away; and though they have had some tastes of his presence by the Spirit and in his ordinances, yet there have been many things to interfere with their enjoyment of his presence, and even to hide him from their souls. But now he *comes;* he himself, in very person, their own loved Saviour and Lord. To know him by faith, to pray to him, to think of him, has long been their best happiness; but now he comes, and they see him, and he knows them and owns them his, and they are to be with him always. "Blessed are those servants." Aye, blessed indeed. Whatever their lot has been hitherto—poor, afflicted, persecuted—at least they are blessed now; for all this is past for ever. No more want, affliction, persecution; no more sorrow or pain; no more of any thing sad or sinful. The Lord is come; that is enough; they want no more. "Blessed are those servants."

But something further is said here about their blessedness: "Verily I say unto you, that he shall gird himself, and make them to sit down to meat, and will come forth and serve them." Generally the servant waits on the master, not the master on the servant. Was not this what the servants in the parable were watching for, to receive their master when he came, and wait on him, and do his bidding? And would it not be happiness enough for the servants of Christ to serve him? Yet in his wonderful condescension and grace he says that he will make them to sit down to meat, and will come forth and serve them. The lord will serve the servants. What does it mean? for of course it is a figure, a part of the parable.

Doubtless it means the great honor and happiness which the faithful servants of Christ will receive at his coming. They will be more than safe. They will be welcomed to happiness and glory. Every want will be supplied. They will receive more than they have ever hoped for or thought of. And what they receive they will receive from their Lord himself. It is he that will supply their wants; he himself will be their shepherd, their light, their portion. "They shall hunger no more, neither thirst any more; neither shall the sun light on them, nor any heat. For the Lamb which is in the midst of the throne shall feed them, and shall lead them unto living fountains of waters: and God shall wipe away all tears from their eyes." "Behold, I stand at the door, and knock: if any man hear my voice, and open the door, I will come in to him, and will sup with him, and he with me. To him that overcometh will I grant to sit with me in my throne, even as I also overcame, and am sit down with my Father in his throne."

At whatever time the Lord may come, such will be the blessedness of those who are found watching. "And if he shall come in the second watch, or come in the third watch, and find them so, blessed are those servants." At whatever period of the world's history, at whatever age in their own life, whenever and however the Lord may come, blessed are those servants. To some he may come early in life, to others late; some may long have been looking for him, others may only lately have been roused to know him and to wait for him. It matters not; "blessed are those servants," *all* those servants, all who are waiting for him with their loins girded about and their lights burning.

At this point our Lord for a moment changes the figure. It was his custom to teach by means of particular things that had happened, as well as by parables drawn from nature and from more usual and general events. Perhaps some man's house had lately been broken into by night, and all who heard him speak were then full of the subject.

Perhaps it was some particular case that he alluded to, when he said, "And this know, that if the good man of the house had known what hour the thief would come, he would have watched, and would not have suffered his house to be broken through." At all events, by this little parable spoken in the midst of the other one, he enforces still more strongly the solemn lesson, "Be ye therefore ready also: for the Son of man cometh at an hour when ye think not." The master of the servants did not tell them at what hour he would return; the thief gave no notice what part of the night he would choose for breaking into the house, or even that he would come at all. The servants therefore watched all night till their master returned, and the householder would have done the same had any warning been given. Let Christians do likewise. They have received warning that their Lord will come, but they have not been told when; nay, they have been told expressly that they are not to know this, but that he will come unexpectedly. "For the Son of man cometh at an hour when ye think not." Their only right posture then is that of "men that wait for their Lord." This is how they are to live always. Thus only can they make sure of being ready. Thus only can they secure a share in this blessedness; "blessed are those servants."

Peter asked whether the parable was spoken to them only—that is, to himself and his fellow-disciples who heard the words, or to all. Our Lord's answer shows that it was meant for all. Whoever should be a faithful and wise steward, whether among those disciples or not, and whether set over much or over little, whoever should be such in any age, that man should have a share in the blessedness of the faithful servants. On the other hand, whoever should be an unfaithful servant, forgetting his master, abusing his trust, wasting his time, misusing his talents, not watching or preparing for his master's return, that servant should find it a terrible return for him. The greater the trust the heavier would be the responsibility; the higher the station, the richer the gifts, the wider the opportunities, so much the greater the condemnation if they should be ill employed. All the servants of Christ do not receive alike; all will not be dealt with alike. Every unfaithful servant will be dealt with according to what he has received. And all have received something.

How solemn, how awful is the warning, "Be ye therefore ready also: for the Son of man cometh at an hour when ye think not!" Be *ye* ready. Who? All. All to whom the message comes, every human being who has heard of Jesus and of the great day. Be ye ready. For blessed beyond all words will ye be, if ye be found watching; and ruined and undone for ever will ye be, if that day find you unprepared. And, knowing this, will you trifle away your life, and waste day after day, and turn a deaf ear to the voice of God, when at any moment, with no further warning, the Lord may come? Do you realize what you are doing? Have you ever considered the eternal consequences of your present life?

It was in mercy that the Saviour spoke this warning, and it is in mercy that it comes to you. He invites you, calls you, as well as warns you. "Blessed is that servant!" Well, such a servant *you* may be. Whatever watch of the night it may now be, how near or how far off soever the Lord's coming may be, or at whatever time of life you may have arrived without seeking him, seek him *now*, begin now at length to wait for him with your loins girded about and your lights burning; and even now the blessedness may be yours. "Blessed are those servants, whom the Lord when he cometh shall find watching."

VI.

The Unfruitful Fig-Tree.

"He spake also this parable: A certain man had a fig-tree planted in his vineyard; and he came and sought fruit thereon, and found none. Then said he unto the dresser of his vineyard, Behold, these three years I come seeking fruit on this fig-tree, and find none: cut it down; why cumbereth it the ground? And he answering said unto him, Lord, let it alone this year also, till I shall dig about it, and dung it: and if it bear fruit, well: and if not, then after that thou shalt cut it down." Luke 13 : 6–9.

THE fig-tree was planted in the vineyard; not growing wild, but set by the hand of man in a cultivated place. Care and pains had been bestowed on it. In this respect it represents our state. We are not heathen men, growing wild as it were, in the wilderness of the world. We have been brought by God's providence within the sound of the gospel, and within reach of the means of grace; we are called by the name of Christ, and in profession at least are his disciples. We are all planted in the vineyard.

God himself is the Lord of this vineyard. And, like the man in the parable, he seeks fruit from it. One particular tree is mentioned in the parable, but doubtless the owner looked for fruit on every tree. So God looks for fruit from every professing Christian; not merely from the church as a body, but from each member of it. The owner of the vineyard came several times seeking fruit on the fig-tree. God's eye is always on us, to see if we are bearing fruit. He needs not to come seeking fruit; "the eyes of the Lord are in every place," and that at every moment.

Nothing but fruit would satisfy the owner of the vineyard, nothing but fruit will satisfy God. But what fruit? Spiritual fruit, the fruits of righteousness, the proper effects of the gospel in heart and life; a contrite and believing heart, a holy and useful life. He looks to see Christians, Christians indeed; adorning their profession, growing in grace, loving and serving their Lord and Master, and so living as to win others to love and serve him too. A clear knowledge and a loud profession will no more content almighty God, than branches and leaves would satisfy the owner of the vineyard. There must be fruit, or the tree is counted worthless.

There was such a tree in the vineyard, a fig-tree that bore no fruit. Three years did the man seek fruit on it, and found none. We may gather from this that it made a fair show, or it would not have been left standing so long. But it was nothing but show; at the end of three years there was still no fruit. Alas! how many are unfruitful in the spiritual vineyard! And how long does God look for fruit from them in vain! Year after year they have a place in the vineyard, receiving gifts from God every day, both temporal and spiritual; hearing the gospel, surrounded by Christian influences,

THE UNFRUITFUL FIG-TREE. 53

and themselves professing to be Christians, yet producing no fruit whatever. Though they have so long heard the gospel, they have never heartily embraced it; and though, like the fig-tree in the vineyard, they have perhaps fruitful trees around them, real Christians who live with them, it may be in the same house, and form part of the same family, yet they remain cold and dead and unprofitable, Christians in nothing but the name.

At length the man in the parable was tired of seeing this useless tree in his vineyard. It did but take up room to no purpose. It did no good, and seemed never likely to do good. It should stand no longer. So he gave orders to the dresser of the vineyard, "Cut it down; why cumbereth it the ground?" We do not hear such a command given with regard to an unprofitable Christian; for God works in secret, and does not make known to us what he is about to do in any particular case. But we know from his word that, sooner or later, every unprofitable servant will be cast out, and will come to eternal ruin. God is long-suffering. He bears long with sinners, sends them his messages again and again, and still waits to be gracious. But not for ever. "If a man will not turn, he will whet his sword; he hath bent his bow, and made it ready." And no impenitent sinner or unfruitful professor is safe for one moment from the word going forth against him, "Cut it down; why cumbereth it the ground?"

How many are condemned by this very word! How many are mere cumberers of the ground!

They may not be grossly wicked, they may even be of moral character and respectable life; but they do no good, they do not use their talents in God's service, they give no help towards advancing the kingdom of Christ, they do but live for themselves. This is not the object for which they were placed in the world, and gifted with means and opportunities. They were meant to act as stewards of God, and to do him service with all that he committed to their charge. They are unfaithful stewards, unprofitable servants; no better than the unfruitful tree which took up room in the vineyard to no purpose.

The order was given; but the dresser of the vineyard put in a word for the tree. He did not deny that it was an unfruitful tree at present, but he asked for one year more for it. He would take more pains than ever with it. He would dig the ground about it, and put fresh manure to its roots. This might make it bear fruit; and if so, it would be well: the time and pains would be well repaid. But if it should still bear no fruit, then let it be cut down; the dresser himself would not ask that it should be spared any longer.

Who is meant by the dresser of the vineyard? The Lord Jesus Christ. He is our Mediator and Advocate. He pleads for us with God. He pleads even for the rebellious. Who among the careless and unprofitable can tell what he may even now be owing to the intercession of the Lord Jesus? It may be that he is alive at this moment, that he still hears the gospel, and that it is preached in his hearing more plainly and powerfully perhaps than ever, just because the Mediator has pleaded for him, and further time has been granted, and further means are being employed. It may be that sorrow has fallen upon one, and sickness on another, for the very same reason: they were careless and unfruitful, and they were about to be cut down, but Jesus pleaded for them, and these are his dealings with them to lead them to God.

If so, how precious is the time which they are now passing! It was only one year more for which the fig-tree was to be spared. You too may be passing through your last stage of life. You may even now be getting to the end of that space of time which was asked for on your behalf by the Friend of sinners. Will you be careless still? Will you still live as a mere nominal Christian, unfruitful, unprofitable, a cumberer of the ground? Think. The moments are slipping away, never to return; the means of grace which you are now enjoying, or which are at least within your reach, have been given you in God's great mercy, in order that you may be led, while yet there is time, to feel your need and to seek Christ, and these too are passing away. What if you should still neglect time and means? What if this last stage of life should pass with you as every former stage has passed? What then? Let the parable answer the question: "Then after that, thou shalt cut it down." How sad! How awful! No more pleading of the Lord Jesus then. Not a word more. And who shall plead for you when Jesus pleads no more? And who shall stand your friend when even the Friend of sinners leaves you to yourself?

Be warned. Be moved. Warned by so fearful a risk, moved by so great forbearance and mercy. Jesus pleads for you, his intercession is heard, time and means are granted, you have them now. Lose not a moment. Rise, and call upon God. Seek Christ as your Saviour. Seek him in earnest. Seek him as your only refuge. Seek him as one ought to seek him who has long neglected him, but who has been spared to seek him at last. Seek him, and pray that all the past may be forgiven through his atoning blood; and that through grace, what remains of life may be heartily given to God, so that you may be found at last not unfruitful, not a cumberer of the ground.

VII.

The Sower.

THE SEED THAT FELL BY THE WAYSIDE.

"And he taught them many things by parables, and said unto them in his doctrine, Hearken; Behold, there went out a sower to sow: and it came to pass, as he sowed, some fell by the wayside, and the fowls of the air came and devoured it up." MARK 4:2-4; see also MATT. 13 and LUKE 8.

THE parable of the Sower is one of the most important. It is fuller than almost any of the others, and more close and particular in its application; and it is one of those which our Lord himself explained. It represents four different kinds of hearers of the word, and each kind forms a subject by itself. We will consider the parable therefore in four readings, taking now the first kind only.

The beginning of the parable applies alike to all the kinds of hearers. The seed and the sower are the same in each case; it is the ground that is different. "The seed is the word of God;" sowing the seed means preaching the word, or teaching it in any way; a sower therefore is any minister or preacher of the gospel.

"There went out a sower to sow;" that is, a

preacher went forth to preach. How often this takes place. Not to speak of other days or other lands, in our own country and on every Lord's day how many sowers go forth to sow, how many thousands of preachers stand up to proclaim the glad tidings of the gospel! The seed they sow is good seed, precious seed. In what the preachers say in explaining the Scriptures there is a mixture of imperfection, for they are but men; but in the word which they preach there is no imperfection, for it is the word of God. The sermon may not be free from fault, but the text is faultless. And even in the sermon the faithful and prayerful minister may look for help from above. The seed therefore is good seed. The word is the word of God, though it is preached by man. It is the great business of the sowers, the ministers of Christ, to sow this seed, to preach this word; and they are constantly doing so.

"As he sowed, some fell by the wayside." This represents a careless hearer. Ground by the wayside is generally trodden hard, so that the seed does not sink in, but rests on the surface just where it fell. The careless hearer's heart is like this ground, hard and cold, not in a state to receive the word. This man has come to the place where the word is preached. Perhaps he was obliged to come there; perhaps he came because it is respectable to come, or because he would not have felt easy in staying away. But he did not come in a spirit of prayer. He did not come for the good of his soul. He did not come to hear God's message to him. He did not come hungering and thirsting after righteousness, desiring "the sincere milk of the word." He listens perhaps, but he does not care for what he hears, or apply it to himself. Perhaps he does not even listen, but lets his mind go off to other subjects, without even an effort to fix his attention. Perhaps even while the most solemn truths are being spoken in his hearing, he is thinking of some mere trifle, or looking around him, or longing for the sermon to be over. Such is a wayside hearer. So he comes, and so he hears. Are there many such? Alas, how many! Doubtless, even when the sower was the Lord himself, some seed fell by the wayside. And seldom, if ever, is the word preached by his servants without being heard by some who are but wayside hearers. There are many such hearers in most congregations. For our Lord was describing not merely what happened under one preaching of the gospel, but what would take place in general. And perhaps he put this class of hearers first, because they are so many and so common.

What became of the seed that fell by the wayside? Just what might be expected: "the fowls of the air came and devoured it up." This is thus explained: "But when they have heard, Satan cometh immediately, and taketh away the word that was sown in their hearts;" "lest," as St. Luke's account adds, "they should believe and be saved."

The object of the preaching of the word is to save souls; the aim of Satan is to destroy souls. Satan therefore is on the watch to hinder the word from finding a place in the heart. Not more ready are the birds to carry off the seed that is left uncovered by the side of the path, than is Satan to snatch away the word from the heart of the careless hearer. The word lies there ready for him. It has not pierced the soil of the heart. It has found no entrance. It is all on the surface. The enemy has but little difficulty in such a case. This, we may believe, is one of his easiest works. If the conscience had been at all touched, if the heart had been ever so little moved, if even the interest had been strongly excited, the work would not have been so easy; for then, so to speak, the seed would have had some covering. But now it lies quite naked and exposed. The word has been heard, and that is all. It is snatched away at once.

Alas, how much precious seed of the word is thus sown in vain! In vain at least as far as the careless hearer is concerned; yet not in vain for all who hear. For it is not with the seed of the word as it is with the natural seed, that a grain that falls by the wayside and is plucked away is quite useless. The very same words that are heard so carelessly by one are listened to with deep attention by another. The message from God which finds no entrance into one heart proves a word of life to another. The careless hearer sits side by side perhaps with one who is eagerly drinking in every sentence. The word is the same, the preacher is the same, but how different are the hearers! This seems to make the case of the careless all the more sad and solemn. The word which is immediately plucked away by Satan might have been the saving of his soul. That which is gone from him in a moment, forgotten as soon as heard, might have been precious spiritual food. It is so to others. It might have been so to him.

The careless hearer will have a heavy reckoning hereafter. The word that he has heard, though plucked away at the very moment of hearing, will rise up and condemn him. The poor benighted heathen, who never in all his life heard the sound of the gospel, and lived and died in darkness and sin, will have a far less heavy account to give than this man. Of those who have received much, much will be required. Ah, how will long-forgotten words then come back to the mind! They were little thought of at the time. It was a weariness perhaps to hear them. Right glad was the hearer when the tedious hour was over and he might leave the house of God. Not one thought of what he had heard was in his mind as he walked away; from that moment it was as if he had not heard; for the seed was snatched away. But *now* solemn words come back to the memory. He remembers that he used to hear such words. He remembers how he used to hear them; with what carelessness and unconcern. The seed that was plucked away seems to be there again; but it cannot grow now. The word that appeared quite gone from the mind is remembered again; but it cannot now save the soul. It is too late. The careless hearer would like to hear again. He would not, he thinks, be a careless hearer now. Alas, it cannot be. The day of grace is past, and the day of reckoning has come.

It is but a little while that separates us from that day. It will soon be here. Yet men are hearing carelessly still. Every time the seed is sown there is some that falls by the wayside; in every congregation there are careless hearers. It is a solemn and awful thing to hear the message of life so; to sit where God's message to souls is being delivered, and to hear it; to be spoken to, appealed to, invited, warned, urged, and all in God's name, and yet to hear carelessly. When this takes place the enemy has his will; for his will is expressed in these words: "*lest* they should believe and be saved."

Oh, beware of careless hearing; beware of the wiles of Satan; come to the hearing of the word with preparation of heart; hear it seriously, earnestly, prayerfully, watchfully. It is the greatest blessing to live within sound of the word, for this word is the gospel of salvation. But every blessing brings responsibility; and a blessing despised or slighted will turn to condemnation. Satan's wiles are dangerous, and his power is great; but God's power is greater. Pray for the gift of the Spirit in the hearing of the word. Watch and pray.

THE SEED THAT FELL ON STONY GROUND.

"And some fell on stony ground, where it had not much earth: and immediately it sprang up, because it had no depth of earth: but when the sun was up, it was scorched; and because it had no root, it withered away." MARK 4 : 5, 6.

THE words "stony ground" do not exactly represent our Lord's meaning; "rocky ground" would represent it better. The passage in St. Luke is: "and some fell upon a rock." The meaning evidently is, that in the field, or perhaps along the edge of it, were rocks, or large ridges of stone, on which some of the seed fell. There was a thin sprinkling of earth on the rock; enough for the seed to take root in, but not enough to give it nourishment afterwards. Indeed, this seed sprang up before any of the rest; for the sun's rays, beating on the rock, made the thin covering of earth warmer than the soil around. The seed therefore sprang up quickly; probably in the night. But when the sun shone out bright and hot, as it does in those eastern countries, the heat proved too great for the tender plant. Having no depth of earth to strike its roots into, and being unable to penetrate the hard rock beneath, it had but little strength; and so it was scorched, and withered away. The warmth of the sun given out by the rock made it spring up quickly; but the sun's burning heat by day made it as quickly wither and die. The plant came to nothing.

Our Lord explains this part of the parable thus: "And these are they likewise which are sown on stony ground; who, when they have heard the word, immediately receive it with gladness; and have no root in themselves, and so endure but for a time: afterward, when affliction or persecution ariseth for the word's sake, immediately they are offended."

These hearers are not careless hearers, like the first class. The word attracts their attention. They listen, and are interested. What they hear pleases, and even affects them. Being probably by nature eager and warm-hearted, they receive the word with joy, and seem heartily to embrace the gospel. Thus far all looks well. So it did at first with the plant that grew up on the rocky ground. But there was a fault there, and so there is here—a want of depth, and therefore a want of root. Like the shallow soil heated by the warmth of the sun, their feelings are easily moved, and an effect seems quickly to follow on their hearing of the word. But there is no deep work in the heart. The effect produced is with them more a thing of feeling than of real impression or principle. There is no counting of the cost, no calm and decided giving up of themselves to Christ, no taking up of the cross and following him. When the time of trial comes, they prove to be but fair-weather Christians.

They "endure but for a time." It may be a longer or a shorter time, according to circumstances. But when they are called to suffer for Christ—when they must submit to being disliked, laughed at, or even persecuted for his sake, then they fail. They are offended; that is, these things are a hinderance or stumbling-block which they cannot get over. They held on while the world smiled on them; but they cannot endure its frown. They could follow Christ through good report; they cannot follow him through evil. They were no hypocrites. They did not *pretend* to hear the word with gladness; they *did* hear it with gladness; they meant to be disciples of Christ, and thought they were so; but they had no root, and so in time of temptation they fall away.

It is a sad case, but not an uncommon one, especially with the young. The young are generally warm and eager in their feelings, quickly worked upon, readily moved; and there is indeed much in the gospel to move the feelings. But something more than this is needed. There must be the work of the Spirit in the heart; a true change wrought within. This alone can give depth and root; this alone can lead one who has received the word with gladness to remain steadfast under affliction or persecution. Without this, however impressible the feelings may be, like the shallow soil on the rock, yet, for any saving reception of the gospel, the heart remains like the hard stone beneath. What then? Did our Lord mean to check the glad hearing of the word, or to damp the ardor of the young disciple? Not so. Let the word be heard with gladness—with even more gladness than ever. The happiest tidings that mortal ear can listen to, the gospel of salvation, the free offer, the sure promise—let it be heard with joy, for well it may. The seed that fell on the rock was doing its rightful office when it sprang up so quickly; the warm earth on the rock's surface was doing its proper work when it cherished the seed and brought forth the plant. So far all was well; the fault was afterwards, in the want of depth of earth to nourish the plant. So it is well that the word be heard with gladness. Let none keep back their hearts from Him who claims them. Let no cold caution be suffered to quench the rising flame. Let there be no delay, no reserve. The gospel calls; let the call be obeyed. It offers pardon; let the offer be accepted. It appeals to the feelings and the affections; let the feelings and affections yield to the appeal, and that at once. The fault was not that the seed sprang up immediately, but that it had no depth of earth. And the reason why some who gladly hear the word afterwards fall away is, not that they heard gladly, but that they had no root. They might have heard gladly, and have had root too.

Do not seek then to stifle those ardent feelings; do not check your delight in the word; do not think that it is wrong or dangerous to have your affections deeply moved by the gospel; only do not build upon feelings or impressions; build upon Christ, and upon him alone; know your own weakness and instability, and pray earnestly for the Holy Spirit. Ask that the work in you may be a real work, a deep work, a lasting work, such as shall abide in the hour of trial.

Will not God hear such a prayer? Surely he will. It was said of our Lord in prophecy: "A bruised reed shall he not break, and smoking flax shall he not quench, till he send forth judgment unto victory." He spoke this parable not to discourage, but to warn. And he himself said that God would give the Holy Spirit to them that asked him. Pray in faith of that promise. "Ask, and it shall be given you; seek, and ye shall find; knock, and it shall be opened unto you." Pray that your heart may not remain hard like the rock, but may be truly softened by the Spirit; and that thus you may receive the word with gladness, not merely in the surface feelings of an ardent nature, but in the deep faith of a believing heart.

THE SEED THAT FELL AMONG THORNS.

"And some fell among thorns, and the thorns grew up, and choked it, and it yielded no fruit." MARK 4:7.

THESE "thorns" were briers or brambles, or something of that sort. The ground had not been thoroughly cleared of them, and so they sprang up with the seed, and being of stronger growth, choked the young plants. Their roots robbed the plants of nourishment, their trailing stems smothered them, and their leaves shaded them from the light and warmth of the sun. Perhaps these plants did not wither and die like the last, but they became weak and sickly, and yielded no fruit.

Here is our Lord's explanation of this part of the parable: "And these are they which are sown among thorns; such as hear the word, and the cares of this world, and the deceitfulness of riches, and the lusts of other things entering in, choke the word, and it becometh unfruitful."

In this case the *world* is the hinderance. A hearer of this class is not careless like the first, and he receives a deeper impression from the word than the second. There may not be in him the same lively pleasure in hearing the word as in the last case, for nothing is said about his hearing with gladness. Perhaps, when cares and riches are mentioned, our Lord's words point rather to those who are older and have more to do with worldly business, as the part before seems especially to describe the young. If so, this hearer has lost somewhat of youthful warmth; he is not so easily impressed as he once was, nor are his feelings so readily excited; he is more calm and grave. Yet the word has made an impression on him—a strong impression; stronger and deeper, it would seem, than in the case before. Through the remainder of the day on which the word has been heard, his thoughts probably are serious, his purposes and resolutions sincere and earnest.

But the day of rest comes to a close, and he wakes on Monday morning to find himself again surrounded by the cares of business. And he is not enough aware of the dangers of the world. He does not watch against being too much engrossed by it. He lets himself give his whole mind to cares and riches. The desire to get on in the world, or to increase his business, or even to provide for his children, (for the word "lusts" does not necessarily mean *wrong* desires,) is suffered to be first with him. He forgets our Lord's words, "Seek ye first the kingdom of God and his righteousness." He is busy from morning till night; his thoughts are wholly occupied. Thus the word is almost forgotten; or if not forgotten, it has lost its life and power in his heart. The serious thoughts, the earnest resolutions have faded away; the word is choked.

St. Luke uses the words "*go forth*, and are choked." The man goes forth into the world again after the retirement and rest of the Lord's day. There is no harm in his going forth. He must go forth, he must mix again with men, he must busy himself again in his worldly concerns; but he need not go forth and forget. He might go forth, prepared by earnest prayer and in a spirit of watchfulness, and thus meet the temptations of the world. He might go forth, armed with the Christian's armor, "the whole armor of God," which each soldier and servant of Christ is to put on; then the seed would not be choked. It is possible, by God's grace, to be in the world, yet not of the world; to be rich and busy, to be engaged in great concerns, to have many cares, and yet to be seeking first the kingdom of God and his righteousness. The word that was heard on Sunday is often choked in the week that follows; but it need not be.

A hearer of this class thus hears the word, and then lets it be choked by the world, not once only, but often. As years roll on, perhaps he becomes even more engrossed in cares and business. Worldly concerns get more and more hold on him. His desires are enlarged, his riches increase, his anxieties increase too. What is the consequence? He hears the word still. He attends perhaps the same ministry, and still approves of what he hears. But the word has lost much of its power over him. He does not even at the time feel it as he used to feel it. He has not room for it, his thoughts are so full of the world. Thus the word is choked, smothered, overwhelmed. This hearer brings no fruit to perfection, no fruit that ripens. There was once a fair promise, and there is still some show of fruit; but the plant is sickly, being choked with other things; it does not get on, it cannot grow; it will come to nothing, and prove unfruitful.

But pleasures are mentioned in St. Luke's account as well as cares and riches—the "pleasures of this life," worldly pleasures; and probably "the lusts of other things entering in," mean the same, in part at least. The seed of the word is as often choked by pleasures as by business. The young are especially exposed to this danger. Many a youthful hearer of the word, who has heard it with deep attention, and has felt at the time strongly drawn to give himself to the Lord, has afterwards gone forth and mixed eagerly in the pleasures of the world, often against the voice of conscience, and thus the seed has been choked. Not all at once, not without many a painful struggle, not without repeated convictions and repeated giving way to temptation; slowly and gradually, yet surely; for it is a dangerous thing to go against conscience; and how can one hope for God's supporting and strengthening grace, who is daily acting against God's voice, the voice within his own heart, and the voice in the word?

But are the young to be always grave? Is youth, the season of joy and gladness, of high spirits and bright hopes—is youth to be debarred of pleasure? Not so. This is a question often asked, or rather a charge often brought by the world; but it has no foundation in the gospel. On the contrary, true religion has pleasures, and pleasures for the young too, such as nothing else can give. It is not merely, as some seem to think, a sad necessity, a way of getting ready for death when life shall come to a close, a wise precaution against what must come. It is not merely this; it is much more. "Godliness is profitable unto all things, having promise of the life that now is, and of that which is to come." Of the life that now is—the present life, the life both of old and young—godliness has promise of it; it can make it happy; it does make it happy. Even in youth, godliness, or true religion, gives pleasure and makes life happy.

True, it calls off the young from the pleasures of sin, shows them the vanity of the world, and bids them not seek their happiness in a vain and thoughtless course of life. But does it give them nothing instead? It tells them of a Saviour, and a Saviour for *them*; speaks to them of the love of God; bids them rejoice. It opens to them in Christ a source of inward comfort and happiness, such as will never fail them, such as will bear thinking of—real, solid, true, and lasting; and, besides, it leaves them in full possession of all right and innocent pleasures of this life. They may be cheerful with all the cheerfulness of youth. They are not debarred from light-hearted merriment. They may enjoy, and enjoy as none else can enjoy them, the works of God. Beautiful scenery, plants, birds, music—they may enjoy all these, and find God in them all. The treasures of knowledge and of science are open to them. They may make full use of all the powers which God has bestowed on them. And lastly, they may do good; they may have the pleasure of giving pleasure to others—pleasure, comfort, and help. They may have the delight of serving Christ. Young as they are, they may even now live and act in such a way as that our Lord's words shall apply to them, "Inasmuch as ye have done it unto one of the least of these my brethren, ye have done it unto me." Is all this nothing? Is it true that the young Christian, who strives that the word may not be choked in him by worldly pleasures, does in fact give up pleasure altogether? Has he not rather the best of pleasures? Are any of the young so happy as he is?

We should judge of worldly things by the effect they have upon us with regard to the word of God. Does such and such a pursuit occupy me too much? Does it deaden or weaken the power of the word in my heart? Do I feel, after indulging in such and such a pleasure, that I do not care for the word as I did, that it has lost its hold on me, that it seems inconsistent and out of place? Do I ever feel so full of business or cares that I have no time or heart for serious things? If so, there is a fault somewhere. Either the thing itself is wrong, or I am wrong in giving myself to it too much. Let the work of self-examination be faithful and strict. Let it be deeply considered how precious the word of God is, and how sad is the case of those in whom it brings no fruit to perfection. No fruit? Then no comfort, no peace, no happiness, no salvation, no life eternal. Yet it is the word of *life*. Alas, that it should be choked!

THE SEED THAT FELL ON GOOD GROUND.

"And other fell on good ground, and did yield fruit that sprang up and increased; and brought forth, some thirty, and some sixty, and some a hundred." MARK 4:8.

WE have seen the seed proving unfruitful in three different ways: some falling by the wayside and devoured by birds, other falling on rocky ground and withering for want of soil, and other choked by thorns. Now at length we come to seed that produced fruit, or corn. This seed fell on good ground; not by the wayside, not where there was no depth of earth, not among thorns, but in good and sufficient soil. There it sprang up, and grew, and brought forth fruit. Not all equally, however: "some thirty, and some sixty, and some a hundred." All bore fruit, but some bore much fruit.

It is happy to find that all the seed did not come to nothing. It is happy also that the word of God is not in every case "of none effect." Our Lord thus explains this part of the parable: "And these are they which are sown on good ground; such as hear the word and receive it, and bring forth fruit, some thirtyfold, some sixty, and some a hundred." Or, according to St. Matthew, thus: "But he that received seed into the good ground is he that heareth the word and understandeth it; which also beareth fruit, and bringeth forth some a hundredfold, some sixty, some thirty." Or, once more, according to St. Luke, as follows: "But that on the good ground are they, which, in an honest and good heart, having heard the word, keep it, and bring forth fruit with patience."

The seed was the same as in the other cases; the difference was in the place in which it fell. So the word is the same word; the difference is in the hearers. In each of the other cases there was something that hindered the word from working its proper effect. Here it did so. Why? Because here it was received in an honest and good heart, and not only received but kept there; heard, but not heard only; heard and attended to, and so understood; received in earnest; received deeply, seriously, and lastingly; not forgotten again, not let slip, not suffered to be snatched away, or choked by other things.

But what does "an honest and good heart" mean? Is any heart such? Is not the heart of man an evil heart?

It may mean simply a heart unlike those of the hearers mentioned before; not indeed in itself *good*, and yet not careless, unstable, or worldly, like them, but sincere and in earnest, desirous to know the truth, and resolved to follow it; humble, teachable, and upright. But probably we are to understand more by it than this. In the full sense of the words, "an honest and good heart" must mean a heart renewed by grace, a heart which the Holy Spirit has prepared to receive the seed of the word. No mere natural sincerity and earnestness will lead to all that follows here—a true receiving of the word, an understanding of it, a keeping of it in the heart, and a bringing forth of fruit in the life, and that with patience or perseverance. This must be the work of the Spirit, making a change, preparing the heart for the word, and applying it with power. Let us pray for this preparation of heart. Whenever we are about to hear the word, let us ask that the Holy Spirit may make us ready to receive it.

The bringing forth fruit hardly wants explanation, and accordingly we find none given by our Lord; the same word, "fruit," is used both in the parable and in the explanation of it. Fruit, it is clear, means all that effect on the heart and life which the word of God is meant to produce; the very same, indeed, as what is elsewhere called "the fruit of the Spirit"—"love, joy, peace, long-suffering, gentleness, goodness, faith, meekness, temperance." Gal. 5:22, 23. The fruitful hearer, in short, is not a hearer only, but a doer of the word—a true believer, a spiritual and practical Christian, living by the word of God, zealous in good works.

But in the parable we find different degrees of fruitfulness: "some thirtyfold, some sixty, and some a hundred." Christians differ much in fruitfulness; and partly, no doubt, because they differ so much in advantages and in the means of grace. But this can hardly be the meaning here, for all this seed was sown at once—it was one and the same preaching of the word. There is a difference even among those who have enjoyed equal advantages. The word, though truly received, does not produce equal effects in all. Our aim should be to produce *much* fruit. Our Lord teaches us this elsewhere: "Every branch that beareth fruit, he purgeth it, that it may bring forth more fruit;" "He that abideth in me, and I in him, the same bringeth forth *much* fruit." And again: "Herein is my Father glorified, that ye bear *much* fruit; so shall ye be my disciples." We must not then rest satisfied with a low standard of holiness, or be content to serve God a little. It is a happy thing, through grace, really to receive the word with the heart, and to bring forth any fruit to his glory; but let us aim high, let us press forward, let our desire be to be among those who bring forth fruit "a hundredfold."

There were three classes of unfruitful hearers, and only one that was fruitful. We may learn from this that, with regard to the hearing of the word, as well as more generally, there are many wrong ways, but only one right way. But we may also learn a yet more solemn lesson, that but few hear with profit compared with the number who hear in vain. Those are striking words of our Lord: "Enter ye in at the strait gate; for wide is the gate, and broad is the way, that leadeth to destruction, and many there be which go in thereat; because strait is the gate, and narrow is the way, which leadeth unto life, and few there be that find it." Many unfruitful hearers, and many travellers along the broad way; but few hearers bringing forth fruit, and few travellers going by the narrow way. This is but the same truth under two different forms. A very solemn truth. It should set us on the work of self-examination.

The seed is sown in *us* continually; often do we hear the word. What kind of hearers are we? Does any one of these classes represent our case? and if so, which? What has the hearing of the word done for us up to this time? What fruit appears in heart and life? Has it humbled our pride? Has it brought us to true repentance? Has it led us in faith to the Lord Jesus Christ? "Faith cometh by hearing, and hearing by the word of God." Has this faith, this saving faith, come to *us* by hearing the word? Do the fruits of faith appear and abound in our lives? Are we bringing forth fruit continually to God's glory—thirtyfold, sixtyfold, or a hundredfold? Are we desiring to bring forth *more* fruit? Are we pressing towards the mark? Are we growing in grace?

The lips of Him who spake as never man spake uttered this parable, and he himself gave the explanation of it. He spoke it for all ages. He spoke it for us. For when he had come to the close he said: "He that hath ears to hear, let him hear." We who read those words in the inspired book may take them as addressed to us by the Lord. They call for our attention, they appeal to our conscience, they speak to us personally and individually. The Lord Jesus himself speaks to us by them. Hear his voice. Hear it all to whom the word is preached, hear it all who read these pages, hear it all whom the message reaches in any way. Hear it as from him, the Lord of life. We are responsible for the gift of hearing, as for every other gift. He seems here to appeal to this responsibility. "He that hath ears to hear," he cries. He to whom God has given this power; he who can hear. Let none who can hear turn a deaf ear to the Saviour's words.

VIII.

THE TARES OF THE FIELD.

"Another parable put he forth unto them, saying, The kingdom of heaven is likened unto a man which sowed good seed in his field; but while men slept, his enemy came and sowed tares among the wheat, and went his way. But when the blade was sprung up, and brought forth fruit, then appeared the tares also. So the servants of the householder came and said unto him, Sir, didst not thou sow good seed in thy field? from whence then hath it tares? He said unto them, An enemy hath done this. The servants said unto him, Wilt thou then that we go and gather them up? But he said, Nay; lest while ye gather up the tares, ye root up also the wheat with them. Let both grow together until the harvest: and in the time of harvest I will say to the reapers, Gather ye together first the tares, and bind them in bundles to burn them; but gather the wheat into my barn. . . . Then Jesus sent the multitude away, and went into the house: and his disciples came unto him, saying, Declare unto us the parable of the tares of the field. He answered and said unto them, He that soweth the good seed is the Son of man; the field is the world; the good seed are the children of the kingdom; but the tares are the children of the wicked one: the enemy that sowed them is the devil; the harvest is the end of the world; and the reapers are the angels. As therefore the tares are gathered and burned in the fire; so shall it be in the end of this world. The Son of man shall send forth his angels, and they shall gather out of his kingdom all things that offend, and them which do iniquity; and shall cast them into a furnace of fire: there shall be wailing and gnashing of teeth. Then shall the righteous shine forth as the sun in the kingdom of their Father. Who hath ears to hear, let him hear." MATT. 13 : 24-30, 36-43.

SUCH is the state of the world still; a mixture of good and evil; "the children of the kingdom" and "the children of the wicked one" living together. All that is evil is the work of Satan; all that is good is of God—every thing that is pure and holy, every renewed heart, every Christian character.

The enemy of the householder wished to spoil his crop. He could not destroy the good seed, but he could mix bad with it; so among the wheat he sowed the seed of a certain weed, still common in the wheat-fields of the East, and very injurious. It is called here "tares," but it is not what we know in this country by that name. In its early growth, the plant is somewhat like wheat; but when the ear is formed, the difference is clearly seen. It is said that if, through carelessness, the seeds of this plant be ground in any considerable quantity with the wheat, the meal is very unwholesome.

The enemy who sowed the tares means the devil, who is the enemy of God and of souls. His great aim is to hinder God's work of grace and to ruin souls. We see this in the fall of Adam; and we may trace it still in numberless ways; not only in what is going on in the world at large, but also in the case of smaller bodies of men, and in the case of individuals. Everywhere, in fact, this aim of Satan may be observed. Hence come suggestions of evil in the heart, snares, temptations, allurements to sin. Hence hypocrites in the church. Hence opposers of the truth. Hence corruptions of the gospel. Hence false doctrine taking the form of truth. Hence partial and distorted views; exaggerated zeal for one doctrine, to the neglect of others. In a thousand different ways the enemy is doing his work, sowing tares among the wheat.

The enemy sowed the tares "while men slept."

This is generally considered to mean in the night; but it is not certain that it does so. For it is still the custom in the East to sleep awhile after the midday meal; and it is wonderful how nearly modern eastern customs are found to agree with those of Bible times. The tares may have been sown during this midday sleep. We can easily imagine the sowers, when their work was done, eating their meal and taking their rest, and then the enemy coming by stealth, and sowing the tares while they were asleep. Indeed the words "while men slept" might be rendered, "while *the* men slept," that is, the men who had just sown the good seed.

Whether, however, it was by night or by day that the tares were sown, it was while men *slept*. Our unwatchfulness is Satan's opportunity. The Scripture says: "Resist the devil, and he will flee from you." But in order to resist, we must be *awake*. "Watch and pray, lest ye enter into temptation;" but watching is the very opposite to sleeping. "Put on the whole armor of God, that ye may be able to stand against the wiles of the devil;" but in sleep the armor is put off.

The tares were not discovered till the blade brought forth fruit; up to that time the wheat and the tares seemed alike. "By their fruits ye shall know them." "Not every one that saith unto me, Lord, Lord, shall enter into the kingdom of heaven, but he that doeth the will of my Father which is in heaven." To hold the same doctrines, make the same profession, and worship in the same church, makes a likeness up to a certain point among men who are perhaps quite different in heart. But when a total contrast is seen between profession and practice, then the sad conclusion is forced upon us that such a person cannot really be one of "the children of the kingdom."

The servants of the householder wished to gather up the tares as soon as discovered. But this they were not allowed to do, lest they should root up the wheat with them. Both must grow together till the harvest. Some servants of God would, in like manner, make a complete separation at once between the "children of the kingdom" and all others, and would have upon earth a perfect church. It cannot be. With the best intentions, we make a thousand mistakes. God has not given us an infallible judgment. We cannot always tell the false from the true. Loud profession and high doctrine and much knowledge will sometimes be accepted, while some humble believer, unable to give account of his faith, may be rejected. And words of stern and undiscriminating rebuke and exclusion, intended for the nominal Christian, may discourage, unsettle, or throw back one of weak, though true faith. The visible church of Christ on earth is a mixed body, and must be so till the great harvest of souls. Not till then will the eternal separation be made. This is God's appointment, and it cannot be altered.

But the separation is only delayed. The wheat and the tares were to grow together till the harvest, but no longer. Then the wheat was to be gathered into the barn, the tares to be burned. Just so "the children of the kingdom" and "the children of the wicked one," though mixed now, will be separated for ever at the judgment-day. Without confusion or mistake, with infallible certainty, the final and eternal division will be made. Not one of the righteous will be left out of "the kingdom of their Father;" not one of the wicked will be admitted. Farther than the east is from the west, by an infinite distance, and by a separation that never can end, the righteous and the wicked will then be parted.

"Who hath ears to hear, let him hear." For this is a matter that concerns every living soul. We shall not be mere lookers on; we shall all have a part in that great division; we shall all be placed on this side or on that. And at this very time, while we are living in the world, with that great day before us, we are all either "the children of the kingdom" or "the children of the wicked one." There were but wheat and tares mentioned as growing in the field; there are but these two classes in the world. "Children of the wicked one!" What an awful title! Who does not shrink from taking it to himself? "Children of the wicked one!" With such a parentage now, such an inheritance hereafter! Yet if one dare not and cannot hope that he is a child of God, what is he but a child of the wicked one? Is this uncharitable? Nay. Nothing is uncharitable that is true; and this is the truth of God.

The harvest of souls is not yet come; the Son of man has not yet sent forth his angels. Do you fear that you are *not* a child of the kingdom? Oh, draw near to Him who now sits on a throne of grace, and beseech him to make you so. Sue for mercy, pardon, life. Cast yourself before the cross of Christ. Plead his blood that was shed for sinners. Ask for his promised Spirit. Pray that for the Redeemer's sake you may even now be numbered among the children of God, and that hereafter you may shine forth as the sun in the kingdom of your Father.

IX.

THE SEED, THE BLADE, AND THE EAR.

"And he said, So is the kingdom of God, as if a man should cast seed into the ground; and should sleep, and rise night and day, and the seed should spring and grow up, he knoweth not how. For the earth bringeth forth fruit of herself; first the blade, then the ear, after that the full corn in the ear. But when the fruit is brought forth, immediately he putteth in the sickle, because the harvest is come." MARK 4 : 26–29.

WHEN the seed has been sown, man's work for the present is over; nature must now do her part. The sower, lately so busy, now sleeps and rises night and day, leaving the seed to itself. But meanwhile nature works. After a time the seed springs up as a plant. First comes the blade, then appears the ear, and the ear grows and swells till the corn is ripe, and then man puts in the sickle and reaps the harvest.

This is a picture of the work of grace in the heart. Some of those parables of our Lord, in which he likens the kingdom of God to various things, represent in a more general way how the gospel spreads in the world; but this parable seems rather to describe its effect in one particular heart. Let us dwell on it in this sense.

The seed sown is the word of God, the gospel. The sowing may be by preaching, or by private reading, or by any other means by which a person is brought to the knowledge of the truth. And in this case the word is not received in vain. It reaches the heart, and brings forth fruit.

But the full ripe fruit does not appear at once. In some instances, it is true, the growth is much quicker and more sudden than in others; but generally, perhaps always more or less, there is a passing from one stage of progress to another, as with the seed. The parable shows us the *usual* course of the work of grace in the heart.

It is God's own work. As the sower casts the seed into the ground, and then sleeps and rises night and day, and the seed springs and grows up, he knows not how, so is it with the spiritual seed. Take the case of the word being received through preaching. The preacher speaks the word to the ear, but can do no more. It is God that causes it to reach the heart, and live there, and spring up and bear fruit. The seed that has been sown in the ground lives and grows by a secret power which we call nature, but which is in fact the power of God put forth in that particular way; and in like manner it is by grace, that is, by the secret work of the Holy Spirit in the heart, that the word becomes effectual. Man's part is to speak the word, and to pray for a blessing upon it; but the blessing is all from God.

Before the blade appears above ground, the seed has sprouted beneath the surface. No eye saw it then, for it was hidden in the earth; but so it was, or no plant would ever have come forth.

So the first work of grace in the heart is also an unseen work. No human eye beholds it. No one knows the secret thoughts, the struggles, the doubts, the fears, the hopes, of one in whom the spiritual life is beginning. No ear but God's hears the prayers he puts up, no human eye marks what takes place within. This unseen work is often for a time a painful work, while there is conviction of sin, but no clear hope in Christ. Yet it is a blessed work notwithstanding, for it is life beginning in the soul.

After the seed has lain for a time in the earth, while this secret growth went on, a tender green blade appears above ground. This is the young plant; and soon thousands of such plants show themselves, and the field that was lately one uniform brown is tinged all over with green. Just so, though the work of grace in the heart is at first beneath the surface, yet it cannot long remain unseen. It shows itself in the life and conduct, in changed desires and tastes, in seriousness of mind, in Christian tempers and behavior, in gentleness, kindness, and love. At first, as befits the young Christian, it comes forth modestly and humbly, in much weakness; yet it is there, and it is seen to be there. Nothing but grace could have wrought this change. This is the work of the Spirit, the growth of the living word in the soul.

As time goes on, the corn-plant grows stronger. The stalk comes after the blade, and soon the stalk bears an ear upon it, not ripe or full at present, but still fruit. In grace the progress is yet quicker.

For no sooner is there a true change of heart than some fruit begins to appear. The blade and the ear in the parable do but represent the continual growth of the soul; but in the spiritual life there never is a mere fruitless leaf or blade, an empty profession. Real fruit is produced at once; in heart, and even in a measure, in the outward life and conduct. But at first, while the Christian is weak and inexperienced, and the inner life is a new thing with him, though there is fruit, yet it is imperfect and unripe. He makes many mistakes, and is guilty perhaps of some acts of indiscretion or extravagance. Many are his shortcomings and inconsistencies, and not seldom does he fall. He is young in grace, if not in years: he has yet much to learn. And now he learns, not merely by the ordinary means of grace, but also by the painful experience of his own weakness. But the work still goes on within him. The same power that caused the seed to live beneath the ground now makes the plant to grow. He who began the good work carries it on still; and, in the diligent use of means, by prayer and watchfulness, through many difficulties, temptations, and trials, the Christian grows in grace.

The season advances, and the plant lives and grows still. The ear, that was at first small and green, gradually becomes full and plump, then changes its color, and hardens. Many a day has the sun shone upon it, many a shower has refreshed it, many a-storm perhaps has blown over it. Through all this it has been growing stronger, and fuller, and riper; and now at length it is quite ripe, "the full corn in the ear." The Christian grows too, making progress in the spiritual life, and bringing forth riper fruit. He also has had experience of sun, and rain, and storms; the grace and love of God, the work of the Spirit, temptations and trials; and he too has thus become stronger, more deeply rooted in Christ, more humble, more loving, more zealous, more fruitful in holiness. He is now no novice. He has learnt much of the spiritual life, and through grace he adorns his profession. He is known by his fruits. As those who now pass by the field say, "The corn is ripening," so do they who observe such a man's life say of him that he is ripening too. And so in truth he is; ripening for heaven, and becoming meet for the inheritance of the saints in light.

At length comes the harvest. When the corn is fully ripe, at once the sickle is put in, and the field is reaped. God only knows when the Christian is ripe for the great change. Some he takes early, some he keeps here long, to do his will and to live to his glory; but we know that in every case it is just at the right moment that the sickle is put in, just when affliction has done its work, when trial and suffering are no longer needed, when the fit time has come for the servant of Christ to go to his rest.

Such is the course of the seed of corn in nature; and such is the progress of grace when all goes well. But is it always so? We cannot forget that other parable of our Lord which describes what happens to the seed of the word more variously. We cannot forget the hinderances, the difficulties, the choking of the plant's growth, the seed failing, and some only of it proving really fruitful. Happy therefore as the picture now set before us is, the picture of a Christian growing, thriving, bearing fruit, and at length taken ripe in grace to the heavenly home, yet there are also solemn questions for self-examination suggested to us by the parable.

In what stage of progress are *you* spiritually? All is progress here, from first to last. Is it so with you? Is there growth? Are you getting on? Do you remember the time when first you had serious thoughts? The grace of God worked within you then; you chose Christ for your portion, and heartily embraced his salvation; you came out from the world, and ranged yourself on the Lord's side. There appeared in you at that time the green blade of an early religious profession—young, fresh, and beautiful. Years perhaps have since gone by. What has taken place meanwhile? What appears in you now? Is there fruit—more fruit? And is the fruit ripening?

Or has there been a check to the growth, a stopping short, a choking of the plant? Has the world gained too great a hold on the heart? Has the love of pleasure proved a snare?

Or again, without any particular hinderance, has your first love been lost, and has your heart grown cold towards God? Have your feelings and affections become more hard and indifferent? Has there been a withering of the spiritual plant, as if the word had never got deep into the heart, as if there had been little or no root, and therefore small growth, if any?

These are solemn subjects for self-inquiry; for the harvest is coming on, and soon may the command be given, "Put ye in the sickle." It is high time to awake out of sleep. Rest not in knowledge or in long acquaintance with the truth. Look well into your soul's state; examine your growth, your progress, your fruit; and seek God in Christ afresh, more humbly and more earnestly than ever. If there be not growth, can there be life?

X.

THE GRAIN OF MUSTARD-SEED.

"And he said, Whereunto shall we liken the kingdom of God? or with what comparison shall we compare it? It is like a grain of mustard-seed, which, when it is sown in the earth, is less than all the seeds that be in the earth: but when it is sown, it groweth up, and becometh greater than all herbs, and shooteth out great branches: so that the fowls of the air may lodge under the shadow of it." MARK 4 : 30-32 ; see also MATT. 13 : 31, 32.

IN this short parable our Lord set forth the spread of the gospel through the world. Beginning in a small and humble way, it would go on increasing till it should become great and mighty.

As was his custom, our Lord chose for his illustration or figure something with which his hearers were well acquainted, a grain of mustard-seed. It is thought to have been not the same as our mustard-seed, though even that grows into a great plant. It was but a small seed, less than any of the seeds commonly sown, such as wheat, or barley; for so we are to understand the words, "less than all the seeds that be in the earth;" but it grew into a much larger plant than the rest; so large, that it became more like a tree than a mere herb or plant, putting forth great branches, and giving shelter to birds. Perhaps such a plant was in sight when our Lord spoke the parable.

The explanation of the parable is not difficult.

THE GRAIN OF MUSTARD-SEED.

Like the grain of mustard-seed, the gospel in its beginning was very small. It was not proclaimed with pomp and show, it did not take its rise in one of the great cities of the world, and it was not preached by learned men. It took its rise in a poor and despised country, its first preachers were humble and unlearned men, and even our Lord himself, great as he was in truth, yet appeared without any outward greatness.

Such was the gospel in its beginning, such it was at the very time when this parable was spoken. We must carry ourselves back to that time, and place ourselves in thought among those who heard our Lord speak, in order fully to see its force. "The kingdom of God" at that time was seen in nothing more than this—a man (for outwardly he seemed no more) attended by a few humble followers, going about from place to place, teaching them and such others as would listen to him. He did indeed so speak as to draw crowds to hear him, and he performed many wonderful works; but those who came to hear him were chiefly poor men like his own followers, and none knew of his wonderful works except the people of that obscure part of the world. It seemed very unlikely that from such a beginning any thing great and mighty should grow. Judging by common rules, no one would have supposed that the history of what was then being done and said, and the very words which were spoken to those humble hearers, would be written in a book which would be read from age to age, in many different languages, by millions upon millions; and that the religion which began so humbly would make its way against all opposition and persecution, and become the professed religion of the greatest nations of the world.

Yet so it has been. We have but to compare the present state of the world, as regards the gospel, with its state at the time when the parable was spoken, and we shall see how wonderfully our Lord's words have been fulfilled. The grain of mustard-seed has grown up and become great, and has put forth great branches. The kingdom of God, by which in this parable we are to understand the outward and professing church of Christ, has spread more or less into almost every part of the world, and in the most civilized and powerful parts has become the prevailing religion. Like the fowls of the air finding shelter under the tree, millions have found a resting-place for their minds in the profession of a true faith; and numbers, receiving the gospel into their hearts, and living in its faith and love, have found true rest to their souls, a refuge in all trouble, a shelter from every storm.

It was most unlikely, humanly speaking, that so great a result should follow so small a beginning. Yet so it is. And this is not all. We have not yet reached the end of the spread of the gospel. A great part of the world still lies in heathen darkness, the followers of Mohammed may be counted by millions, and the Jews as a nation still reject Christ. But we know that the kingdoms of this world are to become the kingdoms of our Lord and of his Christ, and that the earth is to be filled with the knowledge of the Lord as the waters cover the sea. How or when this is to be, and by what means it is to be brought about, we know not; but we humbly receive the word of God, and believe that in his own time and way he will surely bring it to pass.

Some of those who listened to this parable were to be the first preachers of the gospel, the earliest instruments for the spread of the kingdom of God. It must have been a great encouragement to them to be thus assured of the success of their work. Their difficulties and hinderances were many and great, and their own strength was small. When they looked at the humble beginning of the gospel, like a grain of mustard-seed only, they might be tempted to despond. But the promise conveyed in this parable might well encourage them, and probably often did so. Long after the words were spoken—when He who spoke them had long been gone—in the midst of hardships and persecutions, perhaps this parable often came with comfort to the minds of the first preachers of the gospel, and cheered them with the prospect of the triumph of the kingdom of God.

Even so should it cheer those who are now engaged in the same work, and all who take an interest in the spread of the gospel. The hand of man sows the seed in the ground, but it is the hidden power of God in nature that makes it become a great plant. So, though man is made use of as an instrument, yet it is by the power and grace of God that the gospel spreads in the world. This power and grace are promised; we are assured that the gospel shall spread. We see the growth of a seed into a plant, and wonderful as it is, we are not surprised at it; nay, we expect to see it so, because it is according to the course of nature, that is, according to God's appointment. But it is also according to the declared will and purpose of God that the gospel shall spread in the world and his kingdom prevail. Let us believe and look for this as surely. Let us receive all the encouragement of this parable. God causes the seed to grow, and God will cause his kingdom to spread. The one is his will as much as the other. Let every worker for God be cheered in his work by this belief. Let all who long for the reign of righteousness rejoice in this hope.

But let us look to it also that this parable be fulfilled in our own hearts, as well as in the world at large; for though the direct meaning of the parable is more wide and general, yet we may rightly apply it personally too. In hearing the gospel, we have received, as it were, the grain of seed. Let us take care that it be not dead and unprofitable in our minds. And if somewhat of the true light has been given us, and we have experienced through grace the first beginning of spiritual life in the soul— small and feeble, perhaps, yet real—then let us be diligent in seeking that the seed may grow into a plant, and that the plant may flourish and increase more and more. If we humbly and earnestly use the means which God has provided for us, then we may in this way too take comfort from the parable.

God will work in us by his grace, as he is wont to work in nature. He will give us his Holy Spirit, and cause us to grow. The small beginning will increase continually. We should seek this in prayer, always pressing toward the mark, and ever striving for a deeper humility, a stronger faith, a warmer love, a growth in holiness.

And let us seek that, in all difficulty and trouble, and in all our daily life, we may find the full comfort of the gospel, and may lodge continually under its shadow. The more the kingdom of God is established within us, the more shall we find that Christ our Lord is indeed "as a hiding-place from the wind, and a covert from the tempest; as rivers of water in a dry place, as the shadow of a great rock in a weary land." We stand in need of such a shelter every day—a shelter, a refuge, and a defence. Christ will be all this to us; preserving and defending us, comforting us in trouble, helping us in need; and giving us withal such a happy sense of security in him, that in him we shall be enabled to enjoy in large measure that "peace of God which passeth all understanding."

XI.

THE LEAVEN IN THE MEAL.

"Another parable spake he unto them: The kingdom of heaven is like unto leaven, which a woman took, and hid in three measures of meal, till the whole was leavened." MATT. 13:33.

LEAVEN is generally used in Scripture to mean something bad. Thus our Lord bade his disciples beware of the leaven of the Pharisees and Sadducees, meaning their wrong teaching; and St. Paul wrote to the Corinthians that they should purge out the old leaven, and keep the feast, "not with the leaven of malice and wickedness, but with the unleavened bread of sincerity and truth."

Yet leaven does not necessarily mean what is bad; but rather any thing, whether bad or good, which is of such a nature as to spread itself through what it is mixed with. Thus the evil teaching of the Pharisees and Sadducees was likely to spread like leaven through the people; and in like manner the sin which the Corinthians allowed in one of their number, and which thus became mixed up with the ordinances of religion, and with their partaking of the Lord's Supper itself, would, if not checked, spread through and corrupt the whole church.

But in this parable the same figure of leaven is used in a good sense. It means here the gospel; for our Lord said: "The kingdom of heaven is like unto leaven." As leaven spreads through the meal into which it is put, so would the gospel spread through the world. Such was the nature of the kingdom of heaven, the gospel dispensation upon earth.

The general lesson therefore of this parable is the same as that of the parable of the grain of mustard-seed, which goes just before it. But our blessed Lord never spoke needlessly. If he taught the same truth in different ways and by different figures, it was that the truth might be set forth in all its various aspects, and thus a fuller and clearer knowledge of it might be gained. Each parable, however like it may seem to others, carries its own peculiar lesson. If it sets forth the same truth, it puts it in a new light.

"The kingdom of heaven is like unto leaven, which a woman took." The gospel is not left to make its own way in the world, without the use of means. Human instruments are employed — preachers, teachers, writers, workers of various kinds. The woman took the leaven, and mixed it with the meal; and in like manner the servants of God take the gospel, and strive to spread it through the world. Such is God's gracious plan; such is "the kingdom of heaven." It is like, not merely to leaven, but to "leaven, which a woman took."

Perhaps a woman is mentioned rather than a man only because this was more a woman's work. But it may be that there is a further meaning. In the parable of the mustard-seed, a man was the worker; here it is a woman. Perhaps we are meant to learn — and certainly it is the case — that in spreading the gospel there is work for women as well as for men. We have only to read St. Paul's epistles to see how women were made use of in the early church; and in our own time women hold a most important place in the work of the gospel. It is a distinct place from that of the man. This again is clearly to be gathered from the writings of St. Paul. And on no account must woman overstep the bounds which Scripture has set to her work. Man has his work, and woman has her work. The fact of the two being mentioned in different parables seems to draw special attention to this. But every man and every woman to whom the gospel has come in its power is called to use every means and every opportunity for extending it to others. We are all to be sowers of the seed or mixers of the leaven. Not one of us should be idle; not one should be living without an influence for good.

The woman hid the leaven in three measures of meal; that is, mixed it with it. There seems no reason for giving any meaning to the number three beyond this, that the leaven was small in quantity compared with the meal. This little quantity of leaven was mixed with a much larger quantity of meal, and yet the whole three measures were leavened. So the gospel, beginning in a small and humble way, has spread already through a great part of the world, and is to spread yet farther, even till it reaches everywhere. What seemed to the eye of man very weak, has proved to be of mighty power. So again, one who is trying in any way to spread the truth may seem perhaps very weak. In ourselves we *all* are weak, and ought to feel ourselves so: "Who is sufficient for these things?"

But some seem even weaker than others. Their sphere is narrow; their abilities humble; their opportunities few; their knowledge, boldness, and influence small. And deep humility, and perhaps also a desponding spirit, makes them perhaps take even too low a view of the means and talents which God has given them. But grant these to be as low and poor as they esteem them, yet the gospel which they desire to spread is "the power of God unto salvation;" and the strength in which they labor is not their own, but his. Small are the means which they employ, little is it that they can do, like the morsel of leaven which the woman took and hid in the meal; yet who can tell how great an effect may follow? A word spoken for Christ, the simple reading of a few verses to a sick person, in much weakness and fear perhaps, yet in a spirit of prayer and faith, how mighty the change which this may work! And if one heart be turned to God, and one person be brought under the power of the truth, that person himself becomes a fresh instrument for spreading it to others, and those others in their turn will spread it farther—and all from that little beginning, that one humble instrument. Three measures of meal were leavened by one morsel of leaven; numbers yet unborn may be brought to God and to happiness through the humble efforts of some one man or woman.

There is something very peculiar in the nature of leaven; it goes through all that it is mixed with, and makes a complete change in the whole mass. The gospel is like it in this. Wherever it goes, it makes a change; and that not only in those who truly receive it, but also in society in general. In a Christian country there may be many people ignorant of God, sunk in vice, and no better than the heathen in character; yet, taken as a whole, how different is a Christian land from a heathen land! The influence of the gospel is felt throughout the country. It has not changed every heart; far from it; but the general tone and character of the people are the better for the gospel. It is so in our own country. There is much ungodliness among us; yet how different would our country be without the leaven of the gospel! It was so in the time of the apostles, in whatever country the gospel was preached. It is so still in those heathen lands to which the gospel is carried by missionaries. There are many drawbacks and many disappointments in missionary work; but the gospel is not without its effect, and thus we are encouraged to hope and pray for a greater effect still.

But this leavening influence is yet more striking in the case of those who truly receive the gospel into the heart. "If any man be in Christ, he is a new creature: old things are passed away; behold, all things are become new." When the kingdom of heaven is established in the heart, the whole character is changed. For the gospel is not a mere set of doctrines or opinions, but a life-giving principle, "the power of God unto salvation." When truly received, it gives new thoughts and feelings, new hopes and desires, a new ground of trust, a new source of happiness, new and all-pervading principles of action. Every day, and in all his conduct, the Christian is influenced by the gospel; there is a holy consistency in his life. Such is the influence of the gospel, when it does its full work in the heart; and such it is in a measure in every heart that has received it. But alas for human frailty and imperfection! The gospel in itself is like leaven, but in its practical effects it is greatly hindered by man's infirmity and inconsistency, by the sin that still cleaves even to the regenerate heart, and by the temptations and difficulties that beset us from without. The leaven pervades the meal without difficulty or hinderance by the mere force of its nature; the gospel leaven, on the contrary, meets with much to hinder its effect, even in the heart that is under its influence. We must watch and pray. We must watch diligently against all within us or around us that would hinder the gospel; we must earnestly pray for the grace and help of God's Holy Spirit.

Much of the leavening effect of the gospel in the world depends on the consistent lives of Christians. A holy and consistent course may do untold good. For the most powerful preaching is that of the life; and when it is seen that the Christian's whole character and conduct are under the rule of the gospel, a feeling of respect at least will be produced for religion, and perhaps much more. Let us never forget that each of us has an influence on those around us; and let us seek that our influence may be all for good, and that thus we may be doing our part in extending the kingdom of heaven upon earth.

XII.

THE HIDDEN TREASURE.

"Again, the kingdom of heaven is like unto treasure hid in a field: the which when a man hath found, he hideth, and for joy thereof goeth and selleth all that he hath, and buyeth that field." MATT. 13 : 44.

IT has often been a practice in troubled times to hide treasure in some secret place, with the intention of finding it again when peace should be restored. Various are the hiding-places that have been chosen: an old wall, the hollow of a tree, a hole in the ground. But it has happened not seldom that some one else has been so fortunate as to discover the hiding-place, and to possess himself of the treasure, to the bitter disappointment of the owner when he went to look for what he had hidden.

Such a finding is represented in this parable. A man finds treasure hidden in a field. He tells his secret to no one, but, full of joy, takes instant measures to make the prize his own. Carefully hiding it again out of sight, he goes and sells all that he has and buys that field. Now no one can dispute his right. When once the field is his, he may claim all that is in it. He has made a sacrifice, it is true, to obtain it; but he has secured the treasure as his own.

Our Lord likens the kingdom of heaven to this

treasure. He represents to us by this parable the gospel itself, and the conduct of one who truly embraces it.

The gospel is a treasure indeed—better than gold and silver, more precious than rubies, worth more than all the world. A man may have all that the world can give, yet without the gospel he is poor; and he is rich who has the gospel, though he may be in want of almost all besides.

But the gospel has not always been made known: even now it is unknown to a great part of mankind; and where it is known, numbers know it only with the understanding, not with the heart. In all these cases it is like "treasure hid in a field." The heathen are altogether ignorant of it; from *them* this treasure is quite hidden. The nominal Christian knows of its existence, but knows not its preciousness; and it is no treasure to one who feels no need of it, and sees no value in it.

But when the conscience is awakened, and the heart is touched, and a man has been led to feel his sinfulness and need, and to see light and life and salvation in the gospel, then it is as though he had found hid treasure. Many among the heathen, hearing the gospel for the first time, have at once been brought to see its preciousness, and thus have found the treasure. But the change is hardly less, when one who has heard the sound of the gospel all his life first feels his heart affected by it. The treasure was close by him before—in the field with him, as it were; but it was an unknown treasure. It may be that the man in the parable had passed by the spot where the treasure was a hundred times, had trodden it down with his feet, or driven his plough over it; but he never supected what lay so near, till the day when perhaps the ploughshare, in turning up the soil, disclosed what was beneath. So one may have heard the gospel year after year, and yet never have found out its preciousness, till some sermon or some word was brought home to his heart by the Holy Spirit.

When once the heart is thus awakened, then there is a change indeed. Other things lose much of their value; the soul is felt to be of the deepest importance, and the good news of salvation through Christ is prized above all. To gain a share in this great salvation, to be forgiven, reconciled, and saved, this is now felt to be the great concern; and all else seems of comparatively trifling moment. The man in the parable went and sold all that he had, and bought the field where the treasure was. The apostle Paul declared that he had willingly suffered the loss of all things that he might win Christ. Our Saviour taught us that there is but one thing needful. Even so must we embrace the gospel. We must seek salvation as the one thing needful; we must be willing to part with all for Christ's sake; we must count all but loss for him. No bosom sin must be spared, no vain attempt must be made to serve two masters; all that stands in the way of our souls must be freely parted with. Paul never repented the sacrifice he had made. "Yea, doubtless," he said, "and I count all things but loss, for the excellency of the knowledge of

Christ Jesus my Lord." So highly should we prize this treasure, so joyful should we be to find it, that all else will seem to us as dross in comparison.

No earthly treasure can fully represent the preciousness of the gospel. The man in the parable was glad to part with all that he had in order to possess himself of that field; and he did wisely, for the hidden treasure was of far greater value than the price paid to obtain it. Yet it was but earthly treasure after all; the same in kind as what he parted with for it, though larger in amount. But a little while, and all treasure of this kind, whether larger or smaller, whether inherited or earned, or found (as they say) by some lucky chance, must be left for ever. Not so the treasure of the gospel, the true riches. This is a treasure which no moth or rust can corrupt, which no thief can steal, and which even death itself cannot take away. On the contrary, death, which parts us from gold and silver and lands and houses, will but put us in fuller possession of these gospel riches, this heavenly treasure. "To me to live is Christ, and to die is *gain*." He who said this had already found "the unsearchable riches of Christ," but he looked forward to a more perfect enjoyment of them after death.

There are also some other points of difference between the parable and what it is meant to represent.

The man in the parable *bought* the field; but there is no buying the spiritual treasure. We must indeed part with all that comes between us and salvation; but not in the way of a price paid. "The *gift* of God is eternal life, through Jesus Christ our Lord." This is "without money, and without price."

Again, this treasure is enough to supply the wants of all. In the parable, but one could have it; in the gospel it is offered to all. "Ho, every one that thirsteth, come ye to the waters, and he that hath no money." "Come unto me, *all* ye that labor and are heavy laden, and I will give you rest."

He therefore who finds it needs not to hide it, lest another should discover it and rob him of it. On the contrary, the newly-awakened man desires to make all sharers in the blessing he has found. "Come hither, and I will tell you what he hath done for my soul." "The Spirit and the bride say, Come; and let him that heareth say, Come!" One sign of a man's having found the treasure himself is, that he desires to lead others to find it too. He who has found Christ loves Christ; and he who loves Christ, loves all for Christ's sake, and longs that all should know and love him.

XIII.

THE PEARL OF GREAT PRICE.

"Again, the kingdom of heaven is like unto a merchantman, seeking goodly pearls: who, when he had found one pearl of great price, went and sold all that he had, and bought it." MATT. 13 : 45, 46.

THIS chapter is full of parables, all meant to teach us the nature of "the kingdom of heaven." Therefore, all the parables, from the twenty-fourth verse, begin with almost the same words as this one, "The kingdom of heaven is like." This "kingdom of heaven" does not mean heaven above, but heaven below. It means God's government on earth under the gospel, the gospel system, what is taking place now under the gospel, and will take place hereafter. Each parable teaches some particular lesson about "the kingdom of heaven," and throws light on some one point. This parable teaches the great preciousness of salvation in Christ, and that it is worth every sacrifice.

It is a very plain parable, one that all can understand without difficulty. The more so, as the very thing here represented might take place now; for pearls are still precious, and are still bought and sold in this way. They are substances found in certain shells at the bottom of the sea in some parts of the world, and made use of as jewels. The chief pearl-fishery is near the coast of Ceylon, one of the very spots where pearls were sought for in ancient times. The pearls are brought up from the deep by divers, and differ much in size and value. The very finest are worth a large sum of money; but these are rare. There are still merchants whose business it is to deal in pearls, either employing the divers themselves, or buying of those who do so. These customs are probably little changed since the very time when our Lord spoke.

The parable represents a merchant meeting with one pearl of extraordinary value. He had probably never seen or heard of so rich a one before. Could he but get possession of it, his fortune was made. So, without hesitation, he goes and sells all that he has, all his other pearls, all his stock in trade, all his property of every kind, and buys it. Thus he gave up all that he had for it, and thought himself happy to gain it even then.

What does the pearl mean? Evidently salvation. For this is the prize of the gospel, the great blessing of "the kingdom of heaven," the fruit of the coming and sacrifice of Christ. Indeed, Christ himself may be said to be the pearl, in the sense in which the apostle Paul says, "But what things were gain to me, those I counted loss for Christ, ... that I may win Christ." It makes little difference whether we consider the pearl to be the Saviour himself, or the salvation which he wrought out; for to have a part in Christ is to be saved by him; and this is the "pearl of great price."

The merchantman we may take to mean any

person seeking happiness or good for himself. As the merchantman used to go hither and thither, inquiring, seeking, and bargaining, so do people in general seek good for themselves in various ways. Disappointed in one source, they turn to another. Their object is still the same.

Or perhaps we may take him to mean an awakened soul seeking peace. Such a man is not a mere seeker after happiness generally. He has been roused to a sense of religion, his conscience has been touched, he has been led to feel his need. But he has not yet found peace. He is seeking, inquiring, using means.

In whichever sense we take the merchantman, it is clear what is meant by his finding the pearl. This represents a man becoming acquainted with salvation by Christ. He may have known the doctrine before, but it never before arrested his attention and engaged his heart. Perhaps it is now more clearly and forcibly set forth to him, or God's providential dealings have brought him to more seriousness of mind. At all events, the truth now strikes him, and touches his heart. Here the awakened conscience sees just what it wants; here the seeker after happiness finds what he sought. Convinced, impressed, and deeply in earnest, the man parts with all to win Christ. The world is given up, the bosom sin is forsaken, all that stands in the way of his soul is freely sacrificed, self-righteousness is cast away, formal religious observances are trusted in no more. Like Paul, "to win Christ and be found in him," is now all his desire.

As in the parable of "The Hidden Treasure," so here, there is a difference to be noticed between the parable and its interpretation. The merchant *bought* the pearl, but we cannot buy salvation. It is a free gift for Christ's sake. The terms are, "Without money and without price." Yet we must be ready to give up all to gain it. The merchantman parted with all that he had, and paid the value of it as the price of the pearl. We too must willingly part with all that stands in the way of our salvation, though the price has already been paid, and we can add nothing to it.

Paul, we have seen, did this, and gloried in the choice he had made. But we read of one who, though he knew of the pearl, and in some degree felt its value, yet could not make up his mind to give up all for it. "Go and sell what thou hast," said our Lord to the rich young man, "and give to the poor, and thou shalt have treasure in heaven: and come and follow me. But when the young man heard that saying, he went away sorrowful: for he had great possessions." Alas! hearing of the "Pearl of great price" is not enough to make a man choose it, and seek it, and give up all to gain it. Numbers hear of it, yet see no value in it. Numbers who do see something desirable in it, yet love the world better. In a Christian land almost all hear of the pearl, but how many are seeking it in truth?

This merchantman is our example, and that in two points: he set the pearl at its right value, and he sought it without delay.

Our pearl is more precious than his; it is worth more than all besides. Let us value it accordingly. Let us remember those solemn words, "What shall it profit a man, if he shall gain the whole world, and lose his own soul?" Let us be like the merchantman, and like the apostle Paul, not like the rich young man. He went away sorrowful. Ah! well he might.

The merchantman, having made up his mind as to the value of the pearl, lost no time in making it his own. It was not safe to hesitate. While he delayed, another might get it before him. He "went and sold all that he had, and bought it." Time is precious with us too. It is not safe to delay. The pearl may be ours now; but if we now neglect to secure it, it will one day be out of our reach. None can tell how much longer the gospel invitation may be made to him; but this is certain, that he who is hearing it continually, and yet putting off accepting it, is in awful danger. He is trifling with God, and provoking him to cut short his opportunity. The only time for securing the pearl is now; the only time in which God makes the offer, the only time that we are sure of having. Delay may cost us the loss of the pearl, a loss never to be repaired. "Behold, now is the accepted time; behold, now is the day of salvation."

XIV.

The Gospel Net.

"Again, the kingdom of heaven is like unto a net that was cast into the sea, and gathered of every kind; which, when it was full, they drew to shore, and sat down, and gathered the good into vessels, but cast the bad away. So shall it be at the end of the world: the angels shall come forth, and sever the wicked from among the just, and shall cast them into the furnace of fire: there shall be wailing and gnashing of teeth." MATT. 13: 47–50.

SEVERAL of our Lord's disciples were fishermen; much of his ministry was passed by the sea of Galilee; we find him on various occasions making use of a fishing-boat for crossing that inland sea or lake, and once at least he preached from one. Such a scene as that described in this parable might be seen there any day, and may be still. For fishermen still ply their business on those waters; their boats still cross from side to side; their nets are still let down for a draught, and at other times may be seen spread on the rocks.

A net must of necessity gather "of every kind," the bad as well as the good, the worthless as well as the useful. The separation takes place afterwards. Then the bad are cast away and the good are kept. This is done now, wherever net-fishing is practised, just as it was done of old. There are few crafts which have changed less than that of the fisherman.

This parable, therefore, in its story part, is a very plain one, and as plain to us as it was to those who first heard it.

Our Lord has made the spiritual meaning equally clear. He himself explained it.

First, he gives us to understand that the parable is meant to represent "the kingdom of heaven," that is, the visible church of Christ, or God's government on earth under the gospel. In other words, what fishermen do in gathering all kinds of fish into their net, and then separating the bad from the good, is like what almighty God is doing now, and will do hereafter, with regard to men.

The visible church embraces people of every kind. As the net gathers of every kind, so does the gospel. True believers and mere professors, spiritual Christians and heartless formalists, the careless and thoughtless, the undecided, the hypocrite, the deceiver of others and of himself, all these may be found within the visible church, the general body of those who call themselves Christians.

How great a difference there may be even among the members of one congregation! They sit side by side, they unite in the same prayer, they hear the same preaching, yet how vast a difference there may be among them in the sight of God! He sees the hearts of all, and it is by the heart that he judges. Man himself would separate between the grossly wicked and the pious; between the thief, the swearer, the drunkard, the Sabbath-breaker on the one hand, and the man of consistent godly life on the other. But God sees farther than man;

and much that is respectable in the eyes of men is not approved by him. "Without faith it is impossible to please God." Only he who is of a penitent and contrite heart, and rests his hope on his Saviour, and seeks to serve and glorify him, is accepted and approved by God.

But this mixture is only for a time. When the net was full, it was drawn to shore, and the separation was made. When the gospel net shall be full—that is, when God shall see fit to put an end to the present state of things—then likewise a separation will be made. The fishermen would not suffer the bad fish to be among the good. None but good should be put into the vessels. The rest must be thrown away as useless, and worse than useless. In like manner, when the great day shall come, God, by his angels, will "sever the wicked from among the just." They must stay where they are no longer. The hypocrite, the formalist, the careless, the profane, the undecided, may no longer be with the true servants of God. They must now be parted, parted for ever. The righteous will go to their place, the place which was purchased for them by their Redeemer's blood, and which he himself went before to prepare for them; and the wicked must go to theirs. They cannot escape now, for they despised the day of grace, and the day of grace is past. They cannot escape now; they can *never* escape. They must be cast "into the furnace of fire: there shall be wailing and gnashing of teeth."

"But this is for the *wicked*," some may say. "Must all who are not classed among the righteous be placed with the wicked?" Even so. There is no place between the abode of the righteous and that of the wicked; in the sight of God there is no *character* between these two. All the fish gathered into the net were either good or bad; all were either put into vessels, or thrown away. There was no middle sort, not good enough to be kept, yet not bad enough to be thrown away. So every soul will be placed either among the righteous or among the wicked. The angels will leave none but the just among the just. There will be no confusion or mistake in that division. Every one whose name is not written in the book of life will be cast into the lake of fire. There is no middle class, no middle place.

How solemnly does this parable speak to all! How it should lead us to deep searchings of heart! For we are all concerned here. We are all now gathered into the gospel net, and we shall all have a part in that separation; none will be mere lookers-on. Where shall we be placed then? Shall we be numbered among the just? Are we so *now?* Does the all-seeing Eye behold us this very day as true children of God, real believers, Christians in heart as well as in name? Oh, if not, let this parable be as a quickening and awakening voice from God himself. Let there be no self-deception, no stifling of conscience, no vain and unscriptural hope that things may not, after all, be as they are represented. They *will* be. Nothing can alter the word of God. The only wisdom, the only safety, is *now* to seek Jesus with all the heart, and thus to make sure of being found in him at last.

XV.

THE NEW CLOTH, AND THE NEW WINE.

"Then came to him the disciples of John, saying, Why do we and the Pharisees fast oft, but thy disciples fast not? And Jesus said unto them, Can the children of the bride-chamber mourn, as long as the bridegroom is with them? but the days will come, when the bridegroom shall be taken from them, and then shall they fast. No man putteth a piece of new cloth unto an old garment, for that which is put in to fill it up taketh from the garment, and the rent is made worse. Neither do men put new wine into old bottles: else the bottles break, and the wine runneth out, and the bottles perish: but they put new wine into new bottles, and both are preserved." MATT. 9:14-17; see also MARK 2, and LUKE 5.

THIS double parable was spoken by our Lord in answer to a question, and must therefore be considered in connection with it.

"The disciples of John and of the Pharisees," St. Mark tells us, "used to fast." The Pharisees were always trying to entrap our Lord with questions, and it was they probably who set on the disciples of John the Baptist to come and ask our Lord why his disciples did not fast too. As for John's disciples, they most likely asked the question in all sincerity, surprised at seeing the disciples of Christ neglect what they considered a religious duty, and really desiring to know the reason.

Our Lord told them the reason. It was twofold. First, it was not a right time for his disciples to fast, because he was still with them. Fasting is suited to a time of sadness and humiliation, not to a season of joy. He called himself "the bridegroom," and his disciples "the children of the bride-chamber," that is, the bridegroom's friends and companions. While the bridegroom was with them, they could not fast, for it was a time of joy; but soon he was to be taken away from them, and then they might properly fast, for that would be to them a time of sadness and loneliness and need.

The other reason was that our Lord's disciples were at present but young in the faith, and therefore weak. They could not yet bear all that they would be able to bear when more established. Our Lord, therefore, would deal gently with them, and not lay on them too heavy a burden. True, they were to take up the cross and follow him; yet, in his mercy and compassion, he would bring them to it by degrees. When they should have gained more experience, and when they should have received the strengthening grace of the Holy Spirit, then they should fast, then they should learn more completely to subdue the flesh, and to practise the duties of self-denial for his sake.

It is this last reason that our Lord explains more fully by means of the parable.

The new cloth would not match the old, either in look or in strength. The two would not wear evenly; the shrinking of the new stuff would be likely to tear the old, and so the rent would be made worse rather than better. The new cloth would be too new and strong for the old garment.

In like manner it would not be wise to put new wine into old bottles. Bottles were then made, not of glass, but of skins of leather; and the leather in time grew weak, and could not bear the motion and fermentation of new wine, though it might be still strong enough to hold old wine safely. New wine must therefore be put into new and strong bottles.

The meaning of both parts of the parable is the same. As new cloth was ill-suited to an old garment, and new wine must not be put into old bottles, so the disciples, in their weakness, must not have laid upon them at present an unsuitable burden. They were but beginners as yet, "babes in Christ," and must be dealt with accordingly. Just as the garment would be torn worse, and the bottles would be burst and the wine spilled, unless caution and judgment were shown, so these new and inexperienced disciples would be likely to receive injury, to be discouraged, perhaps even to be turned back altogether, if hastily or harshly treated. Such was not our Lord's way of dealing with any. "He shall feed his flock like a shepherd: he shall gather the lambs with his arm, and carry them in his bosom, and shall gently lead those that are with young." "A bruised reed shall he not break, and the smoking flax shall he not quench." "I have yet many things to say unto you, but ye cannot bear them now." "And with many such parables spake he the word unto them, as they were able to hear it." Thus gently and tenderly was it foretold that our Lord would deal, and thus did he in truth deal with his disciples and with all who came to

NEW CLOTH AND NEW WINE. 121

learn of him; not putting a needless difficulty in the way of any, lest they should be discouraged and turn back; feeding them at first with milk, and not with strong meat, as they were able to bear it. In St. Luke's account we find these words added, as spoken by our Lord: "No man also having drunk old wine straightway desireth new, for he saith the old is better."

The ministers of religion, and likewise parents and all who have to do with the training of the young, would do well to follow our Lord's teaching and example here. We must deal gently with beginners. We must remember that children are but children. Our zeal must be tempered with wisdom, and softened by gentleness. Especially in outward observances, such as fasting, and indeed in all the severer duties of religion, much tenderness must be used in dealing with those who are "babes in Christ." Our Lord pronounced a strong condemnation upon those who should "offend one of these little ones." He meant those who should do so wilfully; let us take care lest, though without meaning it, yet through want of gentleness and consideration, we put a stumbling-block in the way of a young disciple.

With regard also to the general question of fasting, we see in this teaching of our Lord the free and merciful spirit of the gospel. The disciples of the Pharisees, and John's disciples too, used to fast often, but our Lord's disciples did not fast at that time. Yet we know that the Pharisees, as a body, were greatly in fault; they were strict in the outward parts of religion, but neglected the religion of the heart and life. We know less about the disciples of John, but it is plain that, while their master himself believed in Jesus and tried to point others to him as the Messiah, these men were still disciples of John only, and had never gone on to believe in Him of whom John testified. There was something faulty therefore in *their* religion too; and it is probable that they, like the Pharisees, had too much of the form and too little of the spirit, and were in some measure in bondage to outward observances. But the religion of Christ is no bondage, and his service is no hard service. True, every thought must be brought into captivity to the obedience of Christ, and the flesh must be subdued, and the body must be brought under, yet all in the spirit of the liberty of the gospel. The disciples of John would doubtless have thought it grievous sin to omit one stated time for fasting; the disciples of Jesus, on the other hand, had no such stated times appointed for them. Their Master taught them much of the spiritual part of religion: he taught them to pray, to be humble and holy, to have faith, to love one another, to be bold in owning him, and to delight in serving him; but he did not teach them much about outward observances. Not that he treated them as of no importance, but he would have his disciples consider them in their proper place; doing them, but not leaving the others undone. And as for fasting, they were not to do that while they had the joy of his presence; for it is not a hard duty, to be performed at all times and under all circumstances. There is a time for all things; and more than that, there ought to be an aim and object in all religious observances. They should not be blindly kept, as if the observances themselves were all; that would be against the whole spirit of the gospel.

Yet it must not be forgotten that our Lord said, "But the days will come when the bridegroom shall be taken away from them, and then shall they fast in those days." The bridegroom, Christ our Lord, is absent from us now in bodily presence, though with us by the Spirit; these words therefore apply to us. Indeed, even while he was with the disciples, there were special occasions on which fasting was right, as when our Lord said of the evil spirit whom they could not cast out, "This kind goeth not out but by prayer and fasting." Fasting is now therefore a scriptural observance. But it must be done in a scriptural spirit; and on that point we are not without our Lord's instruction: "Thou, when thou fastest, anoint thy head, and wash thy face; that thou appear not unto men to fast, but unto thy Father which is in secret; and thy Father, which seeth in secret, shall reward thee openly."

There were some among the Jews who fasted from an ostentatious motive, that they might win a high character for holiness among men. Such fasting must be an abomination to God, whether among Jews or Christians. But the words of our Lord seem to point to something farther still. True fasting is a thing of the heart. There may rightly be such moderation and abstinence in the use of food as will help devotion, by preserving the mind clear, and bringing the flesh more into subjection to the spirit; but there should also be an inward fasting, a humbling of the heart before God, a mortification of pride and self, a restraint upon the inclinations. Thus, in the inward thoughts as well as in the outward act, we should deny ourselves; and in this way we shall be held in the sight of God to fast, even though no change in our habits be seen by men. That fasting has been abused both of old and also in modern times, through formality and superstition, is no reason against a right fasting. Our Lord himself said, "And then shall they fast in those days;" and taught both what to avoid in fasting, and how to fast aright; and we know from Scripture that, when their Lord had been taken from them, the apostles and early Christians did fast as well as pray.

XVI.

True Defilement.

"And he called the multitude, and said unto them, Hear, and understand: not that which goeth into the mouth defileth a man; but that which cometh out of the mouth, this defileth a man.... Then answered Peter and said unto him, Declare unto us this parable. And Jesus said, Are ye also yet without understanding? Do not ye yet understand, that whatsoever entereth in at the mouth goeth into the belly, and is cast out into the draught? But those things which proceed out of the mouth come forth from the heart; and they defile the man. For out of the heart proceed evil thoughts, murders, adulteries, fornications, thefts, false witness, blasphemies: these are the things which defile a man: but to eat with unwashen hands defileth not a man." MATT. 15: 10, 11; 15–20; see also MARK 7.

SEVERAL of our Lord's parables were spoken against the scribes and Pharisees, to expose their errors and correct their false teaching. This is one of them.

The Jewish teachers, among many other such outward points, were very particular about the washing of hands before food. This was one of those "commandments of men" which they had added to the law of God. They made it a matter, not of cleanliness merely, but of religion; and so strict were they about it, that they thought it as wrong to eat with unwashed hands as to commit some great moral crime.

They were much displeased therefore when they saw the disciples eat without first washing their hands, and came to our Lord with this complaint: "Why do thy disciples transgress the tradition of the elders? for they wash not their hands when they eat bread."

Our Lord first answered them by showing how they themselves, on the other hand, put the tradition of the elders before the commandments of God; and then, turning from them, addressed himself to the multitude. The common people were accustomed to hold the teaching of the scribes in much respect, and any objection made by them would have great weight in their eyes; it was necessary therefore that the multitude should hear our Lord's reply as well as the scribes. So "he called the multitude, and said unto them, Hear and understand: not that which goeth into the mouth defileth the man; but that which cometh out of the mouth, this defileth a man."

The words were plain, yet it is probable that the multitude did not understand their meaning, for the disciples certainly did not. Peter afterwards asked for an explanation of what our Lord had said, speaking of it as a parable—"Declare unto us this parable;" and a parable it was, though of the simplest kind—so simple that the disciples ought to have understood it at once. "Are ye also yet without understanding?" said our Lord to Peter and the rest; and there is reproof in the question. However, having thus reproved them for their slowness, he graciously went on to explain to them fully what he had said.

That which goeth in at the mouth, he taught

them, does not defile a man, but that which cometh out of it. The heart is the source and spring of what we say. "Out of the abundance of the heart the mouth speaketh. A good man out of the good treasure of the heart bringeth forth good things; and an evil man out of the evil treasure bringeth forth evil things." Evil thoughts have their birth in the heart, though they are spoken forth by the mouth. False witness, for instance, and blasphemies, are first thought in the heart, and then uttered by the mouth. And such things as murders, adulteries, fornications, and thefts, which have their beginning in the secret thoughts, are talked of by the mouth, and are often planned and carried out by means of the words that pass between one person and another. "These are the things," said our Lord, "which defile a man: but to eat with unwashen hands defileth not a man." There is no sin in the latter; and whatever defilement there may be, it is but an outward defilement, and is quickly got rid of; but there is a real defilement in sin; and evil thoughts, coming forth as they do in evil words and evil deeds, are sin: "These are the things which defile a man." There is a vast difference therefore; and the Jewish teachers were quite wrong in putting such a thing as eating with unwashen hands on the same footing with sins of the heart and life and tongue.

The chief lesson we are to learn from this parable is, that religion does not consist in small outward observances, and that what we are to guard against above all is sin. There is danger of paying so much attention to the outward forms and lesser parts of religion as to have the mind drawn away from its inward and spiritual part. And this is no trifling danger; for an over-scrupulous observance of forms is apt to satisfy the mind, and to lull the conscience to sleep, thus blunting the sense of spiritual need and of moral obligation, and giving a false security. We see this effect very plainly in the case of the Pharisees and the Jewish teachers. They paid tithes of mint and anise and cummin, but omitted the weightier matters of the law, judgment, mercy, and faith. "These," said our Lord, "ought ye to have done, and not to leave the other undone." On the same principle, they thought it exceedingly wrong to eat bread with unwashen hands, but at the same time made comparatively light of real sins. We see their fault; let us guard against any approach to it in ourselves.

The seat of evil is the heart; and in the heart, also, when renewed by grace and sanctified by the Spirit, is the source and spring of good. Let us, to use plain words, begin at the right end. Let us follow our Lord's own rule; not seeking merely to make clean the outside of the cup and of the platter, but cleansing first that which is within, that the outside may be clean also. If the heart be diligently kept, the outward conduct will certainly show the effect; and if the main points in religion be earnestly attended to, then the lesser matters will not be neglected. Inward and spiritual religion will show forth itself in all things, both small and great; and a true and living faith in Christ, and a heart renewed by grace, will produce a watchful walk, and a scrupulous attention to every part of Christian duty.

We cannot have too deep a sense of the defiling nature of sin. The world may think lightly of some sins, but in God's sight all sin is hateful; and some of those sins which are most lightly thought of by men are among those which are most severely condemned in the word of God. Sin indulged defiles the heart, the lips, the life. Nothing but the blood of Jesus can cleanse us from the guilt of past sins, and nothing but the Holy Spirit of God can keep us from the defilement of sin for the time to come. Well may we pray with the psalmist, "Hide thy face from my sins, and blot out all mine iniquities. Create in me a clean heart, O God; and renew a right spirit within me."

XVII.

THE BLIND LEADING THE BLIND.

"Let them alone: they be blind leaders of the blind. And if the blind lead the blind, both shall fall into the ditch." MATT. 15:14; see also LUKE 6:39.

THIS is one of the shortest and simplest of parables. Indeed, we should have rather called it a proverb, had it not been called a parable by St. Luke. It seems to have been spoken by our Lord on two occasions, one recorded by St. Matthew, the other by St. Luke; but the words in the two gospels are almost the same.

As recorded by St. Matthew, the parable was spoken at the same time as the preceding one about defilement: in fact, it comes between that parable and our Lord's explanation of it to his disciples.

Certain scribes and Pharisees who had come from Jerusalem complained to our Lord that his disciples were in the habit of transgressing "the tradition of the elders;" "for," said they, "they wash not their hands when they eat bread." But our Lord in reply brought a much more serious accusation against *them:* "Why do ye also transgress the commandment of God by your tradition?" He then pointed out to them how they put the ordinances of men above the word of God, making the commandment of God of none effect by their traditions; and then, calling the people to him, he warned them, in the presence of the scribes, against such false teaching. Afterwards hearing that the Pharisees were offended by what he had said, he added, "Every plant which my heavenly Father hath not planted shall be rooted up. Let them alone: they be blind leaders of the blind. And if the blind lead the blind, both shall fall into the ditch."

There is no difficulty, therefore, in understanding this short parable. The blind leaders mean the scribes and Pharisees; the blind who were led mean the ignorant Jews whom they taught; and by falling into the ditch we are to understand going astray as to spiritual things, wandering from true doctrine and practice, and so coming to ruin, or at least suffering danger and loss. The people, therefore, were not to follow such teachers; for, not knowing the way of God themselves, they could but lead others astray.

The only true spiritual light comes from God, and this light he has given in his word. The scribes and Pharisees were blind leaders, because they forsook the word of God. This was their fault, and it was this that made them unsafe teachers.

All who forsake or disregard the word of God are but blind leaders, for that word is still the only sure guide. Manners and customs, forms and ceremonies change, but the word of God remains the same. The Jews had but a portion of it; we have the whole. The light which they enjoyed, though true, was but faint and dim, compared with the light of the gospel. So that we may say, with even more confidence than David, "Thy word is a lamp unto my feet, and a light unto my path." For there we find light indeed, and no darkness: the light of truth, the light of God, the light which never misleads, the light which guides, cheers, and comforts all who walk by it.

Yet there are still blind leaders, and for the same reason as of old: they do not take the word of God as their light.

Some pay so much attention to forms of man's invention, that their mind is drawn off from the word of God.

Some refuse to submit their understanding to the word. They doubt and cavil, and find fancied defects, and venture to set up their own little reason against the plain word of Scripture.

Some, though sincere, have never sought the teaching of the Holy Spirit, and therefore the main truths of the word of God are hidden from them. The light is before them, but the eyes of their understanding are darkened.

Some are careless. Though by profession teachers of others, their heart is not in their work. They have no knowledge or love of Christ in their hearts, no concern for souls, no earnest desire to lead them aright.

These are all blind leaders of the blind. They cannot teach what they do not know. They cannot lead others by a way which they have not found themselves. The poor and ignorant who go to them for guidance do not find what they seek; for surely one cannot lead another to Christ who has not sought him for himself, and it is hard to think that a soul can receive spiritual light by means of one who shows no sign of having received it himself.

Where a minister of the gospel preaches the truth of God faithfully, let him be heard, honored, and followed, however small his gifts may be. He may have little power of attracting hearers, his talents may be small, his words void of eloquence, his speech ungraceful; yet, if the love of Christ be in his heart, and he deliver the simple message of the gospel, let him not be despised. He is God's servant, doing God's work. He is no blind leader.

Alas, such a teacher is often neglected for some preacher of showy style and attractive manner, who yet does not preach "the truth as it is in Jesus." There is in our day, perhaps there has been in all days, too much worship of talent, too little regard to truth. Hearers often forget that the object of hearing is, not to be pleased, but to be profited; not to have the mind and the senses gratified, but to learn the way of salvation, to increase in the knowledge of God, and to grow in grace.

The test to which all teaching should be brought is the Bible. "To the law and to the testimony: if they speak not according to this word, it is because there is no light in them." Isa. 8:20. All religious teaching should be judged by this rule. Scriptural truth is the point of first importance; and no teaching can be really good and wholesome in which this is lacking or even obscured. As it would be the height of folly to trust oneself to the guidance of a blind man, so it cannot be right or wise to listen to unscriptural teaching. A proud, captious, criticising spirit must indeed be guarded against by hearers; but, in humility and sincerity, with an earnest desire to know the truth, and to be fed with spiritual food, it is not only their right, but their duty, to judge what they hear by the standard of the word of God.

There is much cause for thankfulness in the great increase of faithful ministers in our land. The pure gospel is preached in thousands of pulpits, and every Lord's-day the glad tidings of a free salvation in Christ Jesus is spread far and wide.

For those who are still "blind leaders" there is one thing which all who love the truth may do: at least they can pray for them. There is not one now walking in the light who did not receive that light from above; and there is not a faithful teacher of the truth who was not himself first taught of God. God can still enlighten those who are in darkness, and cause the "blind leader" to become an enlightened and faithful guide.

Let those who are placed by God's providence where the truth is faithfully proclaimed bless God for this great mercy, and seek earnestly to bring forth fruit to his glory. Let those whose lot is less happily cast make it a matter of continual and persevering prayer that God will give his Holy Spirit, and bring both teachers and hearers into true gospel light. And let their prayer be the prayer of faith.

XVIII.

The Unforgiving Servant.

"Then came Peter to him, and said, Lord, how oft shall my brother sin against me, and I forgive him? till seven times? Jesus saith unto him, I say not unto thee, Until seven times, but, Until seventy times seven. Therefore is the kingdom of heaven likened unto a certain king, which would take account of his servants. And when he had begun to reckon, one was brought unto him, which owed him ten thousand talents. But forasmuch as he had not to pay, his lord commanded him to be sold, and his wife, and children, and all that he had, and payment to be made. The servant therefore fell down, and worshipped him, saying, Lord, have patience with me, and I will pay thee all. Then the lord of that servant was moved with compassion, and loosed him, and forgave him the debt. But the same servant went out, and found one of his fellow-servants, which owed him a hundred pence: and he laid hands on him, and took him by the throat, saying, Pay me that thou owest. And his fellow-servant fell down at his feet, and besought him, saying, Have patience with me, and I will pay thee all. And he would not: but went and cast him into prison, till he should pay the debt. So when his fellow-servants saw what was done, they were very sorry, and came and told unto their lord all that was done. Then his lord, after that he had called him, said unto him, O thou wicked servant, I forgave thee all that debt, because thou desiredst me: shouldest not thou also have had compassion on thy fellow-servant, even as I had pity on thee? And his lord was wroth, and delivered him to the tormentors, till he should pay all that was due unto him. So likewise shall my heavenly Father do also unto you, if ye from your hearts forgive not every one his brother their trespasses." MATT. 18:21-35.

THIS parable is meant to teach us how a Christian ought to forgive. It arose from Peter's question, "Lord, how oft shall my brother sin against me, and I forgive him? till seven times?" Peter thought that beyond a certain number of times he was not bound to forgive one who should have injured him; and probably he thought that to do so as often as seven times would be a great stretch of forgiveness. But our Lord taught him and us that there should be no bounds whatever to a Christian's forgiveness. "I say not unto thee, Until seven times; but, Until seventy times seven:" that is, as often as occasion should arise, however often that might be. And then he went on to enforce the lesson by a striking parable.

Like so many others, this parable begins with the words, "Therefore is the kingdom of heaven likened." It represents what might take place, not among heathen people, but among those to whom the gospel was known. It sets before us a gospel scene, gospel obligations, and a gospel standard of forgiveness. It shows how a *Christian*, as distinguished from all other men, is bound to forgive.

It is hardly necessary to say, that the king means God, the servant a professing Christian, and his fellow-servant another professing Christian, or at least a fellow-man.

The sum owed by the servant to the king was ten thousand talents—a vast sum; equal, according to the lowest reckoning, to nearly ten millions of our money. This enormous debt represents what we owe to God's justice on account of our sins, our shortcomings, our neglected duties, our slighted obligations.

It was impossible that the man should ever pay such a sum. What must be done? According to the practice of that age and country, he must be sold into slavery; "and his wife, and children, and all that he had," must be sold too, to go as far as might be towards payment of the debt. We likewise can never pay what we owe to the justice of God. Of all our countless sins, we cannot make amends for one. On the contrary, through the weakness of our sinful nature, we are continually sinning afresh, and so increasing the debt. We are therefore by nature under condemnation. We must receive the punishment due for our sins. Nothing lies before us but to be banished from the presence of God for ever.

But now the gospel comes in. The king in the parable, moved with compassion for the hopeless misery of his debtor, listened to his prayer; and knowing that, try as he might, he could never pay such a sum, forgave him all. The man did but ask for time: "Have patience with me, and I will pay thee all;" but the king forgave him the whole debt, at once and for ever. Thus does God forgive sinners. Jesus Christ, his dear Son, has made a full atonement for sin by his blood, and in the gospel forgiveness is offered to all—free, full, present, and eternal forgiveness.

The sum which the fellow-servant owed was only a hundred pence, not much more than three pounds sterling—a mere trifle, not to be compared with the vast sum which had been owing to the king. In like manner, the offences which one man commits against another are nothing in comparison with man's offences against God. Let a man have received repeated and undeserved injuries from another; let him have been treated both unkindly and unjustly, and provoked in a thousand ways; yet what does all this amount to, when viewed in comparison with that man's own sins against God? His fellow-man's offences against him, many as they may seem when he counts them over in his mind one after another, have been but few and far between after all. But every day he himself has sinned against God. His offences, his shortcomings, his inconsistent actions, his unguarded words, his unholy thoughts—if he were to set himself to number them, would be found to be beyond all reckoning. Many he has forgotten, of many he took little or no notice; yet all were sins, all items in the great account, all swelling the debt. A hundred pence to ten thousand talents! Such are one man's offences against another man, compared to a man's sins against God.

We are filled with indignation against the servant in the parable. Had he no gratitude? no sense of his own escape? no feeling of the unbounded kindness he had received? With the words of forgiveness still sounding in his ears, how could he go forth from the very scene of his deliverance, and show himself so hard and unforgiving? How was it that even the words of his fellow-servant, "Have patience with me, and I will pay thee all," did not recall to his mind the very same words so lately spoken by him out of the depth of his distress, and so compassionately heard? The feeling is a right feeling; it is no more than a just indigna-

'tion that is thus stirred within us. But let us look to it that we ourselves come not under the same condemnation. We have received forgiveness of that great debt which we owed to the justice of God; at least the offer of forgiveness has been made to us in Christ Jesus. Yet have we never indulged an unforgiving spirit towards a fellow-creature? We may not perhaps have gone so far as to refuse the prayer of one who came with tears and owned his fault, and begged us to forgive him. But how have we *felt* towards those who have injured us? When provoked by others, what is now our conduct? When tried by bitter words, what answer do we return? Do we check the rising anger? Do we strive to overcome the natural feeling of resentment? Do we return good for evil? Do we forgive, even as God for Christ's sake hath forgiven us? It is in this way that we are to apply the parable to ourselves.

What can be more stern and awful than the words of the king to the unforgiving servant? He speaks to him in the severest displeasure. The pardon is revoked. The king would forgive a debt of ten thousand talents, but he would not forgive that hard-hearted ingratitude. Now he must be delivered "to the tormentors till he should pay all that was due from him." Our Lord himself brings home the application to *us:* "So likewise shall my heavenly Father do also unto you, if ye from your hearts forgive not every one his brother their trespasses." God absolutely requires us to forgive one another. By his infinite mercy, his boundless compassion, his free forgiveness, he lays upon us this obligation. Even when he bids us seek forgiveness of him, it is in these words: "Forgive us our debts, as we forgive our debtors." We cannot even seek pardon for ourselves, while we harbor an unforgiving spirit towards another. How then can one who has *received* pardon refuse to pardon another? How can he who has felt the burden of his sins, then gone to the cross of Christ, and there received full and free forgiveness, the purchase of the Redeemer's blood—how can he who has thus been forgiven the ten thousand talents of his countless transgressions feel any thing but a perfect readiness to forgive, freely and fully, a fellow-creature who has done him wrong, a wrong that can be but as a hundred pence, a trifle, a mere nothing, compared with that debt of sin?

The man in the parable was at first forgiven, though the pardon was afterwards revoked; but he who under the gospel refuses to forgive his brother, can never himself have been forgiven. He has received the offer, and that lays him under the obligation, but he can never really have embraced the offer. For wherever Christ's salvation is embraced, there a change of heart takes place too. "We know that we have passed from death unto life, because we love the brethren. He that loveth not his brother abideth in death." 1 John 3:14. It becomes, therefore, a question affecting our own state before God, whether we are of a forgiving spirit or not. If we are unwilling to forgive those who have injured us, are we ourselves forgiven? If we can go forth into the world from hearing the gospel message, and finding there one who has done us wrong, can act, or speak, or think towards him in an unkind or unmerciful way, is it not sadly plain that the message of the gospel has not reached our hearts, and that God's mercy in Christ Jesus has not really been laid hold of by us? Let this question be well weighed, as before God.

XIX.

The Good Samaritan.

"And Jesus answering said, A certain man went down from Jerusalem to Jericho, and fell among thieves, which stripped him of his raiment, and wounded him, and departed, leaving him half dead. And by chance there came down a certain priest that way: and when he saw him, he passed by on the other side. And likewise a Levite, when he was at the place, came and looked on him, and passed by on the other side. But a certain Samaritan, as he journeyed, came where he was: and when he saw him, he had compassion on him, and went to him, and bound up his wounds, pouring in oil and wine, and set him on his own beast, and brought him to an inn, and took care of him. And on the morrow when he departed, he took out two pence, and gave them to the host, and said unto him, Take care of him; and whatsoever thou spendest more, when I come again, I will repay thee. Which now of these three, thinkest thou, was neighbor unto him that fell among the thieves? And he said, He that showed mercy on him. Then said Jesus unto him, Go, and do thou likewise." LUKE 10:30–37.

THIS parable may very likely have been a true story. The road from Jerusalem to Jericho lay in part through a rocky desert, and is said to have been much infested by robbers; and Jericho was the abode of a large number of priests and Levites, who would of course find it necessary from time to time to travel to Jerusalem. The thing here related was therefore by no means unlikely to happen.

Our Lord spoke this parable by way of answer to the question, "And who is my neighbor?" And that question arose from our Lord's reply to the lawyer, "Thou shalt love the Lord thy God with all thy heart, and with all thy soul, and with all thy strength, and with all thy mind, and thy neighbor as thyself."

This man was probably a Pharisee; and the Pharisees, and indeed the Jews in general, held very narrow notions as to whom they ought to befriend. They would own as a neighbor one who was a kinsman or friend, one living in the same place, and perhaps a fellow-countryman or one of their own religion. But a stranger, or one of another belief, or a natural enemy, they would by no means look upon as a neighbor, or feel themselves bound to help.

Our Lord, however, in this parable, taught him, and teaches us, that *all* are our neighbors. Every one who stands in need of our help, and whom it is in our power to help, even if a perfect stranger or an unbeliever or a born enemy, we are to treat as a neighbor, and to help and comfort in case of need.

The parable teaches this in a very striking way. The man who fell among thieves was a Jew, and so were both the priest and the Levite. If they had helped him it would have been according to the common notions of the Jews. But they did not. The one, when he saw him, passed by on the other side, glad to avoid so troublesome a case; the other, though he came and looked on him, yet gave him no relief, but passed by on the other side also. They proved themselves to be no neighbors to the wounded man, though of the same blood and religion. But the Samaritan was a natural enemy of the man; for the Jews and the Samaritans were bitterly opposed, and that on the score of religious forms, which, sad to say, often give rise to more bitter enmity than any thing else. Yet this Samaritan, when he saw a Jewish man lying wounded, helpless, half dead, by the wayside, showed him all the kindness of a brother. He stopped in his journey, bound up his wounds, treating them according to the medical science of the day, set him on his own beast, and brought him to an inn. There he tended him carefully, and on the morrow, after paying what would probably be enough, left him in charge of the host, with the promise to pay any thing further when next he came that way. This man, though a Samaritan, was the true neighbor to the wounded Jew; and so our Lord's questioner was forced to own. "Then said Jesus unto him, Go, and do thou likewise." And these words apply to us also; we are to take the Samaritan as our example.

I. His conduct stands out as different from that of the priest in this: that whereas the priest avoided the wounded man, the Samaritan went to him. Selfishness and indolence would often lead us to try not to see a case of distress. We must not yield to the feeling. We should have an eye for all who are in need, an ear to hear them, a heart to care for them. It is easy to turn away and seem not to notice; and often, doubtless, this would save us much trouble; but it would be to act like the priest, and not like the Samaritan, and it is the Samaritan whom our

Lord bids us follow: "Go, and do thou likewise."
If a Samaritan, with his imperfect religious light,
showed such compassion, how much more should a
Christian! "Whoso hath this world's good, and
seeth his brother have need, and shutteth up his
bowels of compassion from him, how dwelleth the
love of God in him?" We ought not even to feel
vexed when a case of want is brought before us, and
our help is asked; for this would be to turn away
in heart, even though we might not refuse to give.
Rather we should feel thankful for every opportunity of showing kindness for Christ's sake.

II. The conduct of the Levite was different from
that of the priest; but the Samaritan teaches us a
further lesson as compared with the Levite also.
The Levite did not quite disregard the wounded
man. He came and looked on him; and perhaps
if it had been only a little help that he required,
and such as would have caused small trouble or
expense, he might have been willing to give it. But
the case was a serious one. The man lay stripped,
wounded, half dead, and probably senseless. What
was to be done with him? Whither should he be
taken? Any one who should take the case in hand
must make up his mind to unknown delay, trouble,
and expense, and perhaps to being suspected of
having robbed him besides. It was more prudent,
thought the Levite, to let him alone. At least,
whatever he thought, this is what he did. When
he had looked on him, he too passed by on the
other side, and left him there to die, as he must
have supposed. How different the conduct of the

Samaritan! No thought of consequences with him, no reckoning up of delay and trouble and expense. Here was a dying man. That was enough. He must be helped, and if possible saved, at any cost. The greatness of the need, so far from leading him to pass by on the other side, did but make him more earnest in giving help. Such a man would have helped any case of distress; how much more such a case as this.

III. The Samaritan bestowed on this man that which he must have felt the loss of himself. There is nothing to show that he was a rich man, but rather the contrary. No mention is made of his having a servant with him, and he had but one beast for his journey. His thrifty conduct at the inn, in going to no needless expense, though making full provision that the sick man should have whatever he might stand in need of, seems to show him a man obliged to consider expense, though so willing to give. Yet he gave up his own beast to the sufferer's use, and freely bestowed his wine and oil, and grudged nothing that was required. It is little to give what we shall not miss. True Christian compassion will go beyond that, and, in giving to the cause of God, will not spare that which might otherwise be spent on personal comfort. Some of the best of givers are those who have but little to give.

IV. But the Samaritan did more than lay out his goods on behalf of the wounded man. He gave also time and trouble. Money, to those at least who have it in plenty, is the least of all gifts. To give time and trouble is to give far more. Some who do not refuse to help with the purse, are little disposed to take trouble, and practise self-denial in doing good. Yet several of those works of mercy, on which a blessing is pronounced by our Lord in the twenty-fifth chapter of St. Matthew, are such as cannot be done without personal trouble; as to visit the sick and the prisoners. The true Christian, whom God has blessed with means, will spare neither his goods nor his labor; and it is a comfort for those whose means are small that time and trouble can do in many cases what no money can do; and farther, that even a cup of cold water given in the name of a disciple, receives the blessing of the Lord of all.

V. The Samaritan further sets us an example of perseverance in kindness. There are some whose pity is easily moved, but as quickly dies away. They will readily help at the moment when their feelings are worked upon, taking up a case of distress with great eagerness, but soon grow tired of it. Not so the Samaritan. When he saw the wounded man, "he had compassion on him;" and this compassion was not merely a momentary feeling, but a lasting motive. He was as careful about the man on the morrow as he was when first he saw him, and did not leave him till he had made full provision for his wants. In this respect, also, let us go and do likewise; by no means checking the first warm feeling of compassion at the sight of distress, yet taking care that our sympathy and help be continued as long as needed.

VI. Thus the Samaritan sets us an example in various respects. But the special lesson we are to learn from him is this: not to confine our kindness within any narrow bounds, but to show ourselves neighbors to all who want our help. If both men had been Samaritans, or both Jews, the lessons already mentioned might properly have been drawn from the parable; but the wounded man was a Jew, and the man who helped him was a Samaritan: in this lies the special lesson.

As disciples of Christ, we are to be kind not only to those near, but to those far off; not only to kinsmen and friends, but to strangers; not to those only who love us or will be grateful to us, but even to enemies. Our Lord teaches us this same lesson elsewhere: "For if ye love them which love you, what thank have ye? for sinners also love those that love them. And if ye do good to them which do good to you, what thank have ye? for sinners also do even the same. And if ye lend to them of whom ye hope to receive, what thank have ye? for sinners also lend to sinners, to receive as much again. But love ye your enemies, and do good, and lend, hoping for nothing again; and your reward shall be great, and ye shall be the children of the Highest; for he is kind unto the unthankful and to the evil. Be ye therefore merciful, as your Father also is merciful."

There are some who are naturally winning and attractive; it is easy to show kindness to *them:* but we must be kind also to those who are not so. Some, we know, will receive our kindness gratefully and repay it with love: it is a pleasure to show kindness to such; but we must not confine our help to them. Some again are opposed to us in opinions and habits, yet let us help them in their need. And some may even have injured us, yet we must seek to do them good. In all these instances the example of the Samaritan applies. "Go, and do thou likewise."

And when we look abroad into the world at large, far beyond the narrow limits of our own sphere, and hear of vast numbers in need both temporally and spiritually, and especially of the millions of the heathen who know not God, let us not turn away, and plead "home claims," as if their case were no concern of ours. We must be neighbors for them all for Christ's sake. Though separated from them by wide seas; though in this life we shall never see them; though there may seem little in common between us and them; though they may be men of another skin and of other tongues, strangers to our ways and we to theirs; yet let us be neighbors to them, as Jesus meant us to be when he said, "Go, and do thou likewise."

The Samaritan is our example for it, but our Lord himself is a higher example still. "For ye know the grace of our Lord Jesus Christ, that though he was rich, yet for your sakes he became poor, that ye through his poverty might be rich." Such was his example; and his parting words were these: "Go ye into all the world, and preach the gospel to every creature."

XX.

The Importunate Prayer.

"And he said unto them, Which of you shall have a friend, and shall go unto him at midnight, and say unto him, Friend, lend me three loaves: for a friend of mine in his journey is come to me, and I have nothing to set before him? And he from within shall answer and say, Trouble me not: the door is now shut, and my children are with me in bed; I cannot rise and give thee. I say unto you, Though he will not rise and give him, because he is his friend, yet because of his importunity he will rise and give him as many as he needeth. And I say unto you, Ask, and it shall be given you; seek, and ye shall find; knock, and it shall be opened unto you. For every one that asketh receiveth; and he that seeketh findeth; and to him that knocketh it shall be opened." LUKE 11 : 5–10.

WE have here a parable drawn from the conduct of man towards man. There are several of the same kind among the parables of our Lord. But inasmuch as God's ways are higher than our ways, and his thoughts than our thoughts, the parable can represent in part only the truth it is meant to teach; for what man does to man in the way of kindness, is but an imperfect picture of what God does.

In that time and country, when there were not shops and inns as with us, and when travelling was so different, such a thing as is represented in the parable might easily happen. An unexpected visitor arrives in the middle of the night at the house of a friend, and seeks lodging and food; but he finds his friend ill-prepared to receive him, for he has nothing in the house. Hospitality, however, has always been thought a great duty in the East; the friend therefore goes to a neighbor's house, and asks him for bread to set before the stranger. But it is midnight, and the door is shut, and the neighbor and his family have all retired to rest. "Trouble me not," he answers from within: "I cannot rise and give thee." But the other man is not easily sent away. He knocks again, and repeats his request; and this many times, till at length his neighbor, tired of refusing, gets up, though with no good grace, and gives him what he wants. The feeling of friendship was not strong enough to rouse him, but importunity prevails.

By this parable our Lord teaches us to be importunate, or persevering, in prayer. It arose in this way: Jesus himself was praying, and his disciples saw him: and when he left off, one of them came and said, "Lord, teach us to pray, as John also taught his disciples." Then our Lord taught them what we call "The Lord's Prayer," and immediately after spoke this parable to them, thus teaching them not only how to pray, but also that they must persevere in praying, not content with asking once, but asking again and again.

The man in the parable would not get up at the first request. He heard his friend's voice, and knew his wants, but was unwilling to trouble himself to rise. It pleases God sometimes not to answer our prayers at first. It seems as if they were not heard; nay, discouraging circumstances may even lead us to fear that our petition is refused like that in the parable. But there is this great difference: the man was unwilling; God is never unwilling. The man's friendship was but an imperfect friendship. If it had been daytime, and he had been up and about, he would have lent the loaves without grudging; but he would not put himself to the trouble of rising at midnight. The kindness of God, on the other hand, is perfect and unfailing. If, therefore, our first prayers seem to receive no answer, it is not because God is unwilling to grant our request. If it be really for our good, he is quite willing to grant it, and willing from the very first; and he is as able as he is willing. Even the man in the parable was able. His "I cannot" meant, in truth, "I will not." God is both able and willing.

Again, the man would not rise because the time was unseasonable; but no time is unseasonable with God. "Evening and morning and at noon will I pray and cry aloud," said David, "and he shall hear my voice." "At midnight I will rise to give thanks unto thee." Time and place make no difference with God. Every place may be a place of prayer, and every time a time for praying. Prayer to God is never unseasonable. "Call upon me," he says, "in the day of trouble, and I will deliver thee, and thou shalt glorify me." Whenever the day of trouble may come, then and there we are to call upon God. And though he may not deliver us at once, it is not because we have called upon him at a wrong time. There is no wrong time for prayer, provided it is a time of need.

THE IMPORTUNATE PRAYER. 153

But at length the man did rise. Unwilling as he was, yet weary of repeated applications, he at last got up and gave the loaves. How much more then will God attend to the repeated prayers of those who call upon him. In the parable the time was unseasonable, the friend's kindness was but imperfect, and he was unwilling to rise; yet importunity prevailed, and he did rise. No time is unseasonable with God; his kindness is perfect; he is always willing to hear and bless. Surely then he will not turn a deaf ear to us when we call upon him again and again. If persevering prayer prevailed with an unwilling man, it will not fail with a gracious God.

The lesson therefore which our Lord draws from the parable is this: "And I say unto you, Ask, and it shall be given you; seek, and ye shall find; knock, and it shall be opened unto you." To make the exhortation stronger, three different words are used—Ask, Seek, Knock; and to each is joined a promise. And then, lest any humble soul should still fear that the exhortation and promise are not for him, our gracious Lord adds, "For every one that asketh receiveth; and he that seeketh findeth; and to him that knocketh it shall be opened."

It is not to the worthy alone that the promise is given: *every one* that asketh receiveth; every one who asks in the way of the gospel, humbly and sincerely, in the name of Jesus Christ. None are shut out. Whatever they may have done, whatever they may have been, whatever may be their wants, their sins, their sorrows, temptations, infirmities, yet tho exhortation and the promise come to them: "Ask, and it shall be given you; .... for every one that asketh receiveth." The promise is applied more particularly to the gift of the Holy Spirit, but we may apply it also to every blessing, temporal or spiritual, that would really be for our good; to the pardon of sin, to comfort in trouble, to help in difficulty, to guidance in doubt. Whenever we pray, we may do so in the faith of our Saviour's words, "Ask, and it shall be given you;" and the constant remembrance of them will make us more frequent, more earnest, and more believing in prayer.

But these words of our Lord come at the close of the parable, and contain the exhortation which he draws from it; we must therefore take them in close connection with it. We are not to ask once, and then leave off asking, as if the work were done. We are to ask, and ask again; to seek with perseverance; to knock repeatedly: for our Lord does not tell us that the blessing shall come on the first application. He will bless us when he will, and how he will. The Syrophenician woman had to ask three times before she received. The first time Jesus answered her not a word; the second time he seemed almost to refuse her request; and it was only when she still persevered that he said, "O woman, great is thy faith; be it unto thee even as thou wilt." Yet she was heard from the very first; and it was doubtless only to try her faith that the answer was withheld so long.

We too are heard when first we pray, and heard graciously. Even the man in the parable heard the very first knock of his friend, though he would not rise. We are heard at our first cry to God, and heard with no unwillingness to help. If it please our Father, in his infinite wisdom, and for our good, in order to try our faith and thus to strengthen it— if it please him to keep us waiting awhile, that we may pray again and again, more humbly and earnestly, can we not abide his time? Must we have what we desire at the very first cry, or think that God will not give it at all? How often does the psalmist speak of *waiting* on the Lord. "Wait on the Lord: be of good courage, and he shall strengthen thy heart: wait, I say, on the Lord." This is what we are to do: not waiting idly, and not praying once only; but waiting in prayer, praying again and again, and patiently abiding his good pleasure in faith and hope.

For God's promises never fail. "Every one that asketh receiveth; and he that seeketh findeth; and to him that knocketh it shall be opened." Not all at one time, or in one way; some earlier, some later; some in this way, and some in that; but all surely, because God has said it. Let none be cast down or discouraged; let the faith of none fail. "Be instant in prayer." "Ask in faith, nothing wavering." God does hear you already, and hears you graciously, in every prayer you put up, every cry of your heart, every knock at the door of mercy; and in his own good time he will show you that he has heard you. Let faith tell you so even now; and in this assurance "Pray without ceasing."

XXI.

The Father's Gift.

"If a son shall ask bread of any of you that is a father, will he give him a stone? or if he ask a fish, will he for a fish give him a serpent? or if he shall ask an egg, will he offer him a scorpion? If ye then, being evil, know how to give good gifts unto your children: how much more shall your heavenly Father give the Holy Spirit to them that ask him." LUKE 11 : 11-13; see also MATT. 7 : 7-11.

THIS parable—for such it may be considered—follows that of the man who was prevailed upon by importunity to rise and give the loaves, and is upon the same general subject—the subject of prayer.

The first teaches us to persevere in prayer. This shows us that God will not only hear us when we pray, but will give us those very blessings of which we stand in need, especially the gift of his Holy Spirit.

In this parable, as in the one before, our Lord draws the lesson from the conduct of men. What father would give his son a stone instead of bread, or a serpent instead of a fish, or for an egg a scorpion? Men, evil as they are, with many wrong feelings and dispositions, and imperfect both in knowledge and in love, yet know how to give good gifts to their children. When asked by them for necessary food, they will not give them instead what is useless or even hurtful. They know what will supply their children's need, and natural affection prompts them to give it. Much more then will God, who is of perfect wisdom and goodness, give his Holy Spirit to them that ask him.

This is the general meaning of the parable. But let us dwell a little more closely and particularly on the lessons which it teaches.

It has been remarked that in all the three cases there is a certain degree of likeness between the thing asked for and the other thing mentioned. The smooth round back of the scorpion is not unlike in shape to an egg; a serpent is still more like a fish; and a recent traveller in the East writes that at a distance a pile of Egyptian bread, round and dark-colored, might easily be taken for a heap of the flat stones found in the beds of rivers or in the desert. But no father would mock his child by giving him what would do him no good, though like in appearance to what he wanted. Much less will our heavenly Father give us the mere show and mockery of blessings. What the world gives is but a show: what God gives is real and true. Those who seek happiness in the world are but cheated with an empty appearance. Those who seek happiness in God are never disappointed. He gives what the world can neither give nor take away.

The affection of a father to his child is one of the strongest feelings in our nature. It is found even in bad men, and a man must have sunk almost to the lowest depth when he has lost all care for his own offspring. Generally speaking, this love forms a part of our nature, even in its present fallen state, and is strong enough to lead a father not only to give bread to his child, but also to work for it. But what is this love, compared with the love of God? and what is the natural kindness of an earthly parent, compared with the tender compassion and care of our heavenly Father? His is an unfailing compassion and a perfect love. He is always ready to hear us, and to grant our requests. There is no unwillingness whatever in him.

But, besides the willingness, there is a peculiar stress laid on the knowledge; and in this respect again a comparison is made between an earthly father and God. If even an evil parent has natural affection enough to lead him to supply this simple want, so the most ignorant have knowledge enough, not always to do it in the best way, but at least to give what is absolutely necessary, and what is asked for. But we have deeper wants than the want of bread, and wants that require a far deeper knowledge to supply them; yet the infinite knowledge and wisdom of God are sufficient for them all.

Sometimes, for instance, we are placed in difficult circumstances, and know not how to act. In such a case man's knowledge fails, both our own and that of our fellow-creatures. Man cannot help us then: but we seek guidance of God, and find that he knows how to give us just what we want. Our prayer is heard, help and guidance are given, and we are brought through our difficulties. Not perhaps immediately, and not by any strange means; yet in the end we are brought safely through. Our heavenly Father knows how to give us just what we want.

In St. Matthew's gospel the words of our Lord are, "How much more shall your Father which is in heaven give *good things* to them that ask him?" In St. Luke it is the gift of the Holy Spirit only that is mentioned. It is not quite clear whether St. Matthew and St. Luke are relating the same thing, or whether our Lord spoke almost the same words at two different times; but certainly we may receive both promises as his. He assures us in the one place that God will give the Holy Spirit; in the other he tells us more generally that God will give good things to them that ask him. Our heavenly Father therefore will do both.

He will give us "good things"—all that is really good for us—not only guidance in difficulty, but every thing else that he sees us to stand in need of. Does not this very expression, "good things," explain how it is that sometimes our prayers seem to go unheard? We asked, but perhaps we asked amiss; for our knowledge of what is good for us is but imperfect. We thought we were asking for bread, whereas we were asking for a stone. But God knows exactly what is best for us. He does not therefore always answer us according to our prayers; he knows better how to give us good gifts than we know how to ask for them; and surely he does but manifest his fatherly kindness when, instead of giving us what we in our ignorance think to be good, he gives us what he in his infinite wisdom knows to be so.

But the gift of the Holy Spirit is expressly promised: "How much more shall your heavenly Father give the Holy Spirit to them that ask him!"

To those who ask for the Holy Spirit this promise will certainly be fulfilled. We should all ask, and that continually. Bread is not more needful for the body than the gift of the Holy Spirit for the soul. The first beginning of life within is the Spirit's work, and it is only by the same work that it can be maintained. Every spiritual grace is the effect of this work—conviction of sin, repentance, faith, humility, love, holiness. It is through the Spirit that we gain strength for each day's duties and each day's difficulties. It is by the Spirit that our hearts learn more of the truth of God. It is the Spirit that is our Comforter in trouble, our Guide in doubt, our Sanctifier continually. We ought to seek that our hearts may be temples of the Holy Ghost, in which he may always abide. When we pray for this, God will hear us; for there is no doubt that *this* is good. We may feel sure, when we seek the Spirit, that we are seeking according to the will of God, and that he will give to us according to our prayer. Why do we not believe this promise more fully, and pray more constantly, more earnestly, and more in faith, for the Spirit?

But is the promise confined to those who expressly ask for the Holy Spirit? The words are more general: "to them that ask him." God knows what we most want. Perhaps sometimes, when we put up a prayer in all sincerity for something that would not be for our good, God answers it by sending us the Holy Spirit. Perhaps when we, in some hour of deep distress, can only cry, "Lord, help me!" God answers that prayer by the gift of the Spirit. There are times when we cannot find words for prayer, and when even our thoughts refuse to form themselves into petitions. Still let us pray. Even at such times let us cast ourselves upon the love and compassion of God in Christ, and place our hearts, as it were, in the attitude of prayer. Then the Spirit will help our infirmities, making intercession for us with groanings which cannot be uttered. God will give his Holy Spirit to them that ask him, even in the way of helping them to ask him; and the earnest-desires and the broken cries which the Spirit prompts will be answered in a larger outpouring of the Spirit's grace into the soul.

XXII.

CHRIST THE DOOR.

"Verily, verily, I say unto you, He that entereth not by the door into the sheepfold, but climbeth up some other way, the same is a thief and a robber. But he that entereth in by the door is the shepherd of the sheep. To him the porter openeth: and the sheep hear his voice: and he calleth his own sheep by name, and leadeth them out. And when he putteth forth his own sheep, he goeth before them, and the sheep follow him: for they know his voice. And a stranger will they not follow, but will flee from him: for they know not the voice of strangers. This parable spake Jesus unto them: but they understood not what things they were which he spake unto them. Then said Jesus unto them again. Verily, verily, I say unto you, I am the door of the sheep. All that ever came before me are thieves and robbers: but the sheep did not hear them. I am the door: by me, if any man enter in, he shall be saved, and shall go in and out, and find pasture. The thief cometh not, but for to steal, and to kill, and to destroy: I am come that they might have life, and that they might have it more abundantly." JOHN 10:1-10.

If we take the whole passage down to the end of the sixteenth verse as containing one parable and its explanation, still the parable seems naturally to divide itself into two parts, in the first of which our Lord likens himself to the door of the sheepfold, in the second to the shepherd. We will here consider the first part only, keeping the second part for another chapter.

The sheepfold in that age and country was very different from ours. It was enclosed within high walls, and was entered by a door. This door was kept by a porter, who would of course open it to none but those who had a right to go in. If a thief therefore came, he would not try to enter by the door, but would climb up by the wall in some other place; and whoever did so would be proved thereby to be a thief and a robber; for if he were the shepherd, the porter would readily open to him, and he would go in by the door.

It is not difficult to see that by the sheepfold is meant the church of Christ, within which his sheep or people are, as it were, kept and fed. And it is equally plain that "the shepherd of the sheep" means the true minister of the gospel. In the latter part of the parable we shall see that Jesus himself is "the Good Shepherd;" but here, when he says, "He that entereth in by the door is the shepherd of the sheep," he is probably speaking of an under-shepherd, a minister; for there would seem to be some confusion in his speaking of himself in the same sentence both under the figure of a door and under that of the shepherd who goes in by the door—and there is no confusion in the teaching of our Lord.

In explaining the parable, he tells us plainly what is meant by the door: "Verily, verily, I say unto you, I am the door of the sheep." He himself is the door of the sheepfold, and by him every true shepherd goes in. But the Jewish teachers did not go in by him. When once he had come and proclaimed himself as the Son of God, the promised Messiah, they ought to have believed in him and received him, and taught the people to do the same. Then they would have been true ministers of God, going in by the door to tend the flock. Instead of this, they rejected and opposed him. Thus they proved themselves to be no shepherds, but thieves and robbers. For every true shepherd went in by the door, Christ Jesus; but they climbed up another way.

This applies to ministers of the gospel now. If any one does not go in to the flock by Christ as the door, he is no true shepherd. He may bear the name and fill the office outwardly, as even the scribes sat in Moses' seat; but unless he has received Christ himself by faith, and become partaker of his Spirit, and unless he preaches Christ as the way, the truth, and the life, he is no real minister of his. He does indeed appear in the sheepfold, and profess to feed the sheep; but he has not come in by the door; he has climbed up some other way. What is he then? A thief and a robber. If he preach any other doctrine than that of Christ crucified, he is but stealing the hearts of the people, robbing them of the truth, misleading and deceiving them. And if he has undertaken the ministry, and still carries it on, not from faith in Christ, and a desire to spread his kingdom and win souls to him, but from some selfish or worldly motive, then also he is not a true shepherd; for he has gone without being sent, he has taken an office to which he was not called, he has not entered by the door, he has no right to be where he is. "If any man have not the Spirit of Christ," says the apostle, "he is none of his." And if any one who is outwardly Christ's minister be destitute of his Spirit, surely he too is really no minister of his.

"All that ever came before me," said our Lord, "are thieves and robbers: but the sheep did not hear them." Probably he still meant to allude to the Jewish teachers just before his coming and at the very time of it; for he could not be speaking of the ancient prophets. Now it is expressly said that the people were astonished at the teaching of our Lord, "for he taught them as one having authority, and not as the scribes;" showing that the Jewish teachers, not being true teachers, had no weight with the people. They were thieves and robbers, not shepherds, and the sheep did not hear them or follow them. There was nothing in their teaching to touch the conscience or to meet the wants of the soul, for they did not speak from God.

Whether our Lord in this first part of the parable alludes to himself at all as being the chief shepherd, or whether—as before supposed—he here speaks of himself under the figure of the door only, and means by the shepherd a common minister, it is clear that he describes what will be the effect of every true minister's work. All who go in to the sheep by the door, and simply and faithfully preach Jesus Christ, will find that the sheep hear them, and learn to know their voice and to follow them. The faithful ministry of the word will never be in vain. There will, indeed, be many failures and disappointments; yet some at least of those who hear will hear to the saving of their souls, and will be brought into the true spiritual fold of Christ. There is an attractive power in the preaching of the cross which all other preaching wants. Great gifts will often draw a crowd to hear, whatever the substance of the preaching may be; but that which will win hearts is the simple preaching of Christ. God's word does not return to him void.

The parable beautifully shows the close and loving union between a true minister of the gospel and those to whom he ministers. Going in and out among them in his Master's name, he is gladly welcomed by them. "To him the porter openeth." Some think there is a special meaning in these words, and that they signify the entrance which the Holy Spirit gives the minister of Christ into the hearts of the people. I am rather disposed to take the words merely as showing more clearly and forcibly that the true minister enters the sheepfold by the door Christ Jesus, and that when he so enters there is none to hinder him or dispute his right. There was a porter to the ancient sheepfold; but it does not necessarily follow that in the spiritual meaning there should be any person answering to him; for not every part of a parable has its counterpart. But even when taken in this general way, the words express a free and continual intercourse between the minister and his flock. As the shepherd went in and out at the door, and the porter always opened to him, so the faithful pastor, mintering the gospel to his flock, and doing all things in the name and in the power of his Lord, finds a welcome with all who are truly sheep of Christ.

He knows them one by one, and tenderly cares for each. He leads them into the green pastures of the word of God, and feeds them, and tends them, and watches over them. They are not afraid to follow him, for they know him to be faithful and true. He will not teach them false doctrine, or lead them astray. They can trust him well, for they know that he calls them to follow him only as he follows Christ.

With us, the shepherd usually drives the sheep before him; but in many other countries, and especially in the East, the shepherd goes before, and the sheep follow. The parable alludes to this custom: "And when he putteth forth his own sheep, he goeth before them, and the sheep follow him; for they know his voice." The shepherd leads the sheep out to the pasture, and himself shows them the way, while they follow at his call. In like manner the faithful minister not only points out to his people the way, but leads them in it, himself walking before them and showing them a bright example. Let ministers be careful to teach as well by their life as by their words. It is sad when these do not agree. But it is happy indeed when the preacher is himself an example of the truths he preaches, and goes before his flock in the way in which he is continually exhorting them to walk.

But the door of the sheepfold was for the sheep as well as for the shepherd. There was but that one entrance. So Christ is the door both for ministers and for people. None are truly sheep of Christ's flock but such as enter by him. "I am the door: by me if any man enter in, he shall be saved, and shall go in and out, and find pasture." Though Christians will follow, and that rightly, a faithful pastor, yet he is not their hope, their strength, or their way. Christ himself is all this, and Christ alone. They are not only to enter by him at first, and thus become sheep of the fold, but ever after they are to go in and out by him, and through him to be preserved from danger, and receive food for their souls, and grow in grace. Their life is to be in Christ. By him they are to approach the Father; in his name they are to pray; on his merits and mediation to rely. He came that they might have life, and have it abundantly. He *is* their life; for one figure alone can by no means express all that Christ is to his people. He is their door, but he is their life too, and a thousand things besides, for he is in fact their *all*.

Let us make sure that Christ is the door to us. Let us try no other way, but enter by him alone. Then let us go in and out by him, enjoying through him all the safety and happiness of the sheep of his fold. Let the sheep beware of following a stranger, lest he should prove a thief and a robber. Let them be attracted by no outward show, and misled by no strange doctrine; but let them cleave to the simple truth as it is in Jesus, and bring all preaching to that test. And let all who minister in holy things look to it that they prove themselves true shepherds of the flock by entering in at the door, Jesus Christ. Let them not preach themselves, but Christ Jesus the Lord. Let them, both in their souls and in their ministry, know nothing, as a ground of hope, "save Jesus Christ, and him crucified." Let them be simple, faithful, diligent pastors. Let them point all to the Lord Jesus: "Behold the Lamb of God, which taketh away the sin of the world," and strive to build up believers in him. Then their work will not be in vain. "Them that honor me I will honor." Though their gifts may be small, and their sphere narrow, yet they shall have souls for their hire, and in the great day there will not be wanting some who will be their crown of rejoicing.

XXIII.

The Good Shepherd.

"I am the good shepherd: the good shepherd giveth his life for the sheep. But he that is a hireling, and not the shepherd, whose own the sheep are not, seeth the wolf coming, and leaveth the sheep, and fleeth: and the wolf catcheth them, and scattereth the sheep. The hireling fleeth, because he is a hireling, and careth not for the sheep. I am the good shepherd, and know my sheep, and am known of mine. As the Father knoweth me, even so know I the Father: and I lay down my life for the sheep. And other sheep I have, which are not of this fold: them also I must bring, and they shall hear my voice; and there shall be one fold, and one shepherd." JOHN 10 : 11-16.

WE have taken the whole of the passage, beginning with the first verse of this chapter, as one parable, consisting of two parts, in the former of which our Lord represents himself under the figure of the door of the sheepfold, in the latter under that of the shepherd. This latter part we have now to consider.

In the former part he speaks of the shepherd of the sheep as opposed to a stranger, a thief, and a robber. The shepherd, who is the true and faithful minister, enters the fold by Christ as the door; the stranger climbs up some other way. This is the difference. But now, in this latter part, a further distinction appears. The faithful minister was called "the shepherd of the sheep," but Jesus calls

THE GOOD SHEPHERD. 171

himself "the Good Shepherd." The minister is a true minister, because he enters into the fold by Jesus Christ, and ministers in his name and power alone, yet he is but an under-shepherd; the Lord Jesus, on the other hand, is the chief Shepherd, the Lord of shepherds as well as of sheep, of people and of pastors too. Under the one figure he is the door of entrance both for shepherds and for sheep; under the other he himself is the Shepherd, the chief Shepherd, whose servants all the under-shepherds are. The first figure is dropped, and a new one is taken up. This is often found in our Lord's teaching. For, as was said before, one figure alone cannot represent him fully.

"I am the Good Shepherd." Jesus personally is the Shepherd of his sheep. David uses the same figure in the twenty-third Psalm: "The Lord is my Shepherd," and there describes the care, the safety, and the confidence which he thus enjoyed. All that David described, the Lord Jesus, "the Good Shepherd," is to his sheep. He was so at the time when he said, "I am the Good Shepherd," and he is so still. While he was on earth, he used to go about from place to place attended by his disciples. Wherever he went, they went. He led them, taught them, and kept them. He himself said, "While I was with them in the world, I kept them in thy name." We can see the force and beauty of the figure as applied to that time. He was like a shepherd with his flock. He is so still. When going away, he said, "I will not leave you comfortless;" that is, *orphans and destitute*, for so the Greek means—"I will come to you." He is not with us now in bodily presence; but he is with us by the Spirit, and thus the promise is fulfilled. We see not him, but he sees us. We are still his sheep, and he is our Shepherd—our personal Shepherd. Long after his bodily presence had been withdrawn, the apostle Peter wrote, "Ye were as sheep going astray; but are now returned unto the Shepherd and Bishop of your souls." Every humble believer may still say with David, "The Lord is my Shepherd."

But our Lord says, "I am the *Good* Shepherd;" not merely a shepherd, but a *good* shepherd; and not merely *a* good shepherd, as any faithful undershepherd might be called, but *the* Good Shepherd. He separates himself from all others, and speaks of himself as apart and alone, distinct from and far above all other shepherds: "I am the Good Shepherd." And this, not because he is so much higher than they, nor because he is so far better, kinder, more careful and loving, but for another reason: "I am the Good Shepherd," he says; "the good shepherd giveth his life for the sheep." He had not done so then; but he was going to do so very soon. It was in his mind—his fixed and settled purpose. He came to give his life a ransom for many, and nothing could lead him to draw back, because nothing else could save his sheep. It is this, above all, that makes him "*the Good* Shepherd."

Our Lord enlarges upon this in the parable, pointing out the difference between the conduct of a shepherd and a hireling. A hireling, or paid servant, however faithful he may be, does not care for the sheep as the shepherd does, to whom they belong; still less if he be, as our Lord seems to imply, of a hireling spirit, serving only for pay. Such a man may do his duty towards the flock in common times, but he will not expose himself to danger for their sake. In that age and country, when such a man saw the wolf coming, he would leave the sheep and flee. Not so the shepherd himself. The sheep are his. He knows them, and cares for them. He will not shrink from danger in defending them. Should the wolf come, he will not flee, but will expose his own life to save theirs; "the good shepherd giveth his life for the sheep." Our blessed Lord himself went far beyond the parable. A good shepherd might be willing to run some risk of life for his sheep; but Jesus, "the Good Shepherd," gave his life for the sheep, knowing beforehand that this would be required. The faithful shepherd might expose himself to danger, but would probably escape; Jesus freely gave himself to die; and even when the cup of suffering might not pass from him, still he said, "Not my will, but thine be done."

It is the blood of Jesus, shed for sinners, that has rescued them from the enemy, and placed them in safety and happiness. Sin had made a separation between God and man, guilt rested on the conscience, and fallen man lay under the power of the evil one. The blood of Jesus has made a full atonement for sin, and now every believer in him is freed from condemnation, and delivered from the power of Satan. All his salvation rests upon this foundation, that Jesus died for him. "The good shepherd giveth his life for the sheep:" these words express that which every believer takes as the only ground of his hope and trust.

The sense of this redeeming love knits his heart to Christ. As the good shepherd knows his sheep, so do they know him. If the sheep of Christ's flock know the voice of the faithful under-shepherd, who enters in to them by the door, and speaks to them the words of truth, much more do they know and love the voice of the Good Shepherd himself. They hear him speaking to them in his word, in his dealings, by his ministers, by his Spirit. They never forget his love in dying for them, and this makes them hear love in all his words, and see love in all his dealings. Because he first loved them, they now love him. "My sheep hear my voice, and they follow me." He may lead them at times through rough places, yet will they follow him. He may call them to walk in darkness; yet, led by his voice, they will follow him still. He will never lead them wrong, and they know it. The way may at times be rough and dark, but it will conduct them to him, that where he is, there they may be also; for he said, "I give unto them eternal life; and they shall never perish, neither shall any man pluck them out of my hand."

But in following him they want his help. In themselves they are still weak and prone to stray. The Good Shepherd gave his life for them, but they want his grace and guidance still. Still therefore he watches over them as their Shepherd. "I *am* the Good Shepherd," he says. Not merely was he so when he died for them, but he is so now. He loves them now as much as when he gave his life for them. Their safety is as dear to him, and he is as much engaged in providing for their welfare. True, that which marks him especially as the Good Shepherd is that he gave his life for the sheep; but every part of our Shepherd's dealings is of a piece with that. No earthly shepherd is so watchful and tender in his care over his sheep as our heavenly Shepherd is towards us. He knows our dangers, our snares, and our weaknesses. He sees every bypath into which we might wander unsuspecting, and every enemy that is lying in wait for us. He watches over us every moment with a faithful and loving care. Our feeblest cry will bring him to our help. One upward look of the heart will give us the comfort of his presence. Our safety is to keep close to him, listening to his voice, and following where he leads.

There is one other point which the parable sets before us. There are sheep of Christ not yet gathered in. "And other sheep I have, which are not of this fold: them also I must bring, and they shall hear my voice; and there shall be one fold, and one shepherd." Have we any duty towards these wanderers? Have we any thing to do in the work of bringing them in? Yes; our Lord has so ordered it, that every one who is himself within the fold is to do his part towards bringing in others. True, it is the Good Shepherd himself who will bring them in: "Them also *I* must bring." It is his love, his grace, his power, his word, that will do this work. Yet he is pleased to use men as his instruments. "Go ye into all the world, and preach the gospel to every creature." Wherever any are found outside the fold, whether at home or in distant lands, there Christians are to do all they can to bring them in. We pray every day, "Thy kingdom come." We are to act up to our own prayer. Not only are the ministers of Christ, the under-shepherds, to labor for this; but private Christians too—the sheep of the flock. Do we not know that it is the nature of sheep to follow one another? Often they will follow one another into danger; but often, on the other hand, we may hear the shepherd call, and see at first only one or two sheep obey the voice, but soon another and another goes after these few, and presently the whole flock is in motion towards the shepherd. Thus let Christ's sheep lead others to him by following him themselves. Let every Christian be seen following Christ in a holy and consistent life; and let him miss no opportunity of speaking a word that may lead some wanderer home. "Them also I must bring," said our Saviour. Let the servants of Christ be like-minded with their Master; and when they see numbers around them going astray, and feel withal that God has placed those wanderers within their reach, and given them in his providence some special means and opportunities for doing them good, then let them humbly follow their Master's pattern, and

THE GOOD SHEPHERD. 177

say, "Them also *I* must bring." The work by which a sinner is brought to God is God's alone, yet sinful man may be the instrument in his hand. Happy the day, when there shall be "one fold, and one shepherd." And happy then, he who shall have done his part under the Good Shepherd in bringing these wanderers in.

XXIV.

THE STRAIT GATE, AND THE SHUT DOOR.

"Strive to enter in at the strait gate: for many, I say unto you, will seek to enter in, and shall not be able. When once the master of the house is risen up, and hath shut to the door, and ye begin to stand without, and to knock at the door, saying, Lord, Lord, open unto us; and he shall answer and say unto you, I know you not whence ye are: Then shall ye begin to say, We have eaten and drunk in thy presence, and thou hast taught in our streets. But he shall say, I tell you, I know you not whence ye are: depart from me, all ye workers of iniquity. There shall be weeping and gnashing of teeth, when ye shall see Abraham, and Isaac, and Jacob, and all the prophets, in the kingdom of God, and you yourselves thrust out. And they shall come from the east, and from the west, and from the north, and from the south, and shall sit down in the kingdom of God. And, behold, there are last which shall be first, and there are first which shall be last." LUKE 13 : 24–30.

THIS passage, though it can hardly be looked upon as one connected parable, yet contains most solemn teaching in a parable form. It is the answer to a question. One said to our Lord, "Lord, are there few that be saved?" We know not who or what this person was, or why he asked such a question; but the answer is remarkable. It is an answer, and yet it is not an answer. The man is not told in words whether the saved are few or many, but he is solemnly charged, and all others are charged with him, to strive to enter in. It might be idle curiosity that led to the question, or it might be a sincere spirit of inquiry; but even in that case, the great point was not to know about others, but to make sure of finding entrance ourselves.

Let us dwell on three points. I. The strait gate; II. The shut door; III. The striving to enter.

I. The gate is called "strait;" but this is quite a different word from "straight." Straight means that which is not crooked; strait is an old-fashioned word, not much used now, meaning narrow. We find the same word used by our Lord in Matt. 7:13, 14; and there he explains fully what the strait gate means. "Strait is the gate, and narrow is the way, which leadeth unto life." The strait gate and the narrow way mean the way of eternal life, the way of salvation, the gate or entrance to heaven.

But why is it called strait? Because it is difficult, because so many miss it, because there is no room for any to pass, except those who seek to enter by one way, the way which God has appointed. "Strait is the gate, and narrow is the way, which leadeth unto life, and few there be that find it." The way of destruction is broad, and the gate wide; this is an easy course indeed. But not so the way of life.

Never think the way of life eternal to be easy, or the Christian's course to be mere play. It is easy to walk in the broad road, and to go in at the wide gate, for this is only to follow natural inclination; but it is not easy to walk in the way of life, and to go in by the strait gate. For this is a humbling, self-denying course. This requires us to forsake sin, resist temptation, and take up the cross and follow Christ. This requires us to give up all self-righteous trust, and depend entirely on the atoning blood of Christ, coming to him as sinners to be saved by grace alone. We must know our own sinfulness and weakness, we must part with all self-confidence, we must rest every hope on Jesus Christ, we must seek strength from above, we must watch and pray and strive, and that continually, if we would go in at that gate.

Yet the gate is the gate of everlasting glory, and the way is both safe and happy. "Her ways are ways of pleasantness, and all her paths are peace." No gate but the strait gate opens into the place of perfect happiness, no way but the narrow way leads thither. The strait gate, narrow and difficult as it is, is the gate for us to make for; the narrow way is the road for us to tread. Angels in heaven rejoice when a wanderer turns his steps into that way.

The strait gate is also an open gate. Though narrow, we may pass through it. "Strive to enter in," said our Lord. He would not have said so if the gate had been shut. The way is clear, for he himself is the way; "I am the way," he said. All who will are invited to enter. Christ himself has made this gate an open gate to us. He has opened the way, he himself invites us to enter, "Strive to enter in."

II. Thus the case stands at present; the strait gate is open, and we are told to strive to enter in.

But our Lord adds, "For many, I say unto you, will seek to enter in, and shall not be able." What does he mean? Does he make a difference between striving and seeking? Or does he mean that any poor souls will try to go in at the strait gate, while it is still open, and not be able? No, he does not mean this. The reason why some will not find admittance, is that they will not seek to enter till the door is shut.

The door *will* be shut. As surely as the strait gate is open now, so surely will it be shut some day; and once shut, it cannot be opened again. This present time is our day of grace. We may now be pardoned and saved through Jesus Christ. But if we do not flee to him now, our day of grace will slip away and come to an end, and then there will be no more hope for us. This is the meaning of the door being shut.

Even in the figure or parable itself there is something striking and awful in the change from open to shut. One moment, and you may go in; the gate is narrow, but it is open; there is room for you to pass; the way has been cleared for you; you are even invited, persuaded, exhorted to go in. Another moment, and the door is shut. There is no entrance now. A crowd stands without. They knock at the door; they knock again and again; they cry, they pray, they entreat. But all in vain. The door is not opened, and all the answer they obtain is one that drives them to despair: "I know you not, ... depart from me." Yet who are these who thus stand and knock? The very persons who might so lately have freely gone in at the strait gate. It was open to them, and they were told of it, and invited to enter. But they would not. And now it is too late, for the door is shut!

But much more awful is it to consider more closely and plainly what this figure means. The door shut, and the persons standing without, represent those as lost who might have been saved. The Lord Jesus Christ was made known to them as the way; they knew the gospel, and were in the habit of paying an outward attention to religion. This is plain, for they say, "We have eaten and drunk in thy presence, and thou hast taught in our streets." They were not all people of bad lives—drunkards, liars, thieves, and such like. Many of them were respectable as to outward conduct, leading a regular life, church-goers, perhaps even communicants. Yet they are not among the saved; they are shut out. Why? "Depart from me, all ye workers of iniquity." That sentence explains all. Whatever they might be in the sight of men, or in profession or outward observance, they were in God's sight workers of iniquity. For they were sinners, and they did not flee to the Saviour of sinners; though they heard the word, they did not truly lay it to heart; with all their spiritual advantages, and with all their outward attention to religion, they never repented, never sought the Saviour's blood, never gave their hearts to God; they did not seek first the kingdom of God, or strive to enter in at the strait gate. Thus they had no part in Christ, and were therefore yet in their sins—

"workers of iniquity" in the sight of God, and so shut out.

Oh, think what it would be to stand there outside the door, with the door *shut!* To look back on the time past, when the door was open; to remember words heard and read in bygone years, words of warning, of invitation, of mercy, love, and salvation; to think of many a gracious call, and many a heart-searching appeal, and many a solemn warning; and to know that it is now *too late!* No more warnings or appeals, no more calls, no more words of love and mercy; all these are past, the time for them is gone, the door is shut, and shut for ever.

III. The lesson from such a picture, the lesson from the whole subject, is this: "Strive to enter in at the strait gate."

"*Strive* to enter in." This is a very strong word, the strongest word we have, perhaps, to express seeking, trying, endeavoring. In the ancient games of running and wrestling, men used to put forth all their strength and speed, and to do their very utmost to win the prize; and this word "strive" is the word made use of to express this. Thus St. Paul writes of those "that strive for the mastery." In another place, when he is begging the Corinthians to be very earnest in prayer, he uses the same word: "I beseech you, brethren, ... that ye strive together with me in your prayers to God for me." And we ourselves, if we see one very diligent, and very much in earnest in his worldly calling, are apt to call such a man "a striving man." Our Lord bids us strive about our souls, strive to enter in. Many give only half a heart to this work, but we must give a whole heart. Many strive hard about this world, but not at all about the next; active, diligent, persevering in business, but cold and listless in religion. This will not do. "*Strive* to enter in," our Lord says. He would not have said so if we could get in without striving. True, he himself is the way, the living way. He, and he alone, has made open the entrance to us; and whoever enters will owe all his salvation to him. Yet we are to strive. Jesus himself tells us to strive. No one can strive too earnestly. It must be the first concern with us all. Whatever else we are diligent about, we should be *most* diligent about this; whatever else we strive for, we should strive for this most of all: that we may enter in at the strait gate, and find acceptance with God through Christ Jesus. If we should gain the whole world, and lose this, what would it profit us?

But we must not only strive; we must strive *now*. Our Lord teaches us not only that we are to seek above every thing else that we may enter in, but also that we are to be sure to do this while the door is yet open. "For many, I say unto you, will seek to enter in, and shall not be able." Yes, they will seek, and seek earnestly. No more coldness or unconcern then. No more formal worship, no more prayerless prayers. Now at length they are in earnest. They seek to enter in. That is all they care for. Their riches, their business, their pleasures, what are all these to them now? Nothing. Let but the door be opened once more, let but an entrance be given to them. That is all they seek, all they think of now. "Lord, Lord, open unto us!" Ah, why did they not seek thus earnestly before? Why did they not put up such a prayer while yet their day of grace lasted. Time was when not a cry would have been unheeded, not a prayer unheard; why did they put off crying for admittance till the door was shut? Why did they never pray in earnest till the time for hearing prayer was past?

Do not you so. Be not you found among those who will seek to enter in and not be able. "*Strive* to enter in at the strait gate." Strive *now*. If you have not yet begun, begin at once. If you have hitherto put it off—for any thing in all the world, for business, for family cares, for any thing whatever—put it off no more. This is a matter that will not bear putting off. While you are putting it off, the door may be shut. It is open now; and the Lord Jesus himself says to you, "Strive to enter in." He says also, "I am the way, the truth, and the life;" and again, "Him that cometh to me I will in no wise cast out."

XXV.

The Guests who Chose the Chief Rooms.

"And he put forth a parable to those which were bidden, when he marked how they chose out the chief rooms: saying unto them, When thou art bidden of any man to a wedding, sit not down in the highest room; lest a more honorable man than thou be bidden of him; and he that bade thee and him come and say to thee, Give this man place; and thou begin with shame to take the lowest room. But when thou art bidden, go and sit down in the lowest room; that when he that bade thee cometh, he may say unto thee, Friend, go up higher: then shalt thou have worship in the presence of them that sit at meat with thee. For whosoever exalteth himself shall be abased; and he that humbleth himself shall be exalted." LUKE 14:7-11.

THIS is a parable of the simplest kind, a general lesson drawn from a particular instance; the lesson is humility, the instance is the choosing of a place at a feast. Our Lord had gone into the house of one of the Pharisees to eat bread on the Sabbath-day (ver. 1), and it was probably then that he saw the other guests striving for the chief places. This was the common practice of the scribes and Pharisees. Our Lord said of them elsewhere, that they "loved the uppermost rooms at feasts, and the chief seats in the synagogues."

We are not to suppose that the feast was held in different rooms. Probably it was all in one room, but at different tables. The guests sat, or rather reclined, on benches or couches ranged along the tables, and one of these no doubt was the place of honor. There probably the giver of the feast sat, and all tried to be as near to him as possible. By "the highest room," therefore, we are to understand the chief bench or couch.

It does not appear that this eating of bread at the Pharisee's house on the Sabbath-day was any thing more than a common meal, to which the Pharisee had invited our Lord and a number of other guests. Yet even on so common an occasion all sought for the best places. Much more would they do so on greater occasions, such as a wedding-feast. Our Lord therefore draws the lesson, not from the meal of which he was then partaking, but from a wedding-feast: "When thou art bidden of any man to a wedding, sit not down in the highest room," or on the chief seat.

The reason which our Lord gives for their not doing so is one which his hearers would be likely to feel. It would be a great mortification to their pride if, after they had secured the chief place, the master of the house should make them give way to some more important guest. Not only would the chief seat be lost, but by that time the best of the lower places would be filled, and nothing would be left for them but one of the lowest of all. On the other hand, it would be a great honor if, after they had modestly sat down in a low place, the master shoul bid them move to a higher. In that case all the other guests would pay them respect, and the change from lower to higher would bring them even more honor than if they had taken the highest place at first and been able to keep it.

From this supposed case our Lord draws a general warning against self-exaltation and a lesson of humility: "For whosoever exalteth himself shall be abased; and he that humbleth himself shall be exalted." But we are not to suppose that he means us to be influenced by no higher motive than the wish to be moved up higher after having taken a low place. This would be but another way of gaining the same object. This would be to do in a less direct manner the very thing which he bids us not to do. This would be, not humility, but "the pride that apes humility." The truly humble guest would take a low place, from a feeling that it was the right place for him, and from a dislike to putting himself forward, not from the secret hope that he would be seated all the higher for it in the end. In like manner, he who is truly humble in other things not only acts outwardly in a humble manner, but *feels* humble, and *is* humble. He does not calculate what will be the consequence of his taking a low place before men; he does so sincerely and truly; this is the only place of which he thinks himself worthy; and it is often a great surprise to such a man when others take a different view of what he deserves, and bid him "go up higher."

The whole spirit of our holy religion is opposed to self-exaltation. We must become as little children, if we would enter into the kingdom of God. We are to humble ourselves under the mighty hand of God; we are invited to look in faith to the Lord Jesus Christ and be saved, but we are to look as *sinners*. If we do not come to Jesus humbly, we do not really come at all. "God, I thank thee that I am not as other men are!" was a way of addressing God that found no acceptance. "God be merciful to me a sinner!" was a prayer that was heard and answered. The self-righteous will hereafter be covered with shame and confusion of face, and will be abased indeed; while they who shall have truly humbled themselves for sin, and sought the blood of sprinkling, and thenceforth tried to walk humbly with their God, will be exalted far above their highest hopes.

Yet, strange to say, some who hold such doctrines and principles as these, and seem to hold them sincerely, and to feel and act accordingly with regard to their souls' concerns, do yet by no means show a spirit of humility in other things, but are often proud, ambitious, and self-exalting. It seems as if they could be humble before God, but not humble with regard to men. There is something wrong here; there must be something wanting in their contrition before God, their sense of unworthiness, their feeling of the evil of sin. For the heart that is truly humbled before God cannot but be humble towards men also. A broken and contrite spirit cannot dwell in the same heart with a spirit of pride and self-exaltation. A humble man is humble in all things. And one who is vain and ambitious with regard to his fellow-creatures, and desires to have the first place among them, ought to examine himself very strictly as to the state of his heart towards God, lest pride should be lurking there still.

Yet it must be granted that the desire to get on in the world is natural to us, and is not always wrong, even though we must in some measure get on at the expense of others, whom we leave behind and perhaps displace. Life is in this respect like a race; some win, others lose; some are successful and prosperous, others meet with little but failure. There is nothing wrong in doing our best to succeed, if only we maintain a right spirit and act on right principles. In seeking to get on ourselves, we need not desire to keep others back. On the contrary, we may often lend them a helping hand. An honest and moderate endeavor to advance ourselves is not inconsistent with true humility, and we may seek to raise ourselves without any thing of pride, envy, or jealousy.

But all such desires must be *watched;* for the heart is deceitful, and the world is ensnaring. And the words of our Lord must never be forgotten, "Seek ye *first* the kingdom of God and his righteousness;" nor those of the apostle, "Set your affection on things above, not on things on the earth." There, indeed, we cannot desire too much or seek too high a place. There the humblest will be highest, and they who have not sought for themselves the great things of this world will be great indeed. At the marriage supper of the Lamb there will be no misplacing of the guests, no moving up or moving down; none of the proud or self-exalting will sit down there, and not one humble disciple will be missing. Each guest will be placed by the Master himself; none will be mortified or discontented, but all will be satisfied, all thankful, all happy, all glorious. That is what we are to seek first.

XXVI.
THE GREAT SUPPER.

"Then said he unto him, A certain man made a great supper, and bade many: and sent his servant at supper time to say to them that were bidden, Come; for all things are now ready. And they all with one consent began to make excuse. The first said unto him, I have bought a piece of ground, and I must needs go and see it: I pray thee have me excused. And another said, I have bought five yoke of oxen, and I go to prove them: I pray thee have me excused. And another said, I have married a wife, and therefore I cannot come. So that servant came, and showed his lord these things. Then the master of the house being angry said to his servant, Go out quickly into the streets and lanes of the city, and bring in hither the poor, and the maimed and the halt, and the blind. And the servant said, Lord, it is done as thou hast commanded, and yet there is room. And the lord said unto the servant, Go out into the highways and hedges, and compel them to come in, that my house may be filled. For I say unto you, that none of those men which were bidden shall taste of my supper." LUKE 14: 16-24; see also MATT. 22: 1-10.

THIS parable was spoken by our Lord while sitting at meat in the Pharisee's house, by way of answer to what one of those present had said: "Blessed is he that shall eat bread in the kingdom of God." Those words therefore help us to understand the parable. They plainly refer to a spiritual feast, and so does the parable.

The "certain man" means Almighty God: the great supper means the provision which God has made for our souls in the gospel; the "many" who are bidden to it mean all to whom the gospel comes,

THE GREAT SUPPER. 193

I pass over the application of the parable to the Jewish nation, because that concerns us less than its application to ourselves; only remarking that the Jews were invited first, and that when they as a nation refused the invitation, then it was given to others; first to the nations nearest to the Jews, and then to all the nations of the world. Long before Christ came, the Jews knew the will of God, and had the promise of the Messiah; thus, in a general way, they were bidden; when our Lord came, they were invited at once to believe in him, for the spiritual feast was then ready: but they rejected Christ, and then the gospel was preached to the Gentiles. Our Lord's parting command was: "Go ye into all the world, and preach the gospel to every creature."

Passing from this, let us now consider the parable more closely as applying to ourselves.

God has made a great supper, the gospel plan of salvation. It is great in every way. It supplies a great need, it is large enough for all, it will fully satisfy all who partake of it; it is rich and plentiful, and will not only *feed* those who are spiritually hungry, but will make them happy too. It is also a great supper, because the guests are many; for though many refuse, yet great numbers accept the invitation. Already the whole body of believers throughout the world is large; but what will the number be when all the guests of every age and country are gathered together at the feast above?

We are bidden to this supper. The man in the parable bade many. God also has invited many;

he has invited *us*, for we have heard the gospel, and it is in the gospel that the call is given. The invitation is quite free; there is nothing to pay. Just as we are, we are invited to go to Christ; and in him are offered to us freely pardon, life, salvation, peace, heaven.

This invitation has come to us; but, more than that, it does still come to us continually. The parable represents one message only, when the feast was actually spread: "Come, for all things are now ready;" but we are always receiving the message of the gospel afresh. Every time we hear the preaching of the word, every time we open the Bible, the gracious call comes to us again, in one shape or another, "Come, for all things are now ready."

What have we done, and what are we doing with regard to the gospel call? That is the main point in the parable. Those to whom the message was sent, "Come, for all things are now ready," "with one consent began to make excuse." This does not mean that they agreed among themselves what to do and say, for they were not together when the message was brought; it came to each separately. But the meaning is, that they were all of one mind in the matter; none of them had any wish to be at the supper; all alike tried to find an excuse. The excuses were various, but the mind was the same: they would not go.

How exactly this represents what takes place with regard to the gospel. Sinners are invited to go to Christ, but they have no wish to go. They feel no need of him, and see nothing to desire in him. The complaint of the prophet comes true: "Who hath believed our report?" And our Lord's own words are fulfilled: "Ye will not come unto me, that ye might have life." Therefore they make excuse; not in words, perhaps, but in deed. They hear the gospel; that they can hardly help doing. Perhaps some may even feel at times half drawn to accept it. But they do not obey the call. Their will is not that way. Some reason they will find for refusing, or if not refusing, neglecting; and to neglect is really to refuse. And they do find a reason. Whether it satisfies even their own conscience may be a question.

But the excuses in the parable look at first sight like real and good excuses. No doubt the ground and the oxen had been bought, and the wife had been lately taken in marriage. Yet the invitations to that supper ought to have outweighed all. Whatever had happened, they ought to have gone. We see this more clearly in the explanation than in the parable itself. For the supper, as we have seen, means the gospel, and the gospel call must be obeyed in spite of all hinderances, and nothing whatever can form a good excuse for not obeying it. These men did not stay away for the purpose of doing any thing wrong; the things were right in themselves. And, in the same way, the things by which men excuse themselves from obeying the gospel and seeking Christ are not always wrong things. Often, very often, they are, but by no means always.

One of these men had bought a piece of ground,

and thought himself bound to go and see it. Thus it often is, that men of great possessions let their possessions hinder them from attending to their souls. And not only men of great possessions. Here it was but one piece of ground that kept the man from the feast. A very small share of worldly goods will keep a man from Christ, if the heart be too much set upon it. A worldly and covetous mind is not confined to the rich. Such a person does not speak perhaps like the man in the parable, and say in words that he cannot and will not attend to the call of God because of his possessions. But he does in fact let them hinder him. His mind is full of worldly things; his pleasures are all drawn from what he has got; his chief desire is to get more; he has no room in his thoughts for the things of God, far less can he give them, what they *must* have, the first place. He might lawfully look to his property. Nay, he ought to do so. But he ought not to let it stand in the way of his soul. Lands and houses, old possessions and new, all should come second to salvation. When Christ calls, we must be prepared to leave all, if need be, and follow him.

The second man must go and try his new oxen; that was his excuse. He was doubtless a careful and industrious man, and at another time this would have been quite right; but not when he was called to that supper. As worldly possessions must not stand in the way of our souls, no more should worldly business, or work. Yet it often does. Some men are so busy that they cannot find time for religion. They almost say so. Some day, they think, their business will be less engrossing, their work lighter; then they will attend to such things, for they know they ought to be attended to. Alas, that time may never come, or not till it is too late. Some there are who think and speak thus; but perhaps there are more still who act so without saying so. Their life is one almost unbroken course of business, work, and worldly anxiety. Their business may be honestly conducted, their work faithfully done, and their anxieties may but spring naturally from their large concerns. Their fault is, not in being men of business, or working men, but in letting work or business thrust out religion, and keep them back from Christ. "Business must be attended to," such men are wont to say; "work must be done." Another "*must*" may be the answer to them. "The soul *must* be cared for, Christ must be sought, the gospel must be heartily received, or you are undone for ever." And this "must" is the stronger of the two. It never can be right to be kept back from true religion by worldly business or work. It is a very common excuse, but it will no more prevail than did that of the man in the parable.

The third man excused himself by his having lately married a wife. Family reasons are often made an excuse for not attending to religion. The most common instance, perhaps, is that of the mother of a young family. Some young mothers never, or almost never, enter the house of God. They cannot, they say; they have so much to do at home. But other young mothers do, though with difficulty; and, generally speaking, what one does, another may do. The chief difference is in the will. A mother who very much wishes to go to the house of God, will find that she can often do so. One who has no wish at all to go is ready to catch at any excuse. But going to the house of God is not in itself accepting the gospel call, but only going to hear it again and to join in worship. To accept the call of the gospel is something deeper; it is to repent, and believe in Jesus, and close with God's offer of salvation by him. A person may be a steady church-goer, and yet not do this. Family cares are often made an excuse for not thus giving the heart to God. The heart of the careful and anxious mother is quite filled with thoughts of her children. She seems to live but for them. And is not this right? Is she not their mother? Is she not bound to care for them? Yes; but not in such a way as to lead her not to care for her own soul. God never places us in any circumstances in which we may not serve him and do his will. The busiest mother of a family ought still to be seeking God first. No family cares ought to keep her from coming to Christ, as she is invited to do in the gospel. Family duties are very important and very pressing, but *this* is the great concern; and family duties would be all the better done, and children would be better cared for, better brought up, ay, and made happier too, if parents would but seek first the kingdom of God and his righteousness. This is another vain excuse. It looks right, but it is wrong.

But if it is wrong to be kept back from serious religion by family cares, still more so is it to let the love of pleasure be the hinderance. Perhaps the case of the third man may point to this also. He wished to enjoy the society of his newly married wife, and therefore would not go to the feast; many are so bent upon worldly pleasures, often of a less innocent kind, that they cannot or will not give their hearts to spiritual things. This is especially the case with the young. Youth is the season of enjoyment; all looks bright then, and no one would wish to damp youthful spirits, or to interfere with the keen delight which the young take in what pleases them. Yet there is no time of life at which the concerns of the soul ought not to be first. Our chief pleasures, in youth as well as in after years, should be drawn from things spiritual; and that person *must* be wrong, whether young or old, who allows worldly pleasures to keep him from Christ.

The love of pleasure should be watched against even by those who are not thus utterly thoughtless, for they too are in danger from it. Too much indulgence in this way blunts the spiritual affections, and takes away the taste for serious things. And there is danger also of being led to join in things in which a Christian ought to have no part, and thus to seek to serve two masters. Many, who seemed to begin well, have been gradually drawn back to the world by a too great fondness for its pleasures; and many a young and promising disciple has seemed to stop in his growth through the same cause. There is awful danger in such cases of proving at last to have had only "the form of godliness;" for religious habits may, in some degree, be maintained, while yet the heart is kept back from God through the love of pleasure.

The master of the house did not accept these excuses; he was angry with the men who made them. God also is displeased with those who do not accept his offered mercy in Christ. He sees through all their vain excuses. They may deceive themselves, but they cannot deceive him. It is highly displeasing in his sight when those to whom the gospel comes suffer riches or business or family cares or worldly pleasures or any other cause to hinder them from believing and accepting it.

The anger of the master in the parable was shown in his telling his servants to go and call in other guests instead of those who would not come. First they were to go into the streets and lanes of the city, and bring in "the poor, and the maimed, and the halt, and the blind;" and when there was still room left, they were to go "into the highways and hedges, and compel them to come in." As for those who had made excuse, they should not taste of the supper. They who neglect the gospel are in great danger of having the gospel taken away from them. Not to speak of death, which may carry off the worldly and careless in a moment, the faithful preaching of the word may be removed from those who would not attend to it, and taken to some place where it has not hitherto been. Doubtless this often happens in the providence of God. And then, most likely, they who used at times to feel the power of the word, though they would not obey it, become quite careless. Even if the gospel be not thus removed, yet the end of all who excuse themselves from its call must be that they will be shut out at last. They are awful words: "I say unto you that none of those men which were bidden shall taste of my supper." Think what they mean: men invited, refusing or neglecting, and then shut out! This will be the case with those who neglect the gospel invitation.

There is something in the very word "excuse," that seems strange in this case. Men generally excuse themselves from something hard or painful, from a disagreeable duty, or a troublesome task; but in the parable the men excused themselves from a *feast*. And those who excuse themselves from the gospel, excuse themselves from the greatest of all blessings. Yes, the greatest of all blessings; in fact, all blessings are contained in what God offers to us in Christ—a free pardon, a full salvation, a quiet conscience, the peace of God, eternal rest and glory. And this is what men *excuse* themselves from receiving. It is offered as a gift, and they will not have it.

You will never be happy without it. The things which form your excuse do not, cannot make you happy. A little pleasure for a little while is all they can give, and much of vexation and disappointment is mixed with it. Nothing will make you truly happy, nothing will make you even safe, but that which God offers you so freely in Christ. What is it that keeps you from accepting it? What is it that you make your excuse? Whatever it is, put it away. Excuse yourself no longer. Your excuse is a vain one, and you know it. The word of God tells you so, and conscience tells you so too. What will become of your excuses in the great day? Will you dare even to mention them? And if they will be worthless then, must they not be worthless now? They *are* worthless. Be deceived by them no more. God calls you: obey the call. God invites you: accept the invitation. You are not yet shut out, though you have neglected the invitation too long. Go in while you may, and you will still be welcome through Jesus Christ.

XXVII.

THE MAN WITHOUT A WEDDING GARMENT.

"And when the king came in to see the guests, he saw there a man which had not on a wedding garment: and he saith unto him, Friend, how camest thou in hither not having a wedding garment? And he was speechless. Then said the king to the servants, Bind him hand and foot, and take him away, and cast him into outer darkness: there shall be weeping and gnashing of teeth. For many are called, but few are chosen." MATT. 22:11-14.

THE parable of which this passage forms part is almost the same as that contained in the fourteenth chapter of St. Luke. Whether the two accounts relate to the same thing, or whether our Lord spoke the parable on two different occasions, we do not know. At all events, St. Luke does not record the incident of the man without the wedding garment.

The guests here are those who were gathered in from the highways, when those first invited refused to come. The wedding was now at length furnished with guests, and the king came in to see them.

It was the custom on such occasions for the great man who gave the feast to provide each guest with a suitable dress, usually a long white robe, which was put on upon entering the house. Without such a dress no one might appear.

But in the parable, when the king came in to see the guests, he found one who had not on a wedding garment. He at once addressed him, inquiring how he came to be there without one. The man was speechless. He had no excuse to offer. He might have had a wedding garment for the asking, for they were freely bestowed. It must have been pride, or disrespect, or mere careless indifference, that led him to sit down at the feast without one. He could say nothing. Perhaps, before the king came in, he had found plenty to say. His dress was good enough, or he had not had time to change it, or he had forgotten to do so. But now, when the king himself questioned him, he had not a word to say. So he was cast out. He must sit no longer among the king's guests. He was ordered to be bound hand and foot, and cast into outer darkness, as having broken the king's regulations, despised his authority, and treated him with disrespect and insult.

What does this mean? What spiritual lesson does the parable, in this part of it, teach?

The king means God himself; the feast is the gospel with its privileges and blessings; the men first invited were the Jews, those called in afterwards were the Gentiles; and by sitting down at the feast we are to understand having gospel light, belonging outwardly to the church of Christ, and taking part in religious ordinances. The king coming in to see the guests must refer to the day of judgment, when the secrets of all hearts will be disclosed, and the great separation will be made.

And the wedding garment means the robe of Christ's righteousness, implying a state of reconciliation and acceptance; that state, in short, in which the true believer is, as distinguished from the nominal Christian.

The man without a wedding garment represents therefore one who bears the name of Christian, but is no Christian in heart. He takes his place among those who love God, and passes perhaps for a religious man. He attends the house of God, keeps up, it may be, the form of worship in his family, and even goes to the Lord's table. But he has no heart-religion. With all this outward seeming, he has not sought the blood of sprinkling, or the gift of a new heart. He sits among the guests, but the wedding garment is wanting.

The eye of God is upon him all along. God knows the true from the false. In his sight there is an infinite difference between the true believer and the nominal Christian, though both may make the same profession; and in the great day of judgment that difference will be made known, and the righteous and the wicked will be parted for ever. Till then, perhaps, men will not have found out the true character of the mere professor; for he is not a gross sinner, and deceives himself probably as well as others. But in that great day, when the King—the King of kings—will come in to see the guests, and strict and searching examination will be made of all who bear the Christian name, then at last he will be discovered to the eyes of all. He has no wedding garment! He must not stay. He must be cast out. He has seemed indeed to belong to the church on earth, but he cannot be admitted into the church in heaven. He must go to his own place.

There will be *many* such, though but one is mentioned in the parable; many in number and various in character. But they are all alike in this, that they have no wedding garment; and *now* they are all alike speechless. They do not even seek to make excuse. They know it would be vain with Him with whom they have to do.

They were not always speechless. They could make excuses once.

One used to trust in his upright character. When disturbed by conscience, he would take refuge in his honesty and integrity, in his doing no one any harm, in none having a word to say against him. He does not hold this language now, he is speechless.

Another would look around and see numbers living just like himself, and would comfort himself with the thought that he was no worse than others. He does not say that now.

A third had his religion all in the head and on the lips. He was well acquainted with the Bible, kept company with religious people, knew gospel doctrine, and could talk fluently about it. But his heart was unchanged. And now, all his fluent talk is gone, and he too is speechless.

Another felt the need of religion, and was always meaning to seek God in truth. Yes, he would indeed be in earnest; let him but begin another year, and he would be quite different. So he said, year after year. He does not say so now. He too is speechless.

All the old excuses are gone; these, and a thousand more. They have nothing to say. They are speechless. What could they say? They might have had the wedding garment freely. All that their souls needed—pardon, grace, life, salvation—they might have had "without money and without price." Christ might have been theirs. He offered himself to them as their Saviour, and that again and again. But they did not accept the offer. They let slip the day of salvation. It is this that makes them speechless.

This is a matter that concerns us all. We are the guests. We are sitting down at the gospel feast on earth, for we are living in the enjoyment of gospel blessings, and we bear the name of Christian. Oh, let us see that we have the wedding garment! The King has not yet come in to see the guests, the great day of reckoning has not yet arrived. Yet he does see us all continually. What robe does he see on us? The white robe, or the filthy garments? Have you any doubt? Oh, set that doubt at rest. Go to the gracious Saviour; go while yet you may; go just as you are; and ask him to wash you clean, and to clothe you in white. Pray for a new heart, for the gift of the Holy Spirit. Ask for all that is meant by the wedding garment. Ask in faith. The wedding garment of old was free; the wedding garment of the soul is free too. "Ask, and it shall be given you."

XXVIII.

The Tower-Builder.

"For which of you, intending to build a tower, sitteth not down first, and counteth the cost, whether he hath sufficient to finish it? Lest haply, after he hath laid the foundation, and is not able to finish it, all that behold it begin to mock him, saying, This man began to build, and was not able to finish." LUKE 14 : 28–30.

OUR Lord invited all to become his followers, and was willing to receive all who came to him. But he would have none undertake his service without a full knowledge of what they were doing. He would not that any should put his hand to the plough, and afterwards look back.

This parable was spoken at a time when "there went great multitudes with him." There might be among them some who, attracted by his mighty deeds and gracious words, were ready hastily to join themselves to him as his disciples, without sufficient thought. He warned them against this. Let them fully understand what it was to become his followers. Let them be prepared beforehand for what they must meet with in his service. They must be ready to give up all for him. Even the closest and most sacred of natural ties must be held second to his claim upon them as his disciples. Not even father or mother, wife or children, brethren or sisters must be suffered to come in competition with him. They must be prepared, if required, to sacrifice life itself in his service. They must not shrink from hardship and self-denial. They must bear their cross, and follow him.

This lesson our Lord enforced by the simple parable of the man about to build a tower. Would not such a man first count the cost? Would he not calculate his means before laying the first stone? Would he not, as the very first step, ascertain whether he had enough to finish as well as to begin? If he should neglect this, and should find, when he had laid the foundation, that he had not means to finish the building, he would be a laughing-stock to all. The unfinished tower would be perfectly useless. The time and money bestowed upon it would have been quite thrown away. And the building itself, in its unfinished and useless state, would raise a laugh against him from all beholders.

So is it likely to be with those who undertake the service of Christ inconsiderately. They do not think enough of the deep importance of what they are doing. They do not seriously consider what it means, what it requires, and what consequences it will bring. In a moment of excited feeling they profess themselves disciples of Christ, supposing that their feelings will always be as they are now, and not realizing the hinderances, the difficulties, and the discouragements of the Christian course. So when these things come, as come they must, they are disappointed. They find the service of

Christ different from their expectations. And in many cases that service is given up in disgust, and the world is sought again, and perhaps "the last state of that man is worse than the first." Religion is now distasteful to him, and he is not unlikely to give himself wholly to the world, or even to go great lengths in sin.

Alas for the early promise! Alas for the youthful warmth and zeal! Alas for the eager hearing of the gospel, the earnest attention, the deep interest, the seeming impression! Where are they now? Gone, gone, perhaps never to return. The unfinished beginning is useless to the man himself, useless to all. No religion can save that stops short of a coming to Christ and a cleaving to Christ. And no one can be really useful to others, who does but begin well, and then goes back or turns aside.

This brings discredit not only on the person concerned, but also on religion itself, though most unjustly. The world gladly welcomes such a one into its ranks again; yet secretly it thinks the worse of him for turning back from God. "See!" it cries, "this comes of extreme opinions. This is what extravagance and enthusiasm end in. Such strictness could not last."

Thus our Lord warns us against inconsiderately taking up his service. But would he deter us from serving him? Oh, no. He says to all: "Come unto me." But he says further: "Come, take up the cross, and follow me." He invites us to join ourselves to him; but he would have us do it with deep seriousness, with a full sense of what we are doing, and with a real surrender of heart. He would not discourage any. "My yoke is easy," he says, "and my burden is light." "Peace I leave with you, my peace I give unto you." His service is the only happy service, and to be *his* is the only way to be safe. We shall indeed be called to give up sin and the world for his sake, and in following him we shall have to "endure hardness." Yet we shall be no losers; our Master will more than make up to us for all that we shall give up for him. He will give us now pardon and peace, and in the end he will give us a home with him for ever.

It is not too late for those who have turned away from Christ, after once beginning to serve him, to turn to him again. Even the backslider he graciously invites. But let them come to him now, not hastily and inconsiderately as they once did, but humbly, thoughtfully, prayerfully. Unlike the builder of the tower, they have no resources whatever of their own—nothing even to begin with; they must owe *all* to grace. Let them form no rash and hasty purposes, and make no loud professions. Let them seek the Holy Spirit. Let them ask for grace according to their need; grace to choose Christ, grace to cleave to him, grace to follow him; daily grace for daily need. Then they will not be surprised when they meet with difficulties, and will be enabled to face them in a strength not their own. Then, with a truer knowledge of what the Christian course is, they will recognize in trial and temptation, in hinderances and difficulties, the very marks that they are following Jesus. And perhaps others, who used to mock, will learn to respect the consistency of their Christian conduct, and thus will their light shine before men and bring glory to God.

XXIX.

The Lost Sheep, and the Lost Piece of Silver.

"And he spake this parable unto them, saying, What man of you, having a hundred sheep, if he lose one of them, doth not leave the ninety and nine in the wilderness, and go after that which is lost, until he find it? And when he hath found it, he layeth it on his shoulders, rejoicing. And when he cometh home, he calleth together his friends and neighbors, saying unto them, Rejoice with me; for I have found my sheep which was lost. I say unto you, that likewise joy shall be in heaven over one sinner that repenteth, more than over ninety and nine just persons, which need no repentance. Either what woman having ten pieces of silver, if she lose one piece, doth not light a candle, and sweep the house, and seek diligently till she find it? And when she hath found it, she calleth her friends and her neighbors together, saying, Rejoice with me; for I have found the piece which I had lost. Likewise, I say unto you, there is joy in the presence of the angels of God over one sinner that repenteth." LUKE 15 : 3-10.

THIS parable was spoken by our Lord in reply to the Pharisees and scribes. All the publicans and sinners had drawn near to hear him, and the Pharisees and scribes murmured against him because he let them do so. "This man," said they, "receiveth sinners, and eateth with them." The parable was his answer. It is a double one, setting forth the same truth under two different figures. The first is that of a man losing one out of his hundred sheep; the second represents a woman losing one of her ten pieces of silver. The man in the one case, and the woman in the other, mean our Lord himself. The lost sheep and the lost piece of money mean a sinner.

The general lesson to be drawn from the two figures is the same; yet the difference in the things lost is not without meaning.

A lost or wandering sheep is used in other places to represent a sinner: "All we like sheep have gone astray;" "For ye were as sheep going astray." The sheep wanders from the fold and the shepherd, the sinner wanders from God and his ways. The sheep is in great danger, and will be lost if not brought back, yet it probably wanders heedlessly farther and farther. The sinner too is in danger—awful danger—and will be lost for ever if he do not come back to God. He does not feel his danger. The path he has chosen for himself pleases him more than the way of God. He does not see—at least he does not trouble himself to think—whither it leads. Enough for him that it is, as he thinks, a pleasant path. So he too wanders heedlessly on, and gets farther and farther from God. He has no wish to return; nay, he cannot return of himself. He must be sought if ever he is to be saved.

The sheep was lost by its own wilful wandering; the piece of silver by accident, as we should say. It dropped from the woman's hand perhaps, and fell into some crack or corner, where it was overlooked at the time. Now it is possible that our Lord meant to show us here two distinct cases: the one that of a wilful sinner, the other that of one who has fallen—a sinner, it is true, but one who has been betrayed into sin rather than rushed headlong into it. The sheep went astray, the money was simply lost.

But there is another point to be noticed with regard to the piece of silver. It was a thing of value for what it would buy. While in the woman's possession, it might procure for her food or clothing, or any thing she stood in need of; but once lost, it was of no use to her. Somewhere it must be, but it could do her no good till she found it again. So the sinner might be of use in the service of God; but while he is lost, he is of no use whatever. As the piece of money was made of a precious metal, so God has given to him talents, valuable qualities, powers for good, means of usefulness; but at present these are of no avail. For any good that he does, he might as well not be. He is like the lost piece, of no use till he is found. Nay, far from doing good, he is doing harm. Every sinner does harm.

The man in the parable went in search of the lost sheep; the woman lighted a candle, and swept the house, and sought diligently for her piece of money. This represents the Lord Jesus Christ seeking lost sinners. He came on earth to do so. He said himself: "The Son of man is come to seek and to save that which was lost." In all his going about from place to place, preaching and teaching, he was seeking the lost. He was doing so when he let publicans and sinners draw near to him to hear him. The Pharisees were angry that he did so, but it was the very purpose for which he came.

There were among them some at least who were like the lost sheep and the lost piece of silver. He was graciously searching for them when he let them come near and hear his words.

Our blessed Lord, who thus sought out the lost when he was on earth, has long been gone; yet he still carries on the same work. By his word, in which the message of salvation is written; by his ministers, who preach the word; by his Spirit, convincing men of sin and working in the heart, he still goes after that which is lost. Nay more, we are taught that it is for this that he delays his coming: "The Lord is not slack concerning his promise, as some men count slackness; but is long-suffering to usward, not willing that any should perish, but that all should come to repentance." Because there are yet wanderers to be brought home, therefore the Lord has not yet come.

In the parable, the man did not leave off his search for the sheep till he found it; the woman also went on sweeping the house till the piece of money appeared. No pains or trouble was spared. Both persevered till that which was lost was found. In like manner has the Lord dealt with those who are now brought home to God, but who were once wanderers in the paths of sin. It was not once only that he sent them a message of love and mercy. Long were they sought, many and various were the means used. Many a time did he call, and they refused. It was only perhaps after years of gracious waiting and repeated invitations, that the wanderers were brought home, and the lost found.

THE LOST SHEEP.

But, after all, it was but one sheep that the man in the parable had lost, and but one piece of money that was missing: yet for but one all this trouble was taken. This shows us the preciousness of one soul in the Saviour's sight. People sometimes talk slightingly of missionary work and of other efforts to do good to souls, because, say they, the success is so small. If they thought aright of the value of a soul, they would not speak thus. Let it be granted that the number of the heathen converted by the preaching of the gospel is but small compared with the vast number that remain heathen still, and that in all gospel work, whether at home or abroad, we should gladly see hundreds and thousands turned to God instead of tens or ones. Yet even one soul is beyond all price. It is so in God's sight, it ought to be so in ours. Is not each soul to live for ever? Must it not be in endless misery, if not in endless happiness? Then how can it be a light thing, that even one soul should be saved?

In the parable, there was joy when the sheep was brought back, joy when the money was found. Likewise, our Lord tells us there is joy in heaven, "joy in the presence of the angels of God over one sinner that repenteth." Nothing can show more strongly the value of even one soul in the sight of God. Picture the case of a sinner brought to repentance; not a remarkable case, but a common case, such as may happen any day. A poor working man, living, it may be, in some low court in a great town, or in an humble cottage in a country place, unknown beyond the little circle of his own workmates and neighbors, has long lived in neglect of his soul; not a gross sinner perhaps, nor worse than most of those around him, but without God: this man by some means is brought to care for his soul, to repent of his sins, and to seek Christ—in other words, he becomes a Christian man. Very few people care for the change, or even know of it. The minister may thank God for it on bended knee; the man's wife and children may be the happier for it, as they certainly will; and his workmates and neighbors may take notice of the alteration, and some of them may perhaps wonder what has come over the man, and think the change not a change for the better. But meanwhile there is joy in heaven; joy in the presence of the angels of God; joy on account of that poor man, because he has been found at length, because his heart is changed, because he has repented and turned to God. It seems but a small thing to man, but it is not counted a small thing in heaven. Even in that happy place where all is joy, the angels rejoice anew because this one sinner has been brought to repentance.

But even this is not all. The man left the ninety and nine sheep in the wilderness to go after the one that was lost; the woman did not give a thought to the nine pieces that were safe, while she was anxiously searching for the one that was missing; and all the joy that followed was for the one sheep and the one piece of silver. "Likewise," says our Lord, "joy shall be in heaven over one sinner that repenteth, more than over ninety and nine just persons which need no repentance." How are we to understand this?

Some suppose that our Lord spoke of such as *though* they needed no repentance, like those self-righteous scribes and Pharisees. If so, the Saviour's words would yet be true, for there would be no joy at all in heaven over them. But it seems more likely that he meant such as really need no repentance. There is more joy for one repenting sinner than for "ninety and nine just persons who need no repentance." This seems strange at first sight. But what *is* repentance? And why do any not need it? Repentance here means not merely sorrow for sin, which we all need continually, but a change of heart—that very change over which there is joy in heaven in the case of the one sinner. And the reason why the righteous do not need it is that they have experienced it already. They *are* changed, and therefore do not need to be changed. Every one needs this change at one time or another, but those who are here called "just," or righteous, have passed through it. It was by this very change that they became righteous.

Still there seems some difficulty. Why more joy for one than for so many? It is only for the time. There has been joy in heaven over each one of the ninety and nine, as each in his turn repented and came to God; for the moment, each was rejoiced over specially. So it is with this one now. He is brought to repentance, he is added to the number of the righteous; another heart has been led to Christ, another soul has become a partaker of his salvation. Therefore there is joy in heaven; more joy, for the moment, than over those who were already safe.

Has there been joy for *you?* Have you been brought to this repentance, this change of heart? Have you ever learnt that by nature you are lost? See how precious one soul is in the sight of God; *your* soul is thus precious. See how the Saviour seeks the lost. Has he not sought *you?* Has he not sought you again and again? Think of the joy in heaven! Such joy may be felt for *you;* nay, certainly will be felt, if you repent. Your soul is not uncared for above. The Lord Jesus Christ seeks it, and angels would rejoice at its salvation. Wandering from God can only end in ruin; come back at the Saviour's call! It is grievous that talents which God gave to be used for his glory, should be all useless and wasted, like the lost piece of silver. Awake to a sense of what you owe to God, and of the account you must one day give to him. It is not yet too late. You may yet turn to Christ; you may even now do God service.

XXX

THE PRODIGAL SON.

"And he said, A certain man had two sons: and the younger of them said to his father, Father, give me the portion of goods that falleth to me. And he divided unto them his living. And not many days after the younger son gathered all together, and took his journey into a far country, and there wasted his substance with riotous living. And when he had spent all, there arose a mighty famine in that land; and he began to be in want. And he went and joined himself to a citizen of that country; and he sent him into his fields to feed swine. And he would fain have filled his belly with the husks that the swine did eat: and no man gave unto him. And when he came to himself, he said, How many hired servants of my father's have bread enough and to spare, and I perish with hunger! I will arise and go to my father, and will say unto him, Father, I have sinned against heaven, and before thee, and am no more worthy to be called thy son: make me as one of thy hired servants. And he arose, and came to his father. But when he was yet a great way off, his father saw him, and had compassion, and ran, and fell on his neck, and kissed him. And the son said unto him, Father, I have sinned against heaven, and in thy sight, and am no more worthy to be called thy son. But the father said to his servants, Bring forth the best robe, and put it on him; and put a ring on his hand, and shoes on his feet: and bring hither the fatted calf, and kill it; and let us eat, and be merry: for this my son was dead, and is alive again; he was lost, and is found. And they began to be merry. Now his elder son was in the field; and as he came and drew nigh to the house, he heard music and dancing. And he called one of the servants, and asked what these things meant. And he said unto him, Thy brother is come; and thy father hath killed the fatted calf, because he hath received him safe and sound. And he was angry, and would not go in: therefore came his father out, and entreated him. And he answering said to his father, Lo, these many years do I serve thee, neither transgressed I at any time thy commandment: and yet thou never gavest me a kid, that I might make merry with my friends: but as soon as this thy son was come, which hath devoured thy living with harlots, thou hast killed for him the fatted calf. And he said unto him, Son, thou art ever with me, and all that I have is thine. It was meet that we should make merry, and be glad: for this thy brother was dead, and is alive again; and was lost, and is found." LUKE 15:11–32.

THE chief lesson to be learned from this beautiful parable is the perfect readiness of God to receive the returning sinner. It is one of the three parables which our Lord spoke, when the Pharisees and scribes murmured at his allowing publicans and sinners to draw near to him.

The prodigal son represents sinners in general. As he went away from his father, and "wasted his substance with riotous living," so does the sinner depart from God, and misuse the talents intrusted to him. The likeness applies to sinners of every kind and degree, not to those alone who run into great excesses, and lead a grossly sinful life. Every impenitent sinner, though free from gross sin, and even respectable in outward conduct, is a wanderer from God, and misuses his talents, because he does not use them as God would have them used.

Yet the parable applies with peculiar force to one who sins in the very same way as this younger son. Alas, how many such sons there are! Impatient of control, weary of home with its wholesome restraints, and longing to be free, many a youth gladly quits his father's roof, and then runs all lengths in sinful pleasures. Little does he think of the fond and anxious hearts at home, little does he concern himself about a parent's wishes, a parent's prayers, a parent's parting charge. He is now far away, he is his own master, he can do what he likes, he is determined to enjoy himself. Surely it is a double sin thus at once to sin against God and against his earthly parent. The prodigal seemed to feel this: "Father, I have sinned *against heaven*, and in *thy* sight."

The misery to which this young man was brought when he had spent all his money, and the famine came, represents the evil consequences of sin in this life. Not that sin always produces outward ruin: many a man is honest and industrious, and thrives in the world, though his heart is far from God. More than this: many a man thrives, for a time at least, by dishonest gains; and it is not always that, in outward things and at present, sin brings its own punishment. Yet in very many cases it does so. Look at that pale and haggard man, with unsteady hand and tottering limbs, an old man before his time. What has brought him to this? Drink. He has been a great drinker; drunkenness has been his besetting sin, and now it has brought him to this wretched state. See those closed shutters. That was a flourishing shop once; the business was large, the tradesman industrious, few had so fair a prospect as he. But he was in haste to be rich. Not content with honest gains, he allowed himself to be tempted to dishonest courses. And this is the end: he is a ruined man. Covetousness, his besetting sin, has brought him to this. Even in other cases, though all outward things may seem to prosper, yet there may be unhappiness within. An ungodly man is never really happy; and often a smiling face hides an aching heart.

How false are all friendships formed by a companionship in sin; how hollow is the friendship of the world. When the day of want came, where were the friends of this young man's prosperity? Where were they who had feasted with him, drunk with him, laughed with him? They could not all be in the same destitution as himself, "yet no man gave unto him." Often in the day of trouble does a man find that among all his old companions in ungodliness he had not a single real friend, and that it is from those whom he used perhaps to sneer at as "saints" that he must seek a helping hand in his need. Among such he does not seek in vain.

In the parable, want brought the young man to himself: he repented, and returned to his father. It is not always so: trouble hardens some. It is only when the grace of God works with it and by it that trouble leads to God; but often God blesses it thus. Very seldom, if ever, does prosperity lead the heart to God; very often does trouble do so. Whether the trouble be the consequence of sin or not, there is no instrument which God more often uses for bringing the heart to himself.

"He came to himself." He had been, as it were, beside himself till then, blind to his true happiness as well as to his duty, like one out of his mind. And so is the sinner, as long as he is at a distance from God. Satan has blinded him; he is not in his right mind; his judgment and his will are perverted. When the great change is wrought in his heart by the Spirit, it is as though he "came to himself." His eyes are opened. He sees what he has done, how he has been living, whom he has been serving, and what the end would have been. His sin and danger lie open before him. He sees now that sin and the world have never given him real happiness. Peace has not been his. Even if he has prospered, he has had no true satisfaction of mind; all has been "vanity and vexation of spirit." Deeply does he now regret his wasted years and misspent talents, humbly and mournfully does he think of the past.

The past he cannot recall; yet it is not too late to change. The next feeling of the repentant sinner is beautifully represented in this parable: "I will arise, and go to my father." Yes, the wanderer will return to God. Guilty as he has been, undeserving of favor, with no excuse to make for his past sins, he will yet turn to God as his only hope; for he has heard of a Saviour, a Mediator and Advocate. He will seek the Father by him; he will approach the throne of grace as a contrite sinner, owning all, humbling himself before God as utterly unworthy, suing for mercy for Jesus' sake. The prodigal thought himself unworthy to be reckoned again a son: he did but ask to be received and treated as a servant. So the penitent sinner is willing to take the lowest place. Mercy is all he asks. If he may but be forgiven, how happy, how thankful will he be!

Where there is a true change of heart, this feeling does not pass away. No sooner had the prodigal made the determination, than "he arose, and came to his father." So the true penitent is led by the Spirit not only to determine, but to do. He comes to God in Christ. He will make no delay. Awakened at length, he sees there is no time for delay. He is deeply concerned for his soul; he must seek his Saviour at once.

Have his thoughts and feelings, his sorrow for sin, his distress of mind, his self-reproaches, his fears, his hopes, been unnoticed? No: the God who gave them has also seen them. As the father in the parable saw his son while yet a great way off, and had compassion upon him, so does God notice, and notice with pitying love, the first movement of the sinner's heart towards himself. He sees him coming, as it were, and goes forth to meet him by his grace. Some outward means are used to cheer him, or inward comfort is given by the Spirit; and as the father in the parable "ran and fell on his neck, and kissed him," so does God cause the returning penitent to know his love, and speaks to him pardon and peace. No need now to set his sin before him. The work of conviction is already done. Now he shall be cheered.

In the parable the father interrupts his son in his confession. While yet he has scarcely acknowledged his sin, and before he can make his humble petition to be received as a servant, the father breaks in with the joyful command to the servants: "Bring forth the best robe, and put it on him." Thus ready is God *at once* to forgive. The penitent sinner needs not to look upon pardon as a distant blessing, which, after long years of contrition or of penance, he may hope to obtain: God will give it to him *now*. No sooner does he seek than he shall find; no sooner does he come to God in Christ, than the blood of Jesus is applied to wash away his sins, and he is pardoned and accepted in him. It is not a future, but a present salvation that is offered in the gospel. And it is not only present, but *full*. Salvation is more than pardon: it is admission into all the privileges of the sons of God. The prodigal was not made a servant in his father's household, as he had humbly ventured to hope: he was received as a son again. The servants were called forth to wait on him, his rags were taken from him, and once more he was clothed as became the son of his father. The best robe was put on him, and a ring on his hand, and shoes on his feet. He was welcomed home with joy and honor. The fatted calf must be killed, and all must rejoice. Was there not a cause? "This my son," said the happy father, " was dead, and is alive again; he was lost, and is found." Thus graciously and joyfully is the returning sinner welcomed. There is joy in heaven for him, for he was lost, and is found; he was dead, and is alive. Now he is admitted into the family of God; his sins are all forgiven; he is clad in his Saviour's righteousness; peace and love, honor and joy are given to him. He is made an heir of heaven, and already has he a foretaste of his inheritance. Thus does God forgive and bless the penitent sinner who comes to him by Christ.

But whom are we to understand by the elder son? Evidently the Pharisees and scribes, in reply to whose murmuring the parable was spoken. They were like the elder son, as living in outward obedience to the law of God, whereas the publicans and sinners were like the prodigal. And they murmured at our Lord's receiving sinners, just as the elder son was displeased at the father's kind reception of the prodigal.

The elder son, in the true self-righteous spirit of the Pharisee, claimed for himself that he had never transgressed his father's commandment; and in the parable the father acknowledged the claim: "Son, thou art ever with me, and all that I have is thine." Yet we know well that the self-righteous Pharisees were not approved by God, but were, on the contrary, most displeasing to him. In like manner let us feel sure that no one who is a true Christian, and accepted by God, can feel any thing but joy when a sinner is brought to Christ. There can be in such a one no envy or jealousy. The Christian himself is but a sinner who has found mercy; and glad indeed is he when others find it too.

XXXI.

THE UNJUST STEWARD.

"And he said also unto his disciples, There was a certain rich man, which had a steward; and the same was accused unto him that he had wasted his goods. And he called him, and said unto him, How is it that I hear this of thee? give an account of thy stewardship; for thou mayest be no longer steward. Then the steward said within himself, What shall I do? for my lord taketh away from me the stewardship: I cannot dig; to beg I am ashamed. I am resolved what to do, that, when I am put out of the stewardship, they may receive me into their houses. So he called every one of his lord's debtors unto him, and said unto the first, How much owest thou unto my lord? And he said, A hundred measures of oil. And he said unto him, Take thy bill, and sit down quickly, and write fifty. Then said he to another, And how much owest thou? And he said, A hundred measures of wheat. And he said unto him, Take thy bill, and write fourscore. And the lord commended the unjust steward, because he had done wisely: for the children of this world are in their generation wiser than the children of light. And I say unto you, Make to yourselves friends of the mammon of unrighteousness; that, when ye fail, they may receive you into everlasting habitations." LUKE 16:1–9.

A STEWARD is one intrusted with his master's property, and set over his concerns. He is a servant; but being placed in authority over the other servants, and having the management of great affairs, he is in some respects more like a master, especially if he be the steward of a rich man, such as the man in the parable. Only there is always this that makes him a servant still: he is accountable to his master.

We are all stewards, and God is our Master. He has intrusted us with his goods—some with more, some with less. Whatever we have is not ours, but his; and we are accountable to him for the use of it. It is to be used, not for our own pleasure merely, but in the service of God and in doing good.

It is more easy to understand this with regard to a rich man than a poor man, especially for those who are poor themselves. We sometimes hear it said about one who is very rich indeed, but has not learned to make a right use of his riches, "He does not do much good with his money;" as if he were bound to do good with his money *because* he has so much. But why the rich man only? Why not the poor also? Both are God's stewards. To the rich man God has committed much, to the poor man little; but the poor man is just as much bound to spend his little aright as the rich man is to spend his wealth. Besides, money is not all. A steward has goods of all sorts in his charge, and so have God's stewards. Money is one sort, but time and health and strength are goods also. Every one has something. Every one is a steward of God.

The steward in the parable was a dishonest one. He had wasted his master's goods. Probably he had done so for a long time; but now at length it came to his master's ears, and he was accused of it. It is not said that he had stolen his master's property, or spent his money in any thing wicked, but simply that he had wasted it. A steward's business is to look after his master's concerns carefully, so that no loss may befall him, and that his goods may be turned to the best account. This man had not done so. He had been careless and neglectful, indifferent to his master's interests, not strict and conscientious in his management. Thus he had wasted his master's goods, and now he was called to account for it, and was told that he must lose his place.

Some people make it their boast, or at least their excuse, that they do no one any harm. Now in the first place this is not the truth, if they are not doing good; for we are all doing either good or harm to those around us by our example, if not in any other way. But even supposing it to be true, yet if this were all such people could say, their own words would condemn them; for they would thus own themselves to be unjust and unfaithful stewards. God has given them means of usefulness; if they are not doing good with them, they are wasting their Master's goods. Whoever is leading an idle, self-indulgent life, with no serious thought of life's duties, no conscientious regard to the will of God, no desire and endeavor to serve him and to do good—whoever is living so, though he may be free from gross sin, and may be outwardly moral and respectable, is yet an unfaithful steward; for those means and opportunities of which he is making no use, or which he is using only for himself, are the goods which God has intrusted to him as a steward, and he is wasting them. I need not say how much more strongly this applies to those who are spending money, time, and strength in actual sin.

This was enough. The man must lose his post: "Give an account of thy stewardship, for thou mayest be no longer steward." God does not always deal so with men. Though he stands in need of no one to accuse us to him, though his eye is always on us, and he knows exactly how we are using his goods, yet he does not in general put us out of our stewardship at once, even when he sees us to be unfaithful stewards. God's dealings are various. Sometimes indeed a sudden call is sent, and the unfaithful steward has to face his Master unexpectedly; but generally speaking, the unfaithful steward is continued in office as long as the faithful; the man who does no good with what he has remains in possession of it as long as he who is a blessing to all around him; the careless and selfish live as long as the conscientious and godly. But with all of us the present stewardship is but for a time. Putting aside for the moment the case of the faithful, the unjust and unfaithful steward is put out of his stewardship sooner or later. He was always one who wasted his Master's goods, and his Master knew it all along, but he bore with him awhile; now, however, he may be no longer steward. If by no other means, such as loss of health or loss of fortune, yet by death he is at last put out, and a sad account he has to give.

The steward in the parable, when put out of his employment, had to consider what to do for a livelihood. We read of no defence made; the case was too clear. "What shall I do?" thought he, "for my lord taketh away from me the stewardship:

I cannot dig; to beg I am ashamed." How false is the rule of the ungodly as to what is disgraceful! This man was ashamed to beg, yet he had not been ashamed to wrong his master. Outward debasement he could not face, yet he had gone on long in secret unfaithfulness. It was the being found out, and losing his place, and having to seek his bread, that troubled him, not the thought of his wrongdoing.

So far was he from being sorry, that he determined to wrong his master yet more by dishonestly providing a home for himself at his expense.. His mind was soon made up. It was necessary that it should be; for his time was short. Yet a little time did remain; just enough for his purpose. It was not yet known that he was to be steward no longer; so before it should get abroad, he would make use of his authority to provide himself friends against the time of need. No sooner thought of than done. He called to him those who were in debt to his master, and when he had asked of each how much he owed, told each debtor to put down in his account a smaller sum; the man who owed a hundred measures of oil was to make it appear that he owed only fifty; and he who owed a hundred measures of wheat was to put down fourscore instead. The debtors seem to have been almost as dishonest as the steward; for they must have suspected that, in some way or other, he was robbing his master; but they had always been used to do business with the steward, and not with his lord, so they gladly did what he told them now. Thus he secured their friendship. He had done them a good turn, and might look to be received into their houses when he should be put out. See how sin leads to sin. Probably this was the worst piece of dishonesty he had ever been guilty of. Before he had wasted his master's goods; now he deliberately robbed him. A man who wilfully does one wrong thing will not scruple to do another more wrong still in order to hide it or to shield himself from its consequences.

But the master's eyes were opened now. He had trusted his steward in times past, but now that he had found out his character, doubtless he narrowly watched what he did. So, though the plan seems to have succeeded, yet it soon came to his master's knowledge. Ah, little do God's unjust stewards think that all their schemes and plans are known to him every moment. "All things are naked and opened unto the eyes of him with whom we have to do."

But we read in the parable that "the lord *commended* the unjust steward," that is, praised him. This however does not mean the Lord Jesus Christ, but the lord or master of the steward. When he learned the trick his steward had played him, he praised him. But for what? Only for his forethought and shrewdness. Justly displeased as he was with his long unfaithfulness and with this last piece of dishonesty, yet even in the act of turning him off he could not but admire his prudence and quickness. He was a rogue, it is true, but a clever rogue. "He had done wisely." Having a very short time left, he had made the most of it. Instead of giving himself up to vain lamentations for the loss of a good place, he had instantly bethought himself of what he could best do to make up for the loss. Being about to lose his home, he had looked forward to that time, and made provision for it. Thus he had done wisely; that is, wisely for his own interest. Even his master did not say that he had done *well*. And there is no true wisdom except in doing well. This was but the lowest sort of wisdom—worldly and selfish wisdom.

The parable ends here; what follows is our Lord's application of it. "For the children of this world," said he, "are in their generation wiser than the children of light. The children of this world mean worldly people; the children of light mean godly people. The children of light walk by the light of God's word, and live with a view to eternity; the children of this world, on the other hand, have no thought but for the present time and for worldly things. They are quite wrong in this—quite wrong, and by no means wise, but on the contrary miserably foolish; but "in their generation," that is, with regard to this life—which is all they care for—and to the objects which they have in view, they are wiser than the children of light; for they show more diligence, prudence, and forethought in seeking worldly things than religious people show in seeking spiritual things. The children of light have made a right choice in choosing God for their portion; but, alas, they are often cold and slothful, showing but little zeal and earnestness, though eternity is their aim. The children of this world have made a wrong choice, but they often show great diligence in pursuing their objects, and thus put to shame the children of light. This is the lesson which our Lord here teaches us.

But this is not all. Our Lord also bids us make to ourselves "friends of the mammon of unrighteousness." We can only understand this by considering what the unjust steward had done. But, first, "the mammon of unrighteousness" means worldly riches, or worldly goods of any kind. The word "mammon" means riches; and they are called riches "of unrighteousness" perhaps because this steward had used them unjustly, or because the love of them does so often lead men into sin, or possibly only by way of contrast to the true riches. We are to make friends for ourselves by means of our riches, or of whatever we have; that is to say, we are to make such a use of it as that we shall not be left friendless in the time of need. This is what the steward did, only he did it wrongly, while we are to do it rightly; for there is a right way of doing it. The faithful steward of God is one who does it, and does it in a right way; for he tries to spend money, time, talents, all that God has intrusted to him, well and faithfully; and his Master will take care that he shall not be friendless or forsaken. Often God raises up unexpected friends for his servants in their time of need, and at last, when they are called to leave the present scene, he himself will be their friend, and provide for all their wants.

"That when ye fail, they may receive you into

everlasting habitations." "That they may receive you," is just the same as "that ye may be received." God himself will receive his faithful stewards into those everlasting habitations. When they fail, that is, when they are put out of their earthly stewardship, they will be gainers, not losers; for their Master will take them to live with him above. Our Lord sets this before us strikingly in the twenty-fifth chapter of St. Matthew. Those on the right hand had been faithful stewards, feeding the hungry, clothing the naked, comforting the afflicted, and thus using in God's service what he had committed to them. What does the King say to them? "Come, ye blessed of my Father, inherit the kingdom prepared for you from the foundation of the world." They had made to themselves friends of the mammon of unrighteousness, and now they were received into everlasting habitations. We are to do likewise.

Let us consider seriously our responsibility to God as his stewards. "It is required in stewards that a man be found faithful." Let us be faithful. Our goods, our time, our strength, let us look on them as not ours, but our Master's. Let us use them as he would have us use them; for he has not left us ignorant of his will. Yet let us be sure that our ground of hope for ourselves is right. Let none think to win salvation by his faithful stewardship. "None but Christ:" let that great truth lie at the root of all we do. Let us look to be saved by him alone, and let our diligent employment of all our talents for God be the fruits in us of a living faith.

We have many opportunities of doing good: let us use them well. We have a great account to give: let us ever bear it in mind. We have a gracious Master, a blessed Saviour, a Father in heaven: let us delight to serve him.

Let us serve him faithfully, diligently, zealously. Let us look to it that the worldly do not shame us. What!. shall they who have not one object beyond this life be more diligent than we whose minds are fixed on eternity? If God through grace has called us to the knowledge and love of himself, let us be heartily in earnest, let us live as those who are seeking a country. What the unjust steward did, he did without delay, for there was no time to lose. Let us also make the most of the passing hour, for it is all we can call our own: "The night cometh, when no man can work."

XXXII.

THE RICH MAN AND LAZARUS.

"There was a certain rich man, which was clothed in purple and fine linen, and fared sumptuously every day: and there was a certain beggar named Lazarus, which was laid at his gate, full of sores, and desiring to be fed with the crumbs which fell from the rich man's table: moreover the dogs came and licked his sores And it came to pass, that the beggar died, and was carried by the angels into Abraham's bosom: the rich man also died, and was buried; and in hell he lifted up his eyes, being in torments, and seeth Abraham afar off, and Lazarus in his bosom. And he cried and said, Father Abraham, have mercy on me, and send Lazarus, that he may dip the tip of his finger in water, and cool my tongue; for I am tormented in this flame. But Abraham said, Son, remember that thou in thy lifetime receivedst thy good things, and likewise Lazarus evil things: but now he is comforted, and thou art tormented. And beside all this, between us and you there is a great gulf fixed: so that they which would pass from hence to you cannot; neither can they pass to us, that would come from thence. Then he said, I pray thee therefore, father, that thou wouldest send him to my father's house: for I have five brethren; that he may testify unto them, lest they also come into this place of torment. Abraham saith unto him, They have Moses and the prophets; let them hear them. And he said, Nay, father Abraham: but if one went unto them from the dead, they will repent. And he said unto him, If they hear not Moses and the prophets, neither will they be persuaded, though one rose from the dead." LUKE 16:19-31.

WHETHER this passage is the description of a real case, or strictly a parable, is uncertain. Whichever it is, assuredly it is one of the most solemn lessons ever given by our Lord.

The most careless can hardly hear or read it without some impression; for all must feel that, whether parable or not, there is deep and awful truth in it.

Here were two men, as different as possible almost in their circumstances. One was rich, living in ease, plenty, and luxury, with great possessions, and enjoying them to the full: the other was as poor as the first was rich—not merely poor, but a beggar; yet not through his own fault, but because he was heavily afflicted—a poor suffering cripple. To make the difference still more striking, the two were brought close together. Far apart as they were in station and circumstances, yet they were near as to place. The beggar was laid at the rich man's gate. While the one was feasting within, the other was lying in want and suffering without. Yet we do not find him envying the rich man: his utmost desire was to be fed with the crumbs which fell from his table. Whether the poor man got his wish, we are not told: there seems reason to fear he did not.

But the want and suffering of this life do not last for ever. At length death came to the poor man's relief. This is sometimes said of people, whether there is reason for a good hope about them or not: it is very often said untruly. But in the case of Lazarus, death really brought relief; for when he died he went to be happy—he "was carried by the angels into Abraham's bosom." That was a common way with the Jews of describing the place to which the souls of the righteous went after death. And so the poor sufferer was at rest: poor no longer, free now from pain and misery, safe and happy for ever.

But death comes to *all*, to rich as well as poor, to the gay and prosperous as well as to the suffering and afflicted. "The rich man also died." Perhaps Lazarus had *wished* to die; perhaps, as he lay in his misery, he had often humbly asked God to take him when he should see fit. But the rich man did not wish to die; for death would rob him of all he had and all he loved. Yet he did die. He could not refuse that call, or hang back when that messenger came. "The rich man also died, and was buried."

"And was *buried*." Nothing is said about Lazarus' burial: it was but a poor one, no doubt. But the rich man was sure to have a grand funeral. We know the look of such a funeral in our own country; the hearse with its nodding plumes, the mourning carriages, the men in attendance, the long procession; people come to see such a burying, as to a grand sight. A funeral in that time and country was not quite like this; yet doubtless the rich man's burying was as grand in its way. The corpse was richly laid out, the paid mourners were many, and made loud lamentations, and a great company followed the remains to the grave. There is something awful in this, when we think of what we are told next. There is always something awful in a great funeral, when we cannot have a good hope about him who is gone.

He was buried. But that was only his body; where was the soul? While the senseless body was being borne to the tomb, and the mourners lamented, and friends wept and bewailed, where was the soul, the part of him that could think and feel? "In hell he lifted up his eyes, being in torments." How awful a change! This was the "rich man." This was he who had been "clothed in purple and fine linen, and fared sumptuously every day." This was he who had been so prosperous, and in men's esteem doubtless so happy. Ah, little do men know what makes happiness. Even while they were living, Lazarus in his rags lying at the gate was more truly happy than the rich man feasting within, for his thoughts were happier; and it is the state of the mind, not the outward circumstances, that chiefly makes happiness or misery. But now, when life was past with both, how happy was the poor beggar, how wretched was the rich man! *He* was the beggar now, and a beggar to no purpose. He who had enjoyed that sumptuous fare, must now beg for a drop of cold water, and beg in vain. He who had so long lived in every kind of comfort and luxury, must now be in torments, from which there could be no relief.

It must have added to his misery to see Lazarus happy—the poor, miserable creature whom he had so often observed at his gate, in Abraham's bosom, while he was in agony. How must past means and opportunities have risen to his memory! If Lazarus could reach that happy place, why might not he have got there too? Probably his learning and knowledge had been far greater than those of Lazarus; yet he was cast out, while Lazarus was taken in. Alas! though he could see Lazarus, it was "afar off." They were separated now more widely far than they had been in life. There was "a great gulf" between them, so that there was no passing from one to the other. Whether the rich man had ever given relief to Lazarus we do not know; at least, he had had the opportunity; but all such opportunities were now passed on both sides. Lazarus could give the wretched man no help, not even a drop of water to cool his tongue. The one could not come near the other, for the great gulf was between them.

Why was there so great a difference between them now? Was it only because the rich man had in his lifetime received his good things, that he was now tormented? And was it because Lazarus had received evil things that he was now comforted? No. People sometimes talk as if, because they have many troubles in this life, they are sure to be happy in the life to come. But that is not true. Happiness and misery hereafter depend, not on being rich or poor now, but on the state of the heart towards God. The beggar might have been shut out from happiness, the rich man might have been taken to Abraham's bosom; for, alas! all the poor and miserable are not on the road to heaven; and, thanks be to God, many of the rich and great have found the true riches, and will be happy for ever hereafter. We are not expressly told the character of these two men, but are left to gather it from the story. The rich man, we may conclude, was worldly and self-indulgent, living in pleasure, not spending his substance as God's steward, and not making provision for eternity. The beggar, on the other hand, was doubtless a patient sufferer under the hand of God, bearing his trials meekly, trusting in God, and looking forward in humble hope to the time when God would take him to rest. In other words, the rich man was worldly and careless, the poor man was a true servant of God. This was why the one was carried to Abraham's bosom, the other to the place of torment.

But the rich man, unable to obtain relief for himself, now makes another request. He had left five brothers, men probably of the same character and way of life as himself. He thinks of them now, and trembles for their state. Now he knows too well the awful end to which such a life as theirs would lead them. He had reached the end—there was no hope for *him*. But *they* were still in life, they might yet escape; so he begs Abraham to send Lazarus to warn them, lest they also should come to that place of torment. Ah, why did he not care for them in this way before? Why did he not, while yet living, seek safety for his own soul, and try to turn them also into the right way? Doubtless, in life, care for their souls had been as far from his mind as care for his own. He had feasted with them many a time, but never sought God with them. Now at length he cares for them in another way, but not till it is too late.

Oh, ye who have ungodly brothers, children, relatives, friends, make use of the present time to warn them. Be not so cruel as to hold your peace, while yet your words may reach them. No wonder the rich man did not warn his brethren, for he had no sense even of his own danger. But if God by his grace has led you to repent and believe, then you ought to have a deep and awful sense of the danger those are in who are without Christ, and to leave no means untried for bringing them to him. True, the work must be God's, but you may seek to be his instruments. Do not put this off; use the opportunities which you now have. Do not wait till the great gulf lies between you and them, or till that other great and unpassable space be placed between you which separates the living from the dead.

And you who are living without God, see that you do not refuse to hear the word of warning which those who love you and care for your souls may give you. It costs them much perhaps to give it, far more than you think; and perhaps it is only after much conflict and prayer that they can bring themselves to speak. Be not angry with them, do not turn away in displeasure, and thus wound their hearts and rob yourselves of good. Take what they say as a message from God; for it comes to you by his providence. The time will come when those who now warn you will be able to do so no more; hear them while you may. One who warns you in love is a friend indeed.

The miserable man's second request met with no better success than the first. His brothers, Abraham reminds him, had Moses and the prophets: "let them hear *them*." The word of God and the appointed means of grace were within their reach, and were sufficient, if rightly used, to serve as a warning, and to lead them into the right way.

But he still pleaded. He too had had Moses and the prophets, but he had not attended to them; and well he knew that his brothers were living in like neglect. But let Lazarus go to them, let one appear from the place of the dead, and carry them a message from the unseen world, and then surely they would repent. The word of God and the usual means of grace they might neglect; but a voice from the dead they could not disregard.

So one would think; yet it is not so. Abraham's answer is remarkable: "If they hear not Moses and the prophets, neither will they be persuaded, though one rose from the dead." If the careless and ungodly despise God's message when it comes to them in his appointed way, there is no reason for thinking that they would attend to it however it might come. A voice from the dead would startle, yet it would not of itself convert. An impression it would doubtless make, but not a lasting and saving one, unless God wrought by his Spirit in the heart; and the Spirit can work by the gentlest and quietest means, and does in fact make use of those that are usual and common far more often than of those that are strange and startling.

Let us lay this solemn parable to heart. There is no one more solemn: for here our Lord does, as it were, lift the veil that hides from our view the world to come. The rich man and Lazarus had their time on earth, and each had his appointed lot, and means, and opportunities; and then they died, and were separated for ever. We are now passing through life, and each of us has his own peculiar lot, and before us lies the eternal world and the great separation. Where are our hearts? What is our life? Whether we be rich or poor, strong or sickly, is a question of comparatively little moment: the great question is, what is the state of our souls in the sight of God? They of old time had "Moses and the prophets:" we have far more, for we have Jesus and the gospel. "How shall we escape, if we neglect so great salvation?" Abraham's bosom and the great gulf may be figures, but what they represent is plain, solemn truth. There is a happy place to which all true believers go when they die, and there is an endless separation between them and all others. The only safety is to flee in faith to the Lord Jesus Christ; and then, in watchfulness and prayer, and in the daily endeavor to do the will of God, to wait for his appearing. "Blessed is that servant whom his Lord when he cometh shall find so doing."

XXXIII.

The Unjust Judge.

"And he spake a parable unto them to this end, that men ought always to pray, and not to faint; saying, There was in a city a judge, which feared not God, neither regarded man: and there was a widow in that city; and she came unto him, saying, Avenge me of mine adversary. And he would not for a while: but afterward he said within himself, Though I fear not God, nor regard man; yet because this widow troubleth me, I will avenge her, lest by her continual coming she weary me. And the Lord said, Hear what the unjust judge saith. And shall not God avenge his own elect, which cry day and night unto him, though he bear long with them? I tell you that he will avenge them speedily. Nevertheless when the Son of man cometh, shall he find faith on the earth?" LUKE 18 : 1–8.

THIS parable is different from most. Here the dealings of God are compared with those, not of a good man, but of a bad man. This is remarkable; but as we shall see presently, it does but add force to the lesson of the parable.

Our Lord's object was to teach *perseverance in prayer;* and this he did by showing that God will certainly answer prayer, though he may seem for a time to disregard it.

The parable represents a judge in a certain city, or town. There are such still in all the towns of the East; they are much the same as our magistrates. This man was a man of no principle: he feared not God, nor regarded man; he had no wish to do justice. A widow of the place had been injured by some one, and brought her cause before him. We are evidently to understand that it was a just cause; yet the judge paid no attention to her; and though she came again and again, he would still do nothing for her. He cared nothing whether she had justice done her or not. But the widow kept on coming continually, till the judge was quite tired of her and her cause; and so at last he determined to see her righted, not because he cared for justice, but merely that he might get rid of her. He did not even pretend to have a better motive: "Though I fear not God, nor regard man, yet, because this widow troubleth me, I will avenge her, lest by her continual coming she weary me."

Now follows the application: "And the Lord said, Hear what the unjust judge saith. And shall not God avenge his own elect, which cry day and night unto him, though he bear long with them? I tell you that he will avenge them speedily." Shall the unjust judge at length attend to the widow's cry, merely to rid himself of her; and shall God, the righteous Judge, refuse to hear those who call upon him? Shall a mere selfish feeling prevail with this bad man, and shall the God of mercy and truth be deaf to prayer? Impossible. If the unjust judge heard, much more will God hear. If importunity and perseverance at length prevailed even in this case, much more will they prevail with God, who has told us to pray, and has promised to hear. This is the lesson of the parable.

But our Lord adds: "Nevertheless when the Son of man cometh, shall he find faith on the earth?" Notwithstanding all the promises to prayer, will the Lord Jesus Christ, when he comes again, find men living in dependence upon God, seeking the Saviour in faith, trusting in him, and looking for his coming? Will such be the state of the world at large? Will it be the general state of those to whom the gospel has come?

Leaving this question unanswered, as our Lord leaves it, though it is plain what answer he means us to supply, let us seek to learn for ourselves practically the lesson of perseverance in prayer, which the parable is meant to teach.

I. "Men ought *always* to pray;" that is, continually; and that for the same blessing. Once let us be sure that our prayer is according to the will of God, and we are told then to "be instant in prayer." Day after day this widow approached the judge's house with the same petition; day after day should our wants, and especially the one want— whatever it may be—that chiefly presses upon us, be laid before the throne of grace.

II. "And not to faint." We are apt to faint. We pray, and seem to receive no answer; we speak to God, and yet no voice replies; and so we become discouraged; we faint; we are ready to leave off praying. But not if faith be strong. There must be faith, or we cannot really pray at all; and faith leads us to persevere in the face of discouragement. True, we see nothing, we hear nothing; yet faith enables us to realize God's nearness, God's presence, God's blessing. If we walk by sight, we shall faint; if we walk by faith, we shall persevere. This is what God would have us to do. He could bless us in a moment with all that we want. If he is pleased to keep us awhile still praying, shall we think despondingly that he hears us not?

III. "And shall not God avenge his own elect?" This question is a strong assurance that God *will* avenge them. And this particular answer to prayer seems drawn directly from the parable. Even the unjust judge at length did justice to the widow: so will God, in answer to their prayers, help all his people who labor under injustice and oppression, sooner or later, in his own good time. But he will also hear prayer of every kind, and help and comfort and bless in all need. There is not a want which he cannot supply, not one which he *will* not supply, if it be really a want. Earnest, persevering prayer in the name of Jesus Christ, a crying day and night unto God, will never be unheard.

IV. Yet our Lord shows that the blessing may be long withheld: "though he bear long with them." It often is so. See that pale and care-worn face. That mother has a son, an ungodly son, and it is care for him that has saddened her face and dimmed her eye. Yet she is a woman of prayer: day and night she lays her son's case before God, and pleads for him with a mother's heart. Let her not doubt, let her not faint. God is bearing long with her, yet he hears her. Only let her pray, and pray again, and wait, and believe. Ah, it is easy to say this, but it is not easy to do it. To hope against hope, to endure the heart-sickness of hope deferred, to see no change, no token for good, and yet to pray—this is not easy. Yet it is what God calls us to, and what God promises to bless. We are to cry day and night unto him, though he bear long with us.

V. Faith is what is wanted—*more* faith. Whether he find it in many or in few when he comes, let our Lord see faith in us now. Let us lay hold of the promises, and set them against all discouragements. There would be no room for faith if there were no waiting, if we could see all, and see it at once. But faith is the very thing that God requires, and that he is working in us continually. Oh that our faith may be increased! Oh that the Holy Spirit may teach us to believe more and to pray more! Oh that all God's promises and all his dealings may lead us to prayer, to trust, to peace, to joy! We have to do with no unjust judge, no unkind lord. When we pray, we go to more than a judge, even the justest and kindest. We go to our Father, our reconciled Father in Christ Jesus. Shall we doubt him? He has given us his Son; shall he not with him also freely give us all things?

XXXIV.

The Pharisee and the Publican.

"And he spake this parable unto certain which trusted in themselves that they were righteous, and despised others: Two men went up into the temple to pray; the one a Pharisee, and the other a publican. The Pharisee stood and prayed thus with himself. God, I thank thee, that I am not as other men are, extortioners, unjust, adulterers, or even as this publican. I fast twice in the week, I give tithes of all that I possess. And the publican, standing afar off, would not lift up so much as his eyes unto heaven, but smote upon his breast, saying, God be merciful to me a sinner. I tell you, this man went down to his house justified rather than the other: for every one that exalteth himself shall be abased; and he that humbleth himself shall be exalted." LUKE 18 : 9-14.

THESE two men went to the same place, at the same time, and for the same purpose; yet how different were they in heart and character. There is much difference now also among those who meet together in the house of God, and often even among those who come together in a more private way for prayer and for the hearing of the word. God only knows the heart.

But though these two men both went up into the temple, yet they did not worship in the same part of it. It may have been because the Jewish law did not allow the publican to be where the Pharisee was—for there were different courts, to which different classes of people might come—or it may have been through his deep humility that the publican "stood afar off," while the Pharisee worshipped in the inner part. There are no different courts in the Lord's house now. High and low, male and female, Jew and Gentile, may worship together. The gospel has made all one. Whatever differences there may be in other places, in the house of God all stand on one footing.

Thus these two men prayed in different places; but their prayers were more different still.

"The Pharisee stood, and prayed thus with himself." Some think the meaning to be that he stood by himself and prayed; and this would quite agree with the general character and practice of the Pharisees, who thought themselves peculiarly holy, and wished to keep others at a humble distance from them. At all events, he stood up boldly in his proud self-righteousness, and spoke the words of prayer apart.

Prayer? It is called prayer, because it professed to be so; but there was nothing of real prayer in it. The words were addressed to the Almighty: "God, I thank thee;" but his thoughts were upon himself. He was really speaking to himself, rather than to God. And what words they were! True, the opening words show nothing wrong: "God, I thank thee." Fit words indeed with which to begin prayer; but we judge of the feeling from which they sprang by what follows: "God, I thank thee, that I am not as other men are."

In the solemn hour of prayer, how could his

THE PHARISEE AND PUBLICAN. 255

thoughts be fixed upon the faults of others? Had he no sins of his own to confess? What had he to do with "other men" at such a moment? Who had taught him to compare himself with his neighbors, rather than with God's holy law? If he had but looked into that perfect law, and compared himself with it, how different would his feelings and his prayer have been. We can hardly think of any thing less like prayer than the words of this proud Pharisee, standing as in the very presence of God, and thanking Him that he was so much better than others.

It may be that there was truth in his words: he may not have been an extortioner, or unjust, or an adulterer; he may have been free from some sins of which the publican, whom he noticed at that moment in a distant part of the temple, had been guilty. But little did he think that, at that very moment, when engaged in the outward act of prayer, he was guilty of a sin quite as great in the sight of God as extortion, injustice, or adultery. The same word which condemns these, condemns pride also; and we may believe that there is nothing more displeasing to God than a haughty self-righteousness, and a proud despising of others.

This was all his prayer. There was not a word of confession of sin, not one cry for mercy, no acknowledgment of need, not a petition of any kind, nothing asked for, either temporal or spiritual. In his blind self-satisfaction, he flattered himself, doubtless, that he was doing something meritorious in praying, and thought that he was bringing something to God, whereas he ought to have gone to God to receive all from him.

Now let us turn to the other man. How different a prayer is his. Even in outward appearance all is different. There he stands, the poor publican, afar off. His head is bowed, his eyes are downcast, he smites upon his breast, and the words of prayer that burst at once from heart and lips are these: "God be merciful to me a sinner!"

This was prayer indeed. The publican had learnt what the Pharisee had never learnt. He had come to the knowledge that he was a sinner, and in need of mercy. Doubtless the Pharisee was far superior to him in learning; with every part of the Jewish law he was well acquainted; he knew probably every fact in Old Testament history, and was well versed in the ceremonial of his religion; but how much more did this despised and ignorant publican really know than he. All the Pharisee's knowledge was in the head; the publican's heart had been taught of God.

If the publican had been like the Pharisee, he might have said: "God, I thank thee that I am not so bad as others of my trade. I am not wholly set upon gain. I have some care for religion. I come up to thy house to pray." But his thoughts were not upon others, but upon himself; and not upon his fancied excellence, but upon his sins. He is smitten with a sense of sin; it weighs upon his soul. He seeks not to hide his sin; he comes to God just as he is, and sues for mercy. How humbly he sues; with downcast eye and smitten breast, hardly daring to pray, yet finding in prayer his only relief. "Can such a one as I hope to be forgiven?" Yes, poor publican; yes, all who are of the publican's spirit. You may hope; for Jesus himself speaks comfort and forgiveness to you.

"I tell you, this man went down to his house justified rather than the other." Justified; that is, pardoned, acquitted, accepted. The Pharisee confessed nothing, asked nothing, received nothing. Proud he came up from his house, proud he went back again—unhumbled, unblest. The publican went up to the house of God with a heavy burden, the burden of his sins. Did he lose that burden there? Surely we may believe that he did. God, who heard his prayer, and granted him mercy, doubtless gave him in his heart the sense of forgiveness. The publican went down to his house comforted as well as justified. His burden was gone, his sins were forgiven.

This comfort, this blessing was not for him alone: "For every one that exalteth himself shall be abased; and he that humbleth himself shall be exalted." There is no comfort for the proud and self-righteous; but there is all comfort for the humble and contrite. Jesus has died for sinners: here is the source of all our hopes. It is when we cast aside all thought of our own goodness, and approach God as sinners, pleading the merits of Christ alone, then it is that we receive pardon and peace. There are still some who try to comfort themselves with the thought of their religious observances, their moral life, their being not so bad as others. But this is not the way to pardon, this is not the way to peace. Christ is the way, the only way. We must go to him, casting aside all other hope and dependence. "God, be merciful to me a sinner," should be our prayer; and *we* may add, "for Jesus Christ my Saviour's sake;" for we have a blessing that the publican had not. Jesus has died, and we now know clearly that God is "just, and the justifier of him which believeth in Jesus."

Oh, let us beware of proud, heartless, prayerless prayers, with no sorrow for sin, no sense of need, no real asking of God. How much we want; yet not more than God is willing to give. Just as we are, in all our nakedness and need, let us go continually to the throne of grace. Our Advocate is there, the all-prevailing Advocate. We need not stand afar off. Through him we may draw near, and come boldly to the throne of grace.

XXXV.

THE LABORERS IN THE VINEYARD.

"For the kingdom of heaven is like unto a man that is a householder, which went out early in the morning to hire laborers into his vineyard. And when he had agreed with the laborers for a penny a day, he sent them into his vineyard. And he went out about the third hour, and saw others standing idle in the marketplace, and said unto them: Go ye also into the vineyard, and whatsoever is right I will give you. And they went their way. Again he went out about the sixth and ninth hour, and did likewise. And about the eleventh hour he went out, and found others standing idle, and saith unto them, Why stand ye here all the day idle? They say unto him, Because no man hath hired us. He saith unto them, Go ye also into the vineyard; and whatsoever is right, that shall ye receive. So when even was come, the lord of the vineyard saith unto his steward, Call the laborers, and give them their hire, beginning from the last unto the first. And when they came that were hired about the eleventh hour, they received every man a penny. But when the first came, they supposed that they should have received more; and they likewise received every man a penny. And when they had received it, they murmured against the good man of the house, saying, These last have wrought but one hour, and thou hast made them equal unto us, which have borne the burden and heat of the day. But he answered one of them, and said, Friend, I do thee no wrong: didst not thou agree with me for a penny? Take that thine is, and go thy way: I will give unto this last, even as unto thee. Is it not lawful for me to do what I will with mine own? Is thine eye evil, because I am good? So the last shall be first, and the first last: for many be called, but few chosen." MATT. 20 : 1-16.

THE key to this parable is to be found in the words that go before and that follow it; they are almost the same.

The parable begins with the word "for," which joins it to the words that go before:

"But many that are first shall be last; and the last shall be first;" and at its close these words are repeated, in almost the same form, with others added: "So the last shall be first, and the first last: for many be called, but few chosen." The explanation must clearly be looked for in these words. Bearing this in mind, let us first go through the parable, and then consider its application.

Vineyard work was as common in that country as field work is with us. Laborers were often hired by the day only, and it is still the custom in some parts of the East for men to stand in the market-place to be hired. The penny was equal to about sevenpence halfpenny, and a penny was probably the usual day's wages.

The day was reckoned by the Jews to begin at six o'clock: it was probably at that hour that the first laborers were hired, and the rest were hired at nine o'clock, twelve o'clock, three o'clock, and five o'clock. When these last were engaged, but one working hour remained.

There was nothing unusual in the hiring. Those hired for the whole day were to be paid the usual day's wages, and those hired afterwards were to receive what was right; that is, as they no doubt understood it, in proportion to the time they worked. But when the time of payment came, the laborers were dealt with by the master in a way that must have greatly surprised them. The first who were called to be paid were those hired last, at the eleventh hour, and they received a whole day's wages. Afterwards those hired at the ninth, sixth, and third

LABORERS IN THE VINEYARD. 261

hour were called in succession, and, though it is not mentioned, they too no doubt received the same. The first hired were the last paid. They had agreed for a penny a day, and that sum they received. But they were discontented. Though it was the sum for which they had bargained, yet they thought themselves unfairly treated, because others who had not worked nearly so long received the same. The master, however, would not listen to their complaint. There was no ground for it. Might he not do what he would with his own? Might he not give to whom he pleased? For a whole day's pay for an hour's work was almost a free gift. What was it to them if he chose to show such kindness? Let them take their due, and depart. He had kept nothing from them of what was their right, though he had given to others what was far beyond their right.

The opening words of the parable show us that it is one of those in which our Lord teaches us about the kingdom of heaven; that is, the gospel dispensation, and God's dealings with men under it. And the particular lesson here taught is that God claims the right of dealing with men according to his sovereign will, and that men's place hereafter, with regard to each other, will by no means always agree with their place now.

There are two distinct times marked out in the parable: the hiring and working-time on the one hand, and the paying-time on the other. The former represents the present state, the latter the future. In the present state, men are called into the outward and visible church at different times in their life, and some enjoy greater advantages and some less, and some fill higher stations and some lower. When the great day of account arrives, many changes will be made, "many that are first shall be last, and the last shall be first." Many a one who was the child of pious parents, and was brought up from his youth in the knowledge of God and in the habits of religion, will be placed below one who had no such early advantages, and was brought to know God only late in life. Many who filled a high station in the church on earth, whose names were well known and whose influence was great, will then have to take their place below some of the poor and unlearned; poor, yet rich in faith and in good works; unlearned in the wisdom of this world, yet truly taught of God. For God judges not by the outward appearance, but by the heart; and even now in his sight many of the first are last, and the last first.

What goes before the parable seems to show that we are to apply this even to worldly advantages. The young man who came to Christ had great possessions, in that respect he was among the first; Peter and the other disciples were poor, for even what they had they had given up for the sake of following Christ, they were therefore among the last: yet, while that unhappy young man would have no treasure in heaven because he would not leave all and follow Christ, Peter and all true disciples should receive a hundredfold, and should inherit everlasting life. Thus the first should be last, and the last first. The first in riches would find those very riches a hinderance in their way, a hinderance from which the poor would be free.

But in the parable all the laborers received the same: how does this fall in with some being first and some last hereafter? The parable and the lesson seem here not to agree. Perhaps they were not meant to agree on this point; for there are many parts in the parables which form only the circumstances, or scenery, so to speak, without teaching any special lesson. Yet there is more agreement here than appears at first sight. For though the men who were hired last received only the same as those who were hired first, the same and no more, yet for the work done they received a great deal more; the first hired received a penny for a whole day's work, the last received the same for one hour; they were paid at a far higher rate, and so were first. Besides, they were paid first in order of time. Whether much weight is to be given to this or not, at least it goes some way to help us out of the difficulty; for certainly the last hired were the first paid, and so the last were first.

Another question arises. What kind of people exactly are we to understand by those who are first now but will be last hereafter? The parable represents them as really called to work in the vineyard, and bearing the burden and heat of the day, and receiving wages. This would lead us to think them true Christians, though not of so high a stamp as those of the other class. But the case of the rich young man seems to prove the contrary; for he, as far as we know, never gained any part in the kingdom of heaven. Again, those who were hired first murmured at the others' receiving as much as they; but will any true Christian murmur at the grace and mercy bestowed on others, or at any of God's dealings under the gospel? The question is by no means without difficulty; but I am disposed on the whole to take the words in the widest and most general sense. Those who are first now comprise those who are foremost in various respects; first in rank, first in wealth, first in gifts and influence, first in point of time, first in religious advantages, first in station in the church. Some such are true Christians, but some are not so; some there are who have nothing of Christ but the name, and though they are outwardly members of his church, and thus by profession working in the Master's vineyard, and that perhaps all their life long, yet are not really his. It must be observed that our Lord's words are, "*Many* that are first shall be last," not *all.*

This view is confirmed by what our Lord says at the close of the parable, "for many be called, but few chosen." The few chosen mean true Christians, real spiritual members of the church of Christ; the many called mean all professing Christians, whether real or nominal only. Those who will be first hereafter must be the chosen; those who will be last must as certainly comprise numbers who are called but not chosen, Christians in name but not in heart.

True, there is another difficulty that meets us here. All the laborers received at the close of the day, and received the same; how then can some of them represent true disciples, and some nominal Christians? We must not forget our *key*. Our Lord's words before and after the parable mark a clear difference between what will be received by the two classes, especially the words that follow the parable, "for many be called, but few chosen." Either, therefore, the equal sum received by all is merely one of the circumstances of the parable, or it has a meaning in agreement with the key. In the latter case the meaning may be somewhat as follows:

Though the sum received by all was the same, yet in some cases it was what had been bargained for, the just wages and no more, in others it was a gift. The penny therefore may be meant to represent to us a different thing in the one case from that which it represents in the other. The laborer hired at the beginning of the day bargained for a penny, and a penny he received. God will never give a man less than his due. The self-righteous man, the formalist, the nominal Christian, the sinner, will receive the due reward of his deeds, though that will not be eternal life. What he receives, such as it is, he has earned. A penny, the usual day's wages, seems fitly to represent this. But the laborer hired at the eleventh hour made no bargain at all, but trusted to the master to give him what should be right, and at the close of the day received far more than he had earned. In the former case, justice paid the wages; in this case, it is grace that confers the gift. We may trace this difference in the very words of the parable: "Friend, I do thee no wrong: didst not thou agree with me for a penny? Take that thine is, and go thy way." Here is not a word of favor, mercy, or giving; it is bare justice: "I do thee no wrong;" that is all. But in the other case how different is the tone! "I will give unto this last even as unto thee." "Is thine eye evil because I am good?" Here we see goodness and grace concerned.

Some have objected that the penny is thus made to mean one thing in the one case, and another thing in the other: in the one case, the gift of eternal life through grace; in the other, that which a man receives as the fruit of his own works. The difficulty is acknowledged; nevertheless it does not seem fatal to this view.

Let a few words of a practical kind close the subject.

I. Let us have a deep conviction that all that God does is right. Even if we cannot see that it is so, let us humbly believe it. Here we see through a glass darkly, but hereafter we shall see face to face.

II. Let us trust in no mere outward advantages, whether temporal or spiritual; riches, station, power, the means of grace, a religious name, a high position of usefulness. Let us seek earnestly, that we may not be of the number of those who are first now, but shall be last hereafter. Let us seek to be humble, true, sincere, and of a spiritual mind.

III. If God has placed us among the last and lowest now, yet let us not complain, nor let us think that we cannot serve him. We may be poor or afflicted; we may have very little knowledge, and very few opportunities of doing good. Let us take meekly and thankfully what God sends. We shall not always be poor; nay, we are not poor now, if we have Christ. Our affliction is but a light affliction, and it is but for a moment. We are drawing near to the world to come, and there we shall find an exceeding and eternal weight of glory. And though our lot be low, yet can we do nothing for our Lord? And though we may but lately have learnt to know him, yet can we not work for him for the rest of our day? Only let us love him, and he will find us something to do, and we shall gladly do it.

IV. Let none put off the great concern. As soon as they were called, at whatever hour of the day it was, these men went into the vineyard. Some, who are continually being called, are still putting off obeying the call. They "will obey later in life, not now." This is dangerous work. Your day may come to a close before you are aware. Now is the accepted time.

V. It was not through their own fault that some, in the parable, stood all the day idle: no man had hired them. But this cannot be said of those who are trifling life away, doing God no service, and making no preparation for eternity. They are standing idle, and some have reached almost the end of their day; yet they have been called again and again, and are called still. Well may the words be addressed to such, "Why stand ye here all the day idle?" Eternity is near. You can never have your day again. Too much of your life has been wasted already, yet some remains. Do not waste what is left. "Go ye also into the vineyard." Join yourselves to Christ by faith. Listen to him. Receive him as your Saviour. Follow him, serve him, do his will. Then he will give you, not wages, but the gift of eternal life.

XXXVI.

The Pounds.

"And as they heard these things, he added and spake a parable, because he was nigh to Jerusalem, and because they thought that the kingdom of God should immediately appear. He said therefore, A certain nobleman went into a far country to receive for himself a kingdom, and to return. And he called his ten servants, and delivered them ten pounds, and said unto them, Occupy till I come. But his citizens hated him, and sent a message after him, saying, We will not have this man to reign over us. And it came to pass, that when he was returned, having received the kingdom, then he commanded these servants to be called unto him, to whom he had given the money, that he might know how much every man had gained by trading. Then came the first, saying, Lord, thy pound hath gained ten pounds. And he said unto him, Well, thou good servant: because thou hast been faithful in a very little, have thou authority over ten cities. And the second came, saying, Lord, thy pound hath gained five pounds. And he said likewise to him, Be thou also over five cities. And another came, saying, Lord, behold, here is thy pound, which I have kept laid up in a napkin : for I feared thee, because thou art an austere man : thou takest up that thou layedst not down, and reapest that thou didst not sow. And he saith unto him, Out of thine own mouth will I judge thee, thou wicked servant. Thou knewest that I was an austere man, taking up that I laid not down, and reaping that I did not sow: wherefore then gavest not thou my money into the bank, that at my coming I might have required mine own with usury? And he said unto them that stood by, Take from him the pound, and give it to him that hath ten pounds. (And they said unto him, Lord, he hath ten pounds.) For I say unto you, That unto every one that hath shall be given ; and from him that hath not, even that he hath shall be taken away from him. But those mine enemies, which would not that I should reign over them, bring hither, and slay them before me." LUKE 19 : 11–27.

IT was long before the disciples learnt that their Master did not come to be a king like other kings, and that his kingdom was not to be fully established immediately. They clung to the notion that he was going to deliver their nation from bondage, and to reign over it himself; and now that they were getting near to Jerusalem, the capital of the country, they persuaded themselves that he was on the very point of doing so. Our Lord spoke this parable to set them right.

The disciples would have been glad to see their Master a king at once, for then doubtless they would have had a share in his power and glory. So they thought, and so they wished; but it was not so to be. He was first going away for a time. Far from reigning with him yet, they were to lose even his presence; and while he was absent they were to *work* for him. No work, no rest; no cross, no crown. They were to pass through much before they should be with him in his kingdom of glory.

It seems likely that in the early part of this parable our Lord alluded to a public event that had actually happened a few years before, and must have been still fresh in the minds of all. The country was at this time under the power of the Romans; but the Romans used to let a Jewish prince reign over a part of it at least, with the title of king, and with some of the power of a king. Archelaus, son of Herod the Great, reigned in this way. About thirty years before this parable was spoken, he "went into a far country, to receive for himself a kingdom, and to return." That is to say, he went to Rome to get his claim to be king allowed and established by the Roman government. This was of course well known to the disciples as being a great public event that had happened in their own country but a few years before. Our Lord likens himself, by way of parable, to this prince. He too was going into a far country, to receive for himself a kingdom, and to return. He was about to go to heaven, to his Father; thence, after a time, he would return, and then his kingdom would be fully set up upon earth, and he would reign as a king indeed. But this was not to be yet; he was not then even gone. Now he has been gone for above eighteen hundred years, but he has not yet returned.

We do not know in whose hands Archelaus left his concerns while he was absent at Rome; but in the parable our Lord represents the nobleman or prince as delivering ten pounds to his ten servants, a pound to each, with this charge: "Occupy till I come." This pound is generally thought to have been equal to about £3 sterling; but some suppose it to have been worth much more. Whatever the value of it was, each servant was to turn his pound to the best account by trading with it; for that is here the meaning of the word "occupy." Thus Christ, our Lord, has left to us his servants that which we are to turn to account in his service. To each of us he has given something; to each he has said, "Occupy till I come." The pound, in our case, does not mean money only, but every thing else that God has given us, and that may be usefully employed. We are to make the most of all, and that with a view to our Lord's return, always bearing it in mind, "Occupy *till I come*." Then he will reckon with us.

In the parable, the citizens or people of the kingdom over whom the nobleman wished to reign, hated him, and when he was gone, sent a message after him, declaring that they did not desire him for their king. This actually took place in the case of Archelaus. He had already exercised authority over the Jewish people for some time, though not yet settled in the kingdom by the Romans; the Jews therefore knew his character, and by no means wished him to be their ruler; so they sent ambassadors after him to Rome, to beg the Roman emperor not to make him king. He was made king, notwithstanding, and we may be sure that on his return he showed little mercy to those who had opposed him. It seems likely that our Lord in the parable alludes to this. As the Jews had refused Archelaus as their temporal king, so would they refuse Christ as their spiritual King and Saviour. True, the cases are not altogether alike, for the Jews had probably good reason for fearing Archelaus, whereas they ought gladly to have welcomed Christ; but the likeness is in the rejection: "We will not have this man to reign over us." This is what the Jews, as a nation, said with regard to Jesus. They would not believe in him, or receive him as the Messiah; they would not submit to him. Not only while he was on earth, but after he was gone, they refused, and they do refuse still. Thus they do, as it were, send a message after him, refusing his authority. Oh, that the day may speedily come when that nation shall turn and acknowledge Jesus as the Christ, and once more enjoy the favor of God. But all impenitent sinners do likewise in fact thus reject Christ. They send no message indeed; few dare to say in words, "We will not have this man to reign over us;" but they say so by their lives. They may call themselves by his name, and acknowledge him in outward form; but they close their hearts against him, and do not seek to do his will. This is the case with thousands who bear the name of Christian. It is the case with them *now*. While Jesus is gone, while yet we wait for his return from that far country, this is their state of heart and life: "We will not have this man to reign over us." It is an awful state; for he will return, and return to reign.

The next event that comes in the parable—no longer probably referring to Archelaus—is the nobleman's return, having received the kingdom. The first thing he does is to reckon with the servants to whom he had given the pounds. Three cases out of the ten are mentioned. The first servant had been most diligent and successful: his pound had gained ten pounds. He received high praise, and was set over ten cities in the newly-gotten kingdom. The second had been diligent also; but his success, and probably his diligence, had not been so great as that of the first. He had, however, gained five pounds, and was made ruler over five cities. But the third servant had nothing to bring to his master save the pound which he had received of him. He had not lost it, but he had done nothing to make it more. He had laid it up in a safe place, and now sought to excuse himself by the character of his lord. "For I feared thee," said he, "because thou art an austere man: thou takest up that thou layedst not down, and reapest that thou didst not sow." A strange reason indeed to give for his conduct. It was the very reason for *not* doing as he had done. "Out of thine own mouth will I judge thee, thou wicked servant," was his lord's reply. If he thought his master so stern and strict, though we are not to suppose him so really, why did he not act accordingly? Why did he not at least put the money out at interest, that some increase might be made against the master's return?

The servants and the citizens were plainly two different classes. The servants meant our Lord's disciples, who required to be taught that they had to wait for their Lord's return, and meanwhile to work diligently in his service; the citizens meant the Jewish nation at large. In applying the parable to ourselves, we may take the citizens to mean people in general, and the servants those who make a profession of serious religion, and do in some measure engage in the service of God. Our Lord teaches us by the case of the two *faithful* servants, not only that all such will be rewarded hereafter, but that their reward will be in proportion to their service. The man who had gained ten pounds was set over ten cities; he who had gained five pounds, over five. Even a cup of cold water given in the name of a disciple will not lose its reward; the smallest service of love will be acknowledged; but large service will be largely rewarded, and a life of peculiar zeal and devotedness will receive a special blessing: yet all of grace, not of debt. The reward given to these servants was a mere matter of favor, for they did no more than they were bound to do. Christ our Master graciously speaks to us his servants of a reward, but it will be his free gift. We shall not have earned it, we shall not deserve it, yet he will give it; and the thought is a great and wholesome encouragement to the servants of Christ in their work.

But what does the case of the *slothful* servant teach? That Christ expects some profitable service from all. It is not enough that we do no harm; we must do good. Our pound is not to be laid up in a napkin, but used diligently in our Lord's service. Life is given us to serve him with, life and all that it brings us. Our Master is not an austere master, but gracious and kind, having compassion on our infirmities, and willing at all times to give us help and comfort; yet his word to us all is, "Occupy till I come;" and he will surely look for a return for what he has given. Let each servant consider where his pound now is; for each has one somewhere, either lying idle, or being used for the Master with more or less of diligence and perseverance.

The pound was taken from the slothful servant, and given to him who had gained ten. Those who had orders to do this objected at first, "Lord, he hath ten pounds;" but their master persisted, giving this reason for so doing: "Unto every one which hath shall be given, and from him which hath not, even that he hath shall be taken away from him." It was the nobleman in the parable who said this. He would deal thus with his servants: the slothful servant should be no more trusted with any of his goods; whereas the faithful should be abundantly rewarded, and trusted with what was taken from the slothful. So, when our Lord returns, nothing will be left in the hands of his unfaithful and unprofitable servants; they will be stripped of all. But the diligent and faithful, who have made the fullest use of what was committed to them here below, will be greatly promoted. They will receive such honor and dignity as will surprise both themselves and others. The King will delight to honor those who shall have honored him by their faithful and zealous service.

Thus the prince acted towards his servants; but there were yet the citizens to be dealt with, who had refused to have him as their king. What was their sentence? "Those mine enemies, which would not that I should reign over them, bring hither and slay them before me." We know not whether Archelaus took such vengeance as this on those who had opposed him, or whether this part of the parable is more general in its meaning: but this we know, that "the Lord Jesus shall be revealed from heaven with his mighty angels, in flaming fire taking vengeance on them that know not God, and that obey not the gospel of our Lord Jesus Christ." He now invites as a Saviour, and will bless as a gracious king all who receive him and submit to him; but it will be a fearful thing to meet him in a state of rebellion. "Kiss the Son, lest he be angry, and ye perish from the way, when his wrath is kindled but a little. Blessed are all they that put their trust in him."

XXXVII.

THE TALENTS.

"For the kingdom of heaven is as a man travelling into a far country, who called his own servants, and delivered unto them his goods. And unto one he gave five talents, to another two, and to another one; to every man according to his several ability; and straightway took his journey. Then he that had received the five talents went and traded with the same, and made them other five talents. And likewise he that had received two, he also gained other two. But he that had received one went and digged in the earth, and hid his lord's money. After a long time the lord of those servants cometh, and reckoneth with them. And so he that had received five talents came and brought other five talents, saying, Lord, Thou deliveredst unto me five talents: behold I have gained beside them five talents more. His lord said unto him, Well done, thou good and faithful servant: thou hast been faithful over a few things, I will make thee ruler over many things: enter thou into the joy of thy lord. He also that had received two talents came and said, Lord, thou deliveredst unto me two talents: behold I have gained two other talents beside them. His lord said unto him, Well done, good and faithful servant; thou hast been faithful over a few things, I will make thee ruler over many things: enter thou into the joy of thy lord. Then he which had received the one talent came and said, Lord, I knew thee that thou art a hard man, reaping where thou hast not sown, and gathering where thou hast not strewed: and I was afraid, and went and hid thy talent in the earth: lo, there thou hast that is thine. His lord answered and said unto him, Thou wicked and slothful servant, thou knewest that I reap where I sowed not, and gather where I have not strewed: thou oughtest therefore to have put my money to the exchangers, and then at my coming I should have received mine own with usury. Take therefore the talent from him, and give it unto him which hath ten talents. For unto every one that hath shall be given, and he shall have abundance: but from him that hath not shall be taken away even that which he hath. And cast ye the unprofitable servant into outer darkness: there shall be weeping and gnashing of teeth." MATT. 25 : 14-30.

THIS parable is in some respects much like the parable of the pounds, and some of the lessons which it teaches are the same; for we have here a master going into a far country, and giving his property into the hands of his servants, and then after a time coming back and reckoning with them; we find here also two faithful servants who traded with their master's property and made it more, and one who kept it in useless idleness; and lastly, we see the talent taken from the slothful servant and given to him who had ten talents, and the slothful servant punished.

In these respects the parables are alike; yet they are not the same.

In the first place, this parable was spoken at or near Jerusalem; the other at Jericho, in the house of Zaccheus. Again, the parables themselves are so different that it is impossible to take the two passages in which they are contained as only different versions of the same parable. Nor does their being alike in some points make any real difficulty. It was not at all unlikely that our Lord should make use of the same figure in his teaching at Jerusalem as he had done shortly before at Jericho; or that, in doing so, he should yet make a difference. Such seems to be the truth of the case. These are two parables, spoken on different occasions, having a general likeness, and yet unlike in several points.

In this parable the sums given to the servants

were different; to one were given five talents, to another two, to another only one. Each received according to his ability, that is, his supposed power to manage the sum profitably. Whatever the value of the talent was, (and it is reckoned to have been worth a great deal more than the pound in the other parable,) the sums were different—the largest was five times as great as the smallest. So God does not give to all alike. Some he places in a high station, some in a low one; each in that for which he sees him to be fit. One man he makes rich, another poor; to one he gives great powers of mind, and the means of getting learning; another has small abilities and few opportunities. We are not therefore to envy one another, or to wish for the gifts or stations of others. It should be enough for us that our heavenly Master has placed us where we are, and given us what we have, be it much or little. He knows best. Our main desire should be, not to have more, but to use well what we have.. If it be but one talent, while others have five, yet much may be done with the one. At all events, it is what our Master has seen fit that we should have.

Why did he who had received the one talent do nothing with it but bury it in the ground? The reason he gave was just the same as that given by the man in the other parable. He was afraid, he said; for he thought his master a hard man, bent upon getting even more profit than could be fairly expected, and therefore little likely to make allowance for failure or loss; so, to guard against these, he hid the money in the earth—there it would at least be safe, though it could make no profit. Ungodly men, and unfaithful servants of Christ, have very wrong notions of Him who is their Master. They fear God, instead of loving him; fear him, not in a scriptural and right way, but with a feeling of dread and alarm. They do not know him as the God of grace and love. They little think how kind he is to his servants, how ready to make allowance for them, and to help them. They have no gratitude and love, leading them to desire to do his will; and being thus without motive, they shrink from responsibilities which they ought to undertake, and are content to do nothing. The man in the parable, when he said that he was afraid, doubtless made the best of his case; and when such persons as I have mentioned refuse to take part in good works, because, as they say, they fear the responsibility of doing so, they are probably much more influenced by mere sloth and self-indulgence.

There is another reason which sometimes leads people to act like the man who buried his talent. Because their gifts are small and their opportunities few, therefore they despise them. If they were richer, or more learned, or if they lived in a different kind of place, and had more people to whom they could do good, or more ways open to them of working for God, how gladly, think they, would they lead an active and useful life! But as it is, it seems to them not worth while to try. They see nothing they can do that is worth doing. Thus, having but one talent, they go and bury it in the earth. If they had five or two, they would trade with them diligently—so they think. But would they? There is no reason whatever to suppose that he who neglects small opportunities, would make use of great ones; or that one who lets his own talent go unemployed, would do any better if he could exchange with his neighbor. The man with one talent was just as much bound to do his best with it as the man with five. The person whose means of serving God seem the smallest, is as much bound to serve Him in his measure as he whose means are largest; and faithful service will receive an equal reward, whether the talents have been many or few.

For, in this parable, the man who brought his master two talents received as rich a blessing as he who brought five. The words of blessing spoken to both are the same. It is not as it was in the other parable. And why? Because here the sums intrusted to the servants were different: one had five talents given to him, the other only two. When therefore this last brought two talents more, he received equal praise with him who brought five, for he had shown equal faithfulness and diligence. Our Master expects from us according to what he has given to us. "If there be first a willing mind, it is accepted according to that a man hath, and not according to that he hath not." This is how God is graciously pleased to accept our offerings, and this is how he will judge of our use of his gifts in general. In the great day of account, many of the poor and humble will doubtless receive as rich a blessing as those who have been far above them in this life, however faithfully these last may have employed their talents.

It was "after a long time," that the master came and reckoned with his servants. Long as the time was, however, the faithful servants never forgot that he was coming back, but persevered in making the most of their talents up to the very hour of his return. Not so the slothful servant. It appears that no sooner was his master gone, than he went and buried his talent. If afterwards he ever had uneasy thoughts about the reckoning, probably the long time helped him to get rid of them. "My lord delayeth his coming"—such was his feeling; and, not being engaged in his service, but occupied in his own concerns, he most likely seldom gave a thought to the buried talent or to his lord's return. It is so now. The faithful servants of Christ are continually looking for his coming, and though the time is long, yet is their faith not shaken; they know that he will come, and while the thought stirs them up to a diligent use of their talents, that very use helps to keep his coming in their mind. The slothful and careless, on the contrary, forget the coming of the Lord, as they forget their talents and their responsibility. The time is long, and yet he does not come. All things go on as usual. They are busied in their own affairs. All besides is forgotten, or almost forgotten. How will they meet him when he comes? And what account will they give?

The slothful servant in this parable was dealt with in the same way as the one in the other parable; he was trusted no longer, he lost all, the talent was taken from him, and he received his master's stern condemnation as a "wicked and slothful servant." But this parable carries us a step farther, and shows us his awful end: "And cast ye the unprofitable servant into outer darkness: there shall be weeping and gnashing of teeth." Whatever this might mean in the parable itself, whatever dark underground dungeon this unhappy man was to be thrust into, we know well what the meaning is with regard to those who are unfaithful to Christ. The outer darkness represents that awful world, where the light of God's countenance never shines, and into which no hope ever comes; the "weeping and gnashing of teeth" describe the despair of the lost.

But is not this, it may be asked, the doom of gross and outrageous sinners—the robber, the murderer, the adulterer, the blasphemer? Can this be what lies before one who is but a slothful servant? Yes, it is so. There is nothing in this parable about the robber, the blasphemer, and such like. It is the case of the man who buried his talent in the earth that is described, and that alone. But he is called *wicked*, as well as slothful; his slothfulness was wickedness in his master's sight, and so is that of the unfaithful servants of Christ. For his servants they are, by right and responsibility, though unfaithful and useless servants.

Oh, how will some wish that they could have their time on earth again, and once more have talents intrusted to them which they might improve! How bitter will be the thought, that once they had gospel offers and gospel means; that they had the service of Christ proposed to them, talents intrusted to them, and the coming of Christ set before them as that for which they should prepare! And now, that time, that state, is past for ever. These thoughts have come too late. They would not think seriously while they might, but trifled life away, with no thought of its responsibilities, till at length the end came. Ah, let not *your* thoughts come too late. Think in time—think now. Consider your talents, your responsibility, your great account, and the coming of your Lord. The time may be long, yet he will come. Let him not find your talent buried, and you not looking for his coming.

XXXVIII.

The Two Sons.

"A certain man had two sons: and he came to the first, and said, Son, go work to-day in my vineyard. He answered and said, I will not: but afterward he repented, and went. And he came to the second, and said likewise. And he answered and said, I go, sir: and went not. Whether of them twain did the will of his father? They say unto him, The first. Jesus saith unto them, Verily I say unto you, That the publicans and the harlots go into the kingdom of God before you. For John came unto you in the way of righteousness, and ye believed him not: but the publicans and the harlots believed him: and ye, when ye have seen it, repented not afterward, that ye might believe him." MATT. 21:28–32.

THIS parable is not difficult to understand, for it is one of those which our Lord himself explained. He had been speaking to the chief priests and elders about John the Baptist. Now many open sinners had repented at the preaching of John; but the priests and elders had not repented. The son who said, "I go, sir, and went not," represented them; the other son, who at first refused to go, but afterwards repented and went, represented the penitent sinners, the publicans and harlots. These last had lived in wilful sin, making no pretence of obeying God, but saying by their conduct, "I will not." The Jewish rulers, on the other hand professed to serve God, and, whatever their lives might really be, probably kept up a decent outward appearance. But they did not really serve God; their hearts were not given to him; they said, and did not. When John came preaching repentance, and preparing the way of Christ, they did not believe or repent; and even afterwards, when they saw numbers turned to God by his means, they still remained impenitent. Thus the despised publicans and harlots entered into the kingdom of God before the proud scribes and Pharisees.

But though this was the first and direct application of the parable, it may properly be applied more widely. There are still sinners who repent at the preaching of the gospel; and there are still people answering to these Jewish priests and elders, professing godliness, but in reality far from the kingdom of God.

Our Lord does not here justify sinners, as sinners; he takes these publicans and harlots in their changed condition, after they have repented and believed, and then declares that they find admittance into the kingdom of God. If they had remained impenitent, they must have perished. The son in the parable was wrong to say, "I will not," though his conduct afterwards was right.

Nor does our Lord condemn a profession of religion, as such, but only a vain and empty profession. The other son was right in what he said, though wrong in what he did. Many people excuse themselves thus for an ungodly life, "I make no profession." We *ought* to make a profession, only it should be a real and true profession.

It is not clear that these Jewish rulers were all hypocrites, though probably many of them were. Some perhaps, mistook profession for reality, and flattered themselves that they were in the right way, because their lives did not show those gross sins which appeared in many around them. There is much danger of this. A gross sinner, when he thinks at all, must know that he is in the wrong, and that he stands in need of a great change. A man of a decent and moral life, on the other hand, who lives in no open sin, and attends to the outward parts of religion, is apt to think that no such change is required in him. His eyes are not opened to see what sin is in its spirit; and, abstaining as he does from its grosser forms, he thus keeps conscience asleep.

But sin has many different forms; and who shall venture to say which is the most offensive in the sight of God? We see two men, one leading a life of gross sin, the other living decently, though showing no sign of spiritual religion. Without giving much thought to the subject, we set down the gross sinner at once as the worse man of the two. But is that judgment certainly right? There are what may be called smooth sins, as well as rough sins; and if that man of decent life be covetous, extortionate, unmerciful, proud, or self-righteous, who can say how God looks upon him as compared with the other? Sin of every kind is condemned in Scripture, and condemned equally, though man has made distinctions.

The great practical point for each to consider

from the parable is this: what is my religion? Is it a mere profession, a decent life, an abstaining from gross sin? Is it no better than the obedience of him who said, "I go, sir; and went not?" Is it a name, or a reality? a thing of the heart, or a thing of the tongue only? Has any change taken place in me, any repenting, any believing, any coming to Jesus, to that very Saviour to whom John the Baptist pointed?

They are very solemn words of our Lord, words that should raise serious thoughts in many a heart; "Verily I say unto you, that the publicans and the harlots go into the kingdom of heaven before *you*." Before whom? Before hypocrites, before mere professors, before those who say and do not, before those who have a name to live and are dead. Great and awful is the danger of all sinners; but that man seems in greatest danger, who is priding himself on a moral life, and wrapping himself up in the fancied security of his own merits. God's grace can change any heart; but, humanly speaking, the gross sinner, who knows himself to be in the wrong way, is more likely to be brought to God than the smooth offender who fancies himself in the right way already.

For both there is but one way, the Living Way, Jesus Christ. His grace can reach all, his blood can cleanse sinners of every shade. He has opened the gate of mercy to publicans and harlots, to self-deceivers, yea, even to the self-righteous, if they will cast aside all other dependence, and simply look to him.

XXXIX.

THE WICKED HUSBANDMEN.

"A certain man planted a vineyard, and set a hedge about it, and digged a place for the winefat, and built a tower, and let it out to husbandmen, and went into a far country. And at the season he sent to the husbandmen a servant, that he might receive from the husbandmen of the fruit of the vineyard. And they caught him, and beat him, and sent him away empty. And again he sent unto them another servant; and at him they cast stones, and wounded him in the head, and sent him away shamefully handled. And again he sent another; and him they killed, and many others; beating some, and killing some. Having yet therefore one son, his well-beloved, he sent him also last unto them, saying, They will reverence my son. But those husbandmen said among themselves, This is the heir; come, let us kill him, and the inheritance shall be ours. And they took him, and killed him, and cast him out of the vineyard. What shall therefore the lord of the vineyard do? he will come and destroy the husbandmen, and will give the vineyard unto others. And have ye not read this scripture; The stone which the builders rejected is become the head of the corner: This was the Lord's doing, and it is marvellous in our eyes? And they sought to lay hold on him, but feared the people: for they knew that he had spoken the parable against them: and they left him, and went their way." MARK 12 : 1-12 ; see also MATT. 21 ; LUKE 20.

THIS parable is found in all the gospels, except that of St. John, and with very little difference.

There is no doubt about its meaning, or about the persons to whom our Lord meant to apply it; for we read that the chief priests and Pharisees themselves "knew that he had spoken the parable against them." Conscience told them so, and they were right; our Lord did not contradict their thought.

The Jewish teachers were well acquainted with their own Scriptures, and this parable no doubt at once brought to their minds the fifth chapter of the prophecy of Isaiah, in which the same figure of a vineyard is used: "My well-beloved hath a vineyard in a very fruitful hill: and he fenced it, and gathered out the stones thereof, and planted it with the choicest vine, and built a tower in the midst of it, and also made a wine-press therein." That parable of the Old Testament was meant, as they well knew, to describe the Jewish nation, "for the vineyard of the Lord of hosts is the house of Israel, and the men of Judah his pleasant plant." When therefore the Jewish teachers heard our Lord use the same figure, (though in rather a different way,) and when they heard him go on to describe conduct which exactly agreed with their fathers' and their own, they well understood that he spoke the parable against *them*.

The vineyard, which the man in the parable planted with so much care, represented the Jewish church established by Almighty God. The rest of the world was in spiritual darkness, but God chose the Jewish nation to be enlightened by his word, and to enjoy religious privileges. Thus this nation occupied, as it were, an enclosed place. While the rest of the world was spiritually in a wild and desert state, the Jews were in a vineyard carefully prepared for them. Every provision was made for their good, their comfort, and their usefulness. As in the parable there were the hedge, the winepress, and the tower, so did God give them laws and ordinances which fenced them off from other nations and their idolatrous practices, and promised them his protection, and taught them how to serve and please him. They were the husbandmen who were to occupy the vineyard. It was not theirs, but it was let out to them as tenants.

But tenants have rent to pay; and in ancient times, and in eastern countries, rent was often paid in kind; no money passed, but a part of the produce of the land went to the landlord as his rent. Accordingly, at the season for gathering the grapes, this householder sent to the husbandmen for his share of the fruit. But, instead of giving it, they ill-treated his servants; and when he sent again and again, they still refused, and only used his messengers worse and worse, "beating some, and killing some." This part of the parable represents the way in which the Jews treated God's messengers, the prophets. God looked for fruit from them, in return for their religious light and knowledge, the fruit of righteousness; and prophets were sent from time to time, as his messengers, to declare his will to them, to speak to them his word, and to call them to repentance. But they would not listen to the messengers of God. Some righteous doubtless there always were among them, but, as a nation, they rebelled against God, and rejected and ill-treated his servants. Our Lord himself reproached them for this: "O Jerusalem, Jerusalem, which killest the prophets, and stonest them that are sent unto thee." The martyr Stephen did the same: "Which of the prophets have not your fathers persecuted?" Thus did the Jews, generation after generation, treat the messengers of God.

The owner of the vineyard, finding it useless to send servants, at length determined to send his only and well-beloved son. "They will reverence my son," said he. But on the contrary, these wicked husbandmen now went farther than ever in crime. Far from reverencing their master's son, no sooner did they set eyes on him than they determined to put him to death. "This is the heir," said they; "come, let us kill him, and the inheritance shall be ours." This plan they carried out at once. "They took him, and killed him, and cast him out of the vineyard." We know what this means. In the fulness of time God sent his Son, his only and well-beloved Son, into the world, and first to the Jewish nation. But the Jews rejected him, and caused him to be put to death. They ought to have reverenced him; for his coming had been foretold, and gracious words and wonderful works, and even a voice from heaven, proclaimed him to be the Son of God. Instead of this, they filled up the measure of their iniquities by crucifying the Lord of glory; the Jewish rulers thinking that they would thus keep the power which they possessed over the people, and that so the inheritance would be theirs. We may perhaps apply these last words in this way; or it may be that this plan of the husbandmen is but the filling up of the story of the parable, and has no application to the Jews; especially as in the parable the husbandmen knew and acknowledged their lord's son, while the Jews, on the other hand, denied that Jesus was the Son of God.

We cannot but be struck with the proof here given that our blessed Lord is the divine Son of God. How great a difference is made in the parable between the servants and the son! Probably the lord of the vineyard sent the highest and best of his servants on such an errand; yet his sending his *son*, his "one son, his well-beloved," is spoken of as a distinct thing altogether; they were but servants— this was his son. In the opening of the epistle to the Hebrews we find the same great distinction made between the ancient messengers of God and the Son of God: "God, who at sundry times and in divers manners spake in time past unto the fathers by the prophets, hath in these last days spoken unto us by his Son, whom he hath appointed heir of all things, by whom also he made the worlds." Prophets and apostles were but men—good, holy, devoted, and even inspired, yet still but men; Jesus Christ is the only-begotten Son of God; himself God as well as man.

The story of the parable leaves off at this point. The husbandmen have slain the son and cast him out of the vineyard. "When the lord therefore of the vineyard cometh, what will he do unto those husbandmen?" Our Lord put this question, and it was answered by those who heard him; not perhaps by the scribes and Pharisees, but by some of the multitude. "He will miserably destroy those wicked men," said they, "and will let out his vineyard unto other husbandmen, which shall render him the fruits in their seasons." Thus we read in St. Matthew. In St. Luke's account it would rather seem that our Lord himself gave the answer to his own question, for it is added: "And when they heard it, they said, God forbid," or, Let it not be so. But it may be that some of the multitude, thinking only of the story, gave that answer, and that then others of those present, who saw that our Lord meant the story to apply to the Jews, said: "God forbid!"

But our Lord pressed the application home to them, reminding them of what was written in their own Scriptures: "The stone which the builders rejected is become the head of the corner; this was the Lord's doing, and it is marvellous in our eyes;" and adding, according to St. Matthew: "Therefore say I unto you, The kingdom of God shall be taken from you, and given to a nation bringing forth the fruits thereof. And whosoever shall fall on this stone shall be broken: but on whomsoever it shall fall, it will grind him to powder." None of those who heard him could any longer be in doubt as to his meaning. As the vineyard in the parable would be taken from the husbandmen, so should God's presence and favor, and the means of grace, and the gospel, be taken from the ungrateful and unbelieving Jews, and bestowed on others, that is, on the Gentiles; because the Jews were about to act like the husbandmen; already they were refusing to acknowledge Christ, and soon they would put him to death.

The passage about the stone hardly belongs to the parable, yet it is mixed up with it. It is taken from the 118th Psalm, and is undoubtedly a prophecy about Christ, whatever other meaning it may have. Jesus was the stone, the chief corner-stone; but the builders, the Jewish rulers, rejected him; yet this stone was to be the head of the corner, Jesus was to be the head of his church. Whoever should fall on this stone, whoever through unbelief should cause Christ to be to them as a stumbling-stone or rock of offence, should be *broken*, should suffer a great injury, to say the least; but on whomsoever it should fall, it should grind him to powder; all obstinate unbelievers, who should set themselves in opposition to Christ, and refuse to the last to obey him, must in the end be crushed by his almighty power, and perish for ever.

But does this relate to the Jews only? Surely not. If they, as a nation, have been cast off for a time on account of their rejection of Christ, how shall the sinner, the careless, the unbeliever, the man who is a Christian in name only, but brings forth no fruit to God, how shall *he* escape? Such a man is in the vineyard now; God in his providence has placed him there. He belongs outwardly to the church of Christ, knows the word of God, and has the means of grace within reach. If he renders no service to God, if he turns a deaf ear to God's ministers, and does in fact reject Christ, because he does not believe on him with the heart, what remains for him? He will lose the blessings which he never valued aright, and for which he has made no return; nay, further, he must look to find Him who would have been a Saviour, an awful Judge, executing vengeance on all who do not receive him.

One more lesson we may learn. The Jewish rulers knew that our Lord was speaking of *them*: yet they did not repent; but were only the more set against him. When the word of God strikes home, it sometimes happens that a man is only made angry. Conscience tells him that the word is true, and true against *him*; yet this does not of itself lead him to repentance, for only grace can do that; on the contrary, it does but make him perhaps uneasy and displeased. If ever *you* are angry at the preaching of the word, ask yourself why you are so. It may be because you know that what is preached is a true witness against you. But do not be angry. Rather be sorry. Pray God to make you so; to give you his Holy Spirit, that you may be led to repentance and to Christ. Why strive against God? why resist the voice of conscience? why "kick against the pricks?" How much better and happier to submit to Jesus as the Lord of grace and mercy and salvation!

XL.

The Budding Fig-Tree.

"Now learn a parable of the fig-tree: when his branch is yet tender, and putteth forth leaves, ye know that summer is nigh; so likewise ye, when ye shall see all these things, know that it is near, even at the doors. Verily I say unto you, This generation shall not pass, till all these things be fulfilled. Heaven and earth shall pass away, but my words shall not pass away." MATTHEW 24:32–35; see also MARK 13; LUKE 21.

OUR Lord was seated on the Mount of Olives when he spoke the long and solemn prophecy of which this parable forms part. On the opposite side of the narrow valley that lay between him and Jerusalem rose the temple in full view; and in the valley itself, and on the slope of the mount, there were fig-trees as well as olive-trees. It was now spring-time, and the fig-tree was beginning to shoot. Its branches were soft and tender from the rising of the sap, and already leaves began to appear. Growth is even quicker in that country than with us; it was plain that summer was near.

Our Lord drew the attention of his disciples to this. The fig-trees were close at hand, and might well serve to teach them a lesson. He bade them notice the budding branches, the sign of the coming summer, and then added: "So likewise ye, when ye shall see all these things, know that it is near, even at the door."

"These things" meant the signs of which he had just been speaking, especially the Roman army surrounding Jerusalem; and the event that was to follow so closely was the destruction of that city, and the dispersion of the Jewish people. For though our Lord, in speaking of this, did also carry on the thoughts of the disciples to his second coming and the end of the world, yet he is not alluding to that here; for he expressly says, "This generation shall not pass till all these things be fulfilled." Some of those who heard him would be still alive at the destruction of Jerusalem, which took place between thirty and forty years afterwards. He warns them, and all his followers who should be then living, to take notice of the signs which were to go before that great event, and to act accordingly. As soon as those signs appeared, they were to leave the city, and thus to escape a share in its destruction. Let them carefully watch those signs, therefore; for as surely as the budding fig-tree foretold the summer, so surely would the city be soon destroyed, and the nation scattered, when once they should appear.

All took place according to our Lord's words. The signs of which he spoke did appear; the Roman army came against Jerusalem, and, in no long time after, the city was taken and destroyed. The disciples of Christ, or at least the greater part of them, acted on the warning he had given them, and left the city in time to escape its destruction. Thus his words were fulfilled, "Heaven and earth shall pass away, but my words shall not pass away."

Kingdoms were shaken, cities were destroyed, great commotions took place in the world, yet nothing could change what he had said. All that he foretold came true.

And so will all else that he has foretold. Every prophecy that has been fulfilled is a pledge and assurance that all other prophecies shall be fulfilled in their time; and the disciples of Christ accordingly are to give heed to his word, and to what is happening around them, and to mark the signs of the times.

Especially we ought to do this with regard to the second coming of our Lord. In this prophecy the two great events of which he speaks, the destruction of Jerusalem and his own coming, are so linked together, that there is some difficulty in knowing when he is speaking of the one, and when of the other, and when perhaps of both. The disciples, who heard him speak, themselves no doubt felt this difficulty; and little did they think that eighteen hundred years at least would pass between the happening of the two things thus foretold together. But this very difficulty is not without its use. The very mingling of the two events in the same prophecy must have led the disciples to look upon both as equally certain; and still more should it lead *us*, now that one of them has taken place, to feel sure that the other also will take place in its time.

The two events are spoken of in the same prophecy; yet, in one important respect, there is a difference to be observed. With regard to the destruction of Jerusalem, our Lord said that the generation of men living when he spoke should not all have died before it should take place; but with regard to his own second coming and the end of the world he said, "But of that day and hour knoweth no man, no, not the angels of heaven, but my Father only." Thus, at the 36th verse, he seems to make a change. He had been speaking of what should take place within the lifetime of some then living; now he speaks of that which should take place quite as certainly, but no one knew when, none but the Father. In applying the lesson of the parable to ourselves, we must bear in mind this difference.

Yet we *may* apply the lesson to ourselves, and that most profitably, with regard to the coming of the Lord; but not so much with reference to its *time* as to its *certainty*.

We are to mark the signs of the times; for the coming of Christ will as surely follow them as summer followed the budding of the fig-tree; not so quickly, but as surely. There have been, and still are, many different opinions as to the signs of the coming of the Lord. There have been probably in all ages serious Christians, who have thought that they saw in events that happened in their day signs of his approach. There are many who think thus now. These thoughts and expectations are not to be lightly regarded, still less to be turned into ridicule. Even if we do not share them, we should nevertheless be led by them to deeper thought and more watchful preparation. The Lord *will* come. It may be, that these very expectations in the minds of his people are among the signs of his coming. Let us mark them accordingly.

But, putting aside the question of time, we should give earnest heed to all the signs which tell that he will surely come. Ancient prophecy, his own words, the state of the world, the case of the Jewish nation, wrong that is to be set right, war that is to be changed into peace, and a thousand things around us that pain and grieve us, as far as we can tell, will never be greatly mended till he come—these are so many signs to us, more or less sure, of his coming. We should mark these things, and ponder them in our minds. We are not created to live carelessly, wrapped up in our own little concerns of the day, and unconcerned about the great things that are to be. As far as the word of God gives light, let us walk in that light. As far as we can find scriptural ground for seeing in things that happen the signs of our Master's coming, let us mark those things narrowly and seriously. While we must beware of indulging baseless fancies and vain imaginations, and above all of twisting Scripture to suit them, let us look to it also that we fall not under our Lord's reproof of the Pharisees and Sadducees, "Ye can discern the face of the sky; but can ye not discern the signs of the times?"

Eighteen hundred years have passed since our Lord spoke of his coming, and still he has not come, and still his words hold good—"Of that day and hour knoweth no man, no, not the angels of heaven." Though so much time has passed, we are still in the same position as the disciples—servants waiting for our Lord, knowing that he will come, and that he may come soon, but not knowing when. But this we are clearly told, that "the day of the Lord so cometh as a thief in the night," and that, to some at least, he will come suddenly. Whatever views may be held on other points, in this there seems no room for difference among the servants of Christ. He says to us all, "Watch therefore, for ye know not what hour your Lord doth come." Season after season has the fig-tree budded, and the summer come. Eighteen centuries ago our Lord's words about Jerusalem were fulfilled; and still the wandering Jew remains a standing witness to the truth of prophecy, and still we look for "that day and that hour" which "no man knoweth." Let us look for it humbly, watchfully, diligently; with a sure hope, a full trust, a solemn yet glad expectation. Let us see that our loins be girded about, and our lights burning; let each servant be about his work; and oh! let each one of us make sure that he *is* a servant of Christ indeed. Let none put off seeking the Saviour till the Lord shall come in his glory. Let none say in his heart, "My Lord delayeth his coming." Let none disregard the warning voice and the signs of the times; lest, coming suddenly, He find them sleeping.

XLI.

THE WISE AND FOOLISH VIRGINS.

"Then shall the kingdom of heaven be likened unto ten virgins, which took their lamps, and went forth to meet the bridegroom. And five of them were wise, and five were foolish. They that were foolish took their lamps, and took no oil with them; but the wise took oil in their vessels with their lamps. While the bridegroom tarried, they all slumbered and slept. And at midnight there was a cry made, Behold, the bridegroom cometh; go ye out to meet him. Then all those virgins arose, and trimmed their lamps. And the foolish said unto the wise, Give us of your oil; for our lamps are gone out. But the wise answered, saying, Not so; lest there be not enough for us and you: but go ye rather to them that sell, and buy for yourselves. And while they went to buy, the bridegroom came; and they that were ready went in with him to the marriage: and the door was shut. Afterward came also the other virgins, saying, Lord, Lord, open to us. But he answered and said, Verily I say unto you, I know you not. Watch therefore, for ye know neither the day nor the hour wherein the Son of man cometh." MATT. 25 : 1-13.

THIS parable, like so many other of the parables of our Lord, represents "the kingdom of heaven," that is, God's spiritual government upon earth under the gospel dispensation; and the particular time intended is the coming of the Son of man, when the present state of things will be brought to an end. This is plain from the opening words, "*Then* shall the kingdom of heaven be likened;" then, that is, at the time just before spoken of, the the time of the sudden coming of the Lord.

The more precise meaning of the parable is not difficult to arrive at, if we bear in mind the customs of that time and country.

Their marriages were very different from ours, and so are marriages among the Jews, and in eastern countries, still. The bridegroom, accompanied by friends and attendants, usually brought his bride from her father's house to his own at night-time. But while some thus went with them, others waited to meet him on his return; and as the time of his return must be in some measure uncertain, especially if the bride came from a distance, it was necessary that those who were to meet him should watch for his coming.

The parable represents ten virgins going forth in this way to meet a bridegroom on his bringing home his bride. Five of them were wise, that is, prudent and thoughtful; and five were foolish. The five wise virgins made provision for having to wait perhaps a considerable time, by taking oil with them to refill their lamps; but the others made no such provision: they took their lamps, but took no oil with them. The night wore away, the bridegroom was later probably than any of them expected, and they all slept. But at midnight they were roused by the cry that the bridegroom was coming. The wise virgins had nothing to do but to trim their lamps with the oil which they had provided, and they were quickly ready. Not so the foolish. Their lamps had gone out, and they had no oil to fill them with again. In their dismay they applied to the wise virgins. But they had none to spare: they had made provision for their own want, but not for that of the rest. There was nothing left for the foolish virgins but to go with all speed to buy more oil. But while they were gone, the bridegroom came. The procession entered the house, joined by the five virgins who were ready; and when the other five returned shortly afterwards, they found the door shut. It could not be opened again. To all their entreaties the master of the house only replied, "Verily I say unto you, I know you not."

The ten virgins represent professing Christians, waiting, or professing to wait, for the coming of Christ. The five wise virgins are *real* Christians. The oil in their lamps means perhaps the grace of God in their hearts; or, more generally, a state of true preparation, through grace, for the coming of Christ. The five foolish virgins are *nominal* Christians, making the same profession as the others, but having no real religion, and no true preparation of heart. By their *all* sleeping we are perhaps to understand that not even true Christians are so watchful as they ought to be for the coming of the Lord. Or it may be that no blame is intended. Perhaps the wise virgins were not wrong in sleeping, seeing they were ready for the summons when it came.

But in the great day true Christians will be able to give no help to those who are found unprepared. Each must answer for himself. Grace is not a thing which we can give to another. The soul that is washed in the blood of Jesus, and made new by the

Holy Spirit, will be saved for ever; but that soul will have no help to give to another.

And when that day shall have come, it will be too late to seek help even of God. Now he is ready to hear and answer prayer. Now he will give his Holy Spirit to them that ask him. Now Jesus will in no wise cast out him that cometh unto him. But we are warned in Scripture again and again that the day of grace is *limited*, and will come to an end. "Strive to enter in;" that is, strive *now;* "for many will seek to enter in, and shall not be able," because they will not seek till it is too late.

"The door was shut." How awful are these words! How sad! How hopeless! Other doors may open again, but not that door. At other times entreaties may prevail, but not then. The day of grace will have passed when that time arrives, and those against whom the door is closed will be shut out for ever.

We are all in the situation represented in the parable. Our Lord is coming, and we have to meet him. And we are all like either the wise or the foolish virgins, for there is no other class. Either we are prepared, or not prepared. What an awful difference! What a solemn question! And all the more so, because outwardly those who are so different may seem much alike. The ten virgins, before the hour of trial, seemed alike. They all went forth to meet the bridegroom; they all had their lamps with them. It was not till the bridegroom came that the difference appeared. So professing Christians may live together now, and worship together; they may hold the same doctrine, and belong to the same church; yet how vast a difference may the coming of Christ disclose! How many will be separated then who have been joined on earth! How many, who seemed in many respects alike, will prove to have been utterly different!

What is our state *now*? The midnight cry may soon be heard; the Lord may come suddenly; how should we be found? Are we like the wise? Have we made provision? Is there oil in our vessels? Have we sought Christ? Are we walking in the Spirit? Are we watching for our Lord? "Watch therefore," he said. Watch *when*? When the trumpet is heard, when the clouds rend, when the Son of man appears? No; watch *now*, this day, this very hour; "for ye know neither the day nor the hour wherein the Son of man cometh." Oh, woe to those whom he will find unprepared!

Is there any peculiar meaning in what the wise virgins said to the foolish, "But go ye rather to them that sell, and buy for yourselves?" Perhaps not. Perhaps we are only to understand that *they* could not help them; they must go to those who could. Nevertheless the words bring this thought to the mind: Grace and salvation in Christ are *free*, "without money and without price;" yet here the advice is to go to them that *sell*, and *buy*. While salvation is to be had at all, it is to be had as a gift only, not to be *bought*, but to be freely received. When the time of grace is past, and salvation can no longer be had, then what would not the poor lost one give to purchase it? Then he would willingly go to them that sell, and buy even at the price of all he ever had. But it will be too late then. "What is a man profited, if he shall gain the whole world, and lose his own soul? or what shall a man give in exchange for his soul?" "Behold, *now* is the accepted time, behold *now* is the day of salvation."

XLII.

THE VINE AND THE BRANCHES.

"I am the true vine, and my Father is the husbandman. Every branch in me that beareth not fruit he taketh away: and every branch that beareth fruit, he purgeth it, that it may bring forth more fruit. Now ye are clean through the word which I have spoken unto you. Abide in me, and I in you. As the branch cannot bear fruit of itself, except it abide in the vine; no more can ye, except ye abide in me. I am the vine, ye are the branches: He that abideth in me, and I in him, the same bringeth forth much fruit: for without me ye can do nothing. If a man abide not in me, he is cast forth as a branch, and is withered; and men gather them, and cast them into the fire, and they are burned. If ye abide in me, and my words abide in you, ye shall ask what ye will, and it shall be done unto you. Herein is my Father glorified, that ye bear much fruit; so shall ye be my disciples." JOHN 15:1–8.

OUR Lord had taught his disciples much by means of parables, especially just before, in those which we find in the twenty-fourth and twenty-fifth chapters of St. Matthew. But now, at the end of the long discourse, of which this parable of the vine forms part, he said: "These things have I spoken unto you in proverbs; but the time cometh, when I shall no more speak unto you in proverbs, but I shall show you plainly of the Father." By proverbs he seems to have meant every kind of proverbial and figurative teaching, including parables. He had then just spoken to them this parable of the vine; he would teach them no more in that way.

From its nature and subject, this parable is well fitted to be the last. Many of the others, especially those spoken just before, relate to the church of Christ at large; but this is more personal. Before he was taken from them, our Lord would lead his disciples seriously to consider what part they had in him, lest they should deceive themselves by taking it for granted that they belonged to that kingdom of heaven of which he had told them so much, while yet they had but an outward union with him. The case of Judas might well be a warning to them. He had been one of the apostles, and so had seemed to belong to Christ. But he was but a fruitless branch, and as such he had been taken away. At the time when our Lord spoke, he had already left the little band of disciples, and had gone out to betray his Master. Yet up to that very night he had seemed to belong to Christ, as a branch to the vine. Let them take warning by so sad a case. Let them not trust in any seeming union. Let them abide in Christ indeed.

Whatever it was that led our Lord to choose the vine as the figure in this parable, there is a special force and meaning in it. The vine is a humble tree, not great and tall like the cedar and the oak. So our Lord came in a humble way, as it was foretold of him: "For he shall grow up before him as a tender plant, and as a root out of a dry ground; he hath no form nor comeliness; and when we shall see him, there is no beauty that we should desire him." Again, the vine is valuable only for its fruit; the wood is of no use. This represents the fruitfulness that is required in Christians. Mere profession is nothing. While any tree therefore would have answered the purpose of showing the union between Christ and his people, as between tree and branch, there is a peculiar fitness in the vine, a humble, yet fruit-bearing tree.

"I am the *true* vine," says our Lord. Perhaps he means, the natural vine is but a figure; I am what the figure represents. Or he may mean to teach us that, though there may be other pretended sources of spiritual life and growth, he is the only true source. Therefore he says, not merely, "I am the vine," but, "I am the *true* vine." It is not even doctrines, however right, that will give us life; doctrines, forms, ceremonies, ordinances, all have their proper use, but they cannot give life; Christ is the true vine, and we must be joined to him as branches, or there is no life in us.

"And my Father is the husbandman;" the owner and cultivator of the vineyard, and the dresser of the vine. It is God who deals with the branches. Every one who bears the name of Christian is under his continual observation. He knows the spiritual state of each, and comes seeking fruit. The work of a husbandman, especially in a vineyard, requires constant watchfulness and care: God never forgets or overlooks even one branch.

The manner of his dealing with the branches is described very particularly by our Lord.

First he mentions the fruitless branch. "Every

branch in me that beareth not fruit, he taketh away." These words have been a difficulty to some. How can any one be in Christ, and yet be unfruitful? But our Lord means those who are in him by profession and in appearance only. Judas was so till he was taken away. Nominal Christians are so. True, the figure and the lesson do not exactly agree here, for in nature the fruitless branch is as much joined to the vine as the fruitful; but this is often the case in our Lord's parables.

"Every branch in me that beareth not fruit, he taketh away." Every vine-dresser does so, and the heavenly Husbandman does so too. Even in the natural vine, though the branch grows out of the tree, yet being fruitless, it is treated as if it did not belong to it: in the case of the spiritual vine, there is no real union at all. The husbandman takes away such a branch as useless. God also, in his own time, takes away the mere nominal Christian, and will not suffer him any longer even to seem to belong to Christ. If nothing else does so, *death* puts an end to this seeming union, and takes away the fruitless branch. But often, before death, God in his providence takes such a one away from the means of grace. He did not profit by them while he had them; he shall now have them no more.

Next we learn how the husbandman deals with the fruitful branches. "And every branch that beareth fruit, he purgeth it, that it may bring forth more fruit." Even the fruit-bearing branches are not left to themselves. The knife is used to them also. But only the pruning-knife. They are not cut off, but purged. Every one is treated so, for there is not one but may become more fruitful still. Thus God deals with his children, the true branches. All the fruit they bear already is of his grace; he will deal with them in grace still, that they may bear more fruit. But how? Chiefly in the way of affliction and chastisement. These form his pruning-knife. Wisely and gently does he use it; not to hurt the branch, but to do it good; not to cut it off, but to rid it of that which is doing it harm, and to make it more fruitful. Sometimes God's dealings with his children seem surprising; when trouble after trouble befalls them, and one comfort after another is taken away. But this is only the gentle care of the Husbandman, pruning the branch. The knife may be sharp, but it will not cut too deep, for it is in the hand of perfect wisdom and love. Every true Christian experiences this treatment more or less. Indeed, chastisement is one of the marks of God's children. "If ye endure chastening, God dealeth with you as with sons; for what son is he whom the father chasteneth not?" "We must through much tribulation enter into the kingdom of God." As an old writer says: "God would rather see his vine bleed, than see it barren." Let it be our comfort under chastisement, that it is he who is dealing with us, and that he is dealing with us for our good and for our fruitfulness.

"Now ye are clean," our Lord continues, "through the word which I have spoken unto you." It has been thought by some that our Lord here alludes to the traitor Judas. He had been, as it were, a blight and stain upon the band of apostles. That blight was now removed by his being gone; and now, as a body, they were clean. But it seems more simple and natural, and more in agreement with the rest of the parable, to take the words in another sense. The word "purgeth," just before, and this word "clean," have the same meaning. Chastisement is not the only way by which God prunes and cleanses; he does so also by his word. Now the disciples had just been listening to the words of Jesus, and those words had had a deep effect on them. Their hearts were full of love to their Lord, they were looking to him in faith, their earnest desire was to do his will, and they were in a state of acceptance and blessing. Thus they were then clean through the word of Christ; he himself pronounced them so: "Now ye are clean," that is, "Now ye are purged." He does not say they were even then *perfect;* but they were in such a state that purging, or pruning by chastisement, was not then needed. Their hearts were at that time truly joined to him, and the fruits of faith and love were shown forth.

Thus these disciples were owned by our Lord himself as living and fruitful branches. But he adds: "*Abide* in me, and I in you." Let this union continue. For "as the branch cannot bear fruit of itself, except it abide in the vine, no more can ye, except ye abide in me." The fruitfulness of the branch depends entirely on its remaining joined to the vine, from which all its life and nourishment comes. The fruitfulness of the Christian equally depends on his being joined by faith to Christ. If any thing could break this union, all fruit, and even the very life of the soul, would come to an end. And as surely as a Christian grows cold and careless, and faith becomes weak, and the union between his soul and Christ is less firm and close, so surely do the fruits of the Spirit grow less in him too. The only way to fruitfulness is to abide or stay in Christ.

Lest the disciples should not apply this to themselves, our Lord now says plainly: "I am the vine, *ye* are the branches." Let us receive those words as if spoken to us. He is the vine, and *we*, in one sense or another, are the branches; for in name and profession at least we are so. All that he has said before therefore concerns us, and the yet more solemn and searching words that follow concern us too.

"He that abideth in me, and I in him, the same bringeth forth much fruit; for without me ye can do nothing." Some begin well, but soon drop off. At first their feelings are excited, and they are full of warmth and zeal, and give every promise of much fruit to God's glory; but these hopeful appearances do not last, just as we often see buds and blossoms come to nothing. Why is this? Perhaps there never was real faith; or perhaps the young Christian began in his own strength, and did not know, or did not remember, that without Christ he could do nothing.

Those are remarkable words: "Without me ye

can do nothing." The meaning is, "separated from me, or apart from me, ye can do nothing"—still carrying on the figure of the vine and the branches. Not only will there not be much fruit, unless the union with Christ be maintained, there will not be any at all. The words seem to throw light too upon the kind of fruit that is meant. "Without me ye can *do* nothing." The fruit is what we do—our conduct, our actions, our service, our life. These words therefore do not mean merely, as they are often supposed to mean, that without Christ's *help* we can do nothing. That is quite true; but these words mean much more. They teach us that *apart* from Christ, that is, if not joined to him by faith, we can bear no fruit, and do God no acceptable service.

But on the other hand, a true and lasting union with him will cause us to bear not fruit only, but *much* fruit. And this is what we should aim at; because this, as our Lord tells us afterwards, is for the glory of God: "Herein is my Father glorified, that ye bear much fruit." A true disciple cannot be satisfied with a little fruit. He is one who hungers and thirsts after righteousness. He feels deeply what he owes to redeeming love; and all that he can do in the service of his God and Saviour seems nothing in comparison with his debt of gratitude and love. Indeed, our Lord makes it the mark of his disciples, not that they bear fruit merely, but that they bear *much* fruit: "so shall ye be my disciples." How can one be a true disciple of such a Master, who will do him a little service, and there stop? How can one be really desirous of living to the glory of God at all, who is content to live so as to promote it but a little only?

Not only does the true disciple desire to bear much fruit to the glory of God, but a close union with Christ enables him to do so. His sphere may be small, and his lot humble, yet his light will shine brightly before men, and they will glorify God. The light indeed is not his, but Christ's, and the grace which appears in him is from Christ alone; he is but a branch, Christ is the vine; yet as in the natural vine the branches bear fruit, though drawing all their nourishment from the stock, so every branch in Christ, even that which grows lowest, bears fruit to the glory of God, and the more the fruit the more the glory. Many of Christ's humblest disciples are, nevertheless, by his grace, bearing rich fruit to God's glory in Christian tempers, and holy lives, and self-denying works of love. Their strength, their comfort, their growth, their fruit, are all drawn from Christ; the work of his Spirit in their hearts, the effect of their union with him by faith. They walk in a strength not their own. They have an unseen source from which they draw all. Their life is a life of prayer, and it is by this mainly that their union with their Lord is maintained. They are not careless or forgetful. The words of Christ abide in them, and they make full and happy use of their access by him to the throne of grace. They go there freely. They ask what they will. Every want, every fear, every sin they take there. And the promise is fulfilled: they ask, and it is done unto them. They receive out of the fulness that is in Christ.

But what becomes of those who do *not* abide in Christ? "If a man abide not in me, he is cast forth as a branch, and is withered; and men gather them, and cast them into the fire, and they are burned." Have we not often seen such a sight in a vineyard or garden? Wherever the pruner has been at work, the ground is strewn with clippings; some are dead wood, others fruitless branches; all lie together, withered or withering, till one comes and takes them away for burning. In the very words of this part of the parable there is an awful likeness between the figure and the reality. Ah, in that outer darkness that is to come, how many will be found who once seemed to belong to Christ! They bore his name, attended his ordinances, and perhaps at one time gave some appearance of fruit in heart and life. But they were not truly joined to him by faith; they did not abide in him; and when the husbandman sought fruit on them he found none. They were not all alike, indeed, for some showed more sign of life than others; but they were all alike in being unfruitful, and now they are all found together.

These are the words of truth. The speaker was the Lord Jesus Christ. His words will come to pass with regard to some who bear his name. Look to it that you be not of the number. Examine your state with regard to Christ. Rest satisfied with nothing short of a living union with him by faith, and seek the proof of it in your heart and life.

"*So* shall ye be my disciples," he said; so, and so only. Judge yourselves by that rule. Is there fruit in you? Is there *much* fruit? At least, is there, amid many shortcomings, the earnest desire, and the daily endeavor and prayer, to glorify God by bearing much fruit?

www.ingramcontent.com/pod-product-compliance
Lightning Source LLC
Chambersburg PA
CBHW030755230426
43667CB00007B/981